Alaska

THE CRUISE-LOVER'S GUIDE

THE CRUISE-LOVER'S GUIDE

Paul & Audrey Grescoe

GREYSTONE
BOOKS

Douglas & McIntyre
Vancouver/Toronto

To our sisters,
Karen, Lorraine, Eleanor, and Donna,
In hope this book will inspire them to take an
Alaskan cruise

Copyright © 1994 by Paul and Audrey Grescoe

94 95 96 97 98 5 4 3 2 1

Greystone Books
A division of Douglas & McIntyre Ltd.
1615 Venables Street
Vancouver, British Columbia
V5L 2H1

Published in the United States by Alaska Northwest Books

Canadian Cataloguing in Publication Data

Grescoe, Paul, 1939–
        Alaska : the cruise-lover's guide

        ISBN 1–55054–129–3
        1. Alaska—Guidebooks.   2.   Ocean travel—
Guidebooks.   I.   Grescoe, Audrey.   II.   Title.
F902.3.G74 1994   917.9804'5   C93–091869–X

Cover design by Rose Cowles
Composition by Eric Ansley & Associates
Cover photo by Pat O'Hara
Printed and bound in Canada by D.W. Friesen & Sons Ltd.
Printed on acid-free paper

Permissions

The quote on page 96 is from *A Guide to the Birds of Alaska* (1991) by Robert H. Armstrong. Reprinted with permission of Alaska Northwest Books, Seattle.

The quotes on pages 112 and 114 are from *Bashful No Longer: An Alaskan Eskimo Ethnohistory, 1778–1988* by Wendell H. Oswalt. © 1990 by the University of Oklahoma Press. Reprinted with permission.

The quote on page 131 is © 1989 by Art Davidson, from *Alakshak: The Great Country* by Art Wolfe and Art Davidson. Reprinted with permission of Sierra Club Books.

The quote on page 154 is © 1988 by Bridget A. Smith, from the book *Death of an Alaskan Princess* by Bridget A. Smith. Reprinted with permission from St. Martin's Press, Inc.

The section on Yukon, Canada, contains material by Paul Grescoe adapted from *Heritage of Canada,* © 1978, 1984 Reader's Digest Association (Canada) Ltd., Montreal. Adapted with permission.

Photo and Art Credits

All maps are by *Dennis & Struthers,* Victoria, B.C.

All photographs are courtesy of *Princess Tours,* unless otherwise noted below:

Alaska State Library: Winter & Pond Collection, 10 (PCA 87-1733), 30 (PCA 87-362), 114 (PCA 87-180), 123 (PCA 87-048); Alaska Purchase Centennial Collection, 117 (PCA 20-59); Skinner Foundation Collection, 147 (PCA 44-5-2).

Anchorage Museum of History and Art: 35 (B69-2233), 136 (B76.118.10)

British Columbia Archives: 51

John K. B. Ford: 72

R. Roy Forster: 109 (top left)

E. Granquist: 169

Mark Kelly: 56

Lon E. Lauber: 91, 98–99

Wayne Lynch: 86–87

Rick McIntyre: 89

Pat O'Hara: 8, 12–13, 106–7

Sheldon Jackson College, Sitka: Stratton Library Collection, 29

Fred and Sandra Tremblay: 39

University of Washington Libraries: Special Collections Division, 178 (UW 14812), 228 (UW 14811), 233 (UW 14809).

Vancouver Public Library: 48 (PA.016w)

John W. Warden: 134–35, 152

ACKNOWLEDGEMENTS

We would like to thank the people of Princess Tours, Seattle, for their wholehearted co-operation in the creation of this book, especially Bill Pedlar, Charles Ernst, and Elizabeth Steen. Our thanks as well to Vivian Greblo of Holland America, Seattle, and to transportation expert Gary Duke of Vancouver. In a project like this, there are so many people who participate in so many ways. Among them: Taras Grescoe, who researched and wrote the section on *Stalking The Land* as well as generally researching for the entire book; Danny Lehman, whose in-the-field knowledge enhanced the section on photography; Roy Corral, photo editor of *Alaska Magazine*, for his kind help in locating photographers; R. Roy Forster, curator of the VanDusen Botanical Display Garden in Vancouver, for identifying Alaska wildflowers; Dave Cormany, the Pribilof Islands program manager, for his insights into those islands; Dr. Richard Morlan of the Museum of Civilization, Hull, Quebec; Robert Sheldon of Friends Church in Kotzebue; Nelson Angapak of the Alaska Federation of Natives; Tracy Green of Alyeska Pipeline Service; the people of the U.S. Fish and Wildlife Service in Anchorage and the Enforcement Division, Pacific and Yukon Region, of the Canadian Wildlife Service; Fred and Sandra Tremblay for their contributions to the Alaska Highway section; Joyce Tiplady for her treasure trove of Alaskana; and Bob and Rennie Ducick for their personal knowledge of Alaska (and countless cappuccinos). And finally, our deepest thanks to Marilyn Sacks, who demonstrated again, through her skill and dedication, why she is our editor of choice.

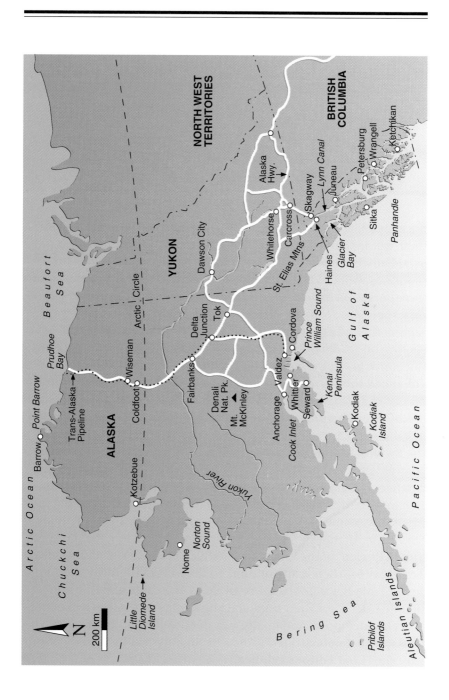

Contents

INTRODUCTION: THE LAST, VAST FRONTIER

A moment that crystallized the Alaskan cruise experience for us happened not aboard ship but in a little yellow float plane skimming over the Misty Fjords Monument. As we left Ketchikan harbor that morning in late May, the low-flying wisps of fog over deeply indented Carroll Inlet and the clouds brooding over the blue mountains helped explain the name of this wondrous 2.3-million-acre wilderness. There were killer whales down there, and brown bear, and mountain goats the color of the snow they scrambled along; bowl-shaped lakes, still unsullied, and rivers and streams thick with fighting game fish; dark-green wildwood and steep-flanked granite canyons, their peaks patchworked with white. But our moment of awareness came with the realization that Misty Fjords, as immense as it seems, covers less than an eighth of the 17-million-acre Tongass National Forest. America's largest federal forestland, larger than West Virginia, Tongass encompasses most of the southeastern Alaska Panhandle.

There was another defining moment, again well away from our cruise ship. A group of us had slipped into yellow slickers and tall blue boots and clambered into helicopters at the Juneau airport. The sextet of choppers took off like a cloud of mosquitoes and climbed over a lake and mountains before landing on the moonscape of Mendenhall Glacier, with its monolithic columns forming a cliff and its frigid meltwater whirlpooling down deep crevasses. In places the glacier was nearly 2,000 feet thick and 1.5 miles wide; and though we were already a mile onto its eerie expanse, Mendenhall wound up the Coast Mountains for another 11 miles.

Nootka lupine flourish in summer, enlivening Alaska's scenic drama.

Yet, alien as the environment was, we realized the face of the glacier was only a brief bus ride away from downtown Juneau.

Most glaciers in Alaska are much less approachable by land, and are best witnessed from the water. Which is how we came to experience yet another moment of revelation. From Juneau we cruised through Icy Strait to Glacier Bay, which hadn't even existed when Captain George Vancouver sailed by here two centuries before. But the world's biggest collection of tidewater glaciers had been in retreat ever since, and now our ship was slowly circling the head of the bay while we stood on deck, watching mighty Margerie calve. Native people had a phrase for the sound of house-sized chunks of ice peeling off a glacier's face: white thunder. Watching them crash into the water, we had a word for Nature's noisy, splashy creation of instant icebergs: astounding.

Alaska is abrim with such moments, and today's cruise-ship passengers can savor them first-hand, up close, by land and from the air as well as on the sea. The 49th state offers some of the world's sublimest adventure holidays to satisfy virtually any kind

Luxury cruising, 1895 style: tourists from the *City of Topeka* ashore at Glacier Bay.

of taste, any level of fitness, any age. Henry Gannett, who sailed with the 1899 Harriman Expedition, which named many of the glaciers of Prince William Sound, had his tongue slightly in cheek when he wrote: "There is one word of advice and caution to be given those intending to visit Alaska for pleasure, or for sight-seeing. If you are old, go by all means, but if you are young, wait. The scenery of Alaska is much grander than anything else of its kind in the world, and it is not well to dull one's capacity for enjoyment by seeing the finest first."

The fact is, there is *so much* scenery and there are so few people. Alaska is 99 per cent uninhabited; the population is only 570,000, half of it residing in Anchorage. At 586,412 square miles, this is the largest state in the Union—a fifth the size of the entire Lower 48. It spreads across two time zones, Alaska and Hawaii-Aleutian. If superimposed on a map of the contiguous states, it would cover an area from California to Georgia and from Mexico to Canada. Or, to put it another way, it's almost double the size of California, Oregon, and Washington combined. More than 20,000 square miles of Alaska's area is water. Its convoluted coast, 6,640 miles measured point to point, has 47,300 miles of tidal shoreline, more than all the other continental states combined. The state has more than three million lakes of 20 acres or more and 39 mountain ranges, including 17 of America's highest 20 peaks. Its landforms range from 25,000 feet below the Pacific in the Aleutian Trench to the 20,306-foot summit of Mount McKinley.

Its list of natural splendors seems endless. All the 1,000 or so glaciers in the western United States would not equal the area of one of Alaska's big valley glacier systems. One of its glaciers, Malaspina, is larger than Rhode Island. The largest federal park in the U.S. is Wrangell–Saint Elias National Park and Preserve, bordering on Canada's Yukon: its 8.1 million acres and 4.1-million-acre preserve make it four times the size of Yellowstone.

There is so much more, including wildlife roaming freely in staggering numbers. The state has 600,000 Barren Ground caribou,

A field of buttercups borders the stunning
sea- and mountain-scape of Sitka's harbor. ➤

for instance, and one estimate suggests an average of more than 70 collisions a year between moose and car in Anchorage alone. Animals that are rare or nonexistent down south flourish here, among them grizzlies, polar bears, and the primitive-looking musk-ox. The landscapes they live on differ dramatically, from the icy desert of the Arctic tundra to the rich green rainforests of Southeast (which is how Alaskans refer to the panhandle-like mainland and hundreds of islands that parallel the British Columbia coastline for about 500 miles between Dixon Entrance in the south and Skagway in the north).

The land is considered a creature of plate tectonics, a theory that says the planet's crust floats on a mantle of molten material, which rings the core of the earth and oozes out from enormous fissures in the ocean basins. The ruptured pieces of the crust, called plates, drift and slowly reassemble themselves. The plates beneath the the northeast Pacific Ocean collided with those of continental North America millions of years ago, moving north along such fault lines in the earth as the San Andreas. Simultaneously, land in the far north of North America drifted westward into the Pacific and perhaps 80 million years ago created a bridge between North America and Asia—the origin of northern Alaska and northeastern Siberia. When the plate sliding to the north along the Pacific struck this land bridge, it squeezed under the continental plate, causing tremendous geologic forces—earthquakes, volcanoes—that continue to this day. One effect of this process called subduction may have been the relatively sudden uprising of the central Alaska Range, including mighty Mount McKinley.

The major mountain ranges help define Alaska while influencing its weather systems. *(See* And Now, The Weather, *page 17.)* The Coast Range in the lush Southeast winds northwest toward Anchorage. The Alaska Range stretches westward for 600 miles to the Alaska Peninsula, creating a rainy and reasonably mild climate, to link with the storm-battered, 1,600-mile-long Aleutian Range, whose 47 active volcanoes are part of what is called the Pacific "ring of fire." The impressive bulk of the Brooks Range, 150 miles wide and 600 long, separates the dry, cold, open Interior from the petroleum-rich, permafrosted North Slope running into the Arctic Ocean.

A land as diverse and theatrical as Alaska is bound to produce a people just as distinctive. As the stories in this book reveal, the state has had (and continues to have) larger-than-life good guys and bad. Like Jimmy Doolittle, a newspaper delivery boy in Nome who grew up to lead Doolittle's Raiders, the U.S. Army pilots who launched their bomb-laden B-25s off Navy carriers to pound Japan and change the course of World War II. Or the volunteer fireman in Ketchikan, a nice young fellow who set large blazes throughout the town in the late 1950s while disguised as a woman in veil and high heels. (He turned himself in and went to prison.) And remember that Alaskans as a whole—a generally libertarian bunch at the time—tolerated legalized marijuana for 15 years, until the nation's most liberal pot law was overturned in 1990. At the same time, the state's gun-control laws are among the weakest in the U.S.

This is a state where the governor from 1974 to 1982 was a bearded homesteader, bush pilot, commercial fisherman, guide, and trapper who lived in a log cabin he built himself. Jay Hammond also created the Alaska Permanent Fund, which since 1982 has given Alaskan residents annual dividend checks from the state's savings-account earnings. As the 1990s began, each eligible resident was receiving almost $1,000 a year from a fund dependent on petroleum revenues—which then accounted for about 85 per cent of Alaska's general fund. These revenues encouraged per-capita state and local spending triple the U.S. average, which directly and indirectly supported one-third of all wage-earners. Alaska has been the only state in the Union to assess no state income tax—a situation that is expected to change by decade's end as North Slope oil continues declining from its peak in 1988.

But Alaskans are optimists, as any breed of people must be to settle in a land that for so long was so isolated and could impose such stern living conditions. All that has changed, of course, with modern transportation, communications, and comforts. Today's ease of travel has helped make tourism the state's second-largest industry, behind petroleum, with the total of annual visitors well exceeding the number of residents. And the most convenient, dramatic—and popular—way to visit Alaska is by cruise vessel.

Which is why we have written this book, the first to combine all the functions of pre-trip planner, on-board and land-tour guidebook, cruise diary, and post-trip souvenir for the Alaskan cruise-ship passenger. Because it's aimed at such a specialized audience, *Alaska: The Cruise-Lover's Guide* has some unique characteristics. This may be the only guide to the state that deals almost entirely with spring, summer, and autumn—making mention of its harsh winter features only when they are relevant and interesting. Because cruise passengers by definition have all their food and lodging needs accommodated automatically, we haven't included distracting, ever-changing listings of restaurants and hotels. This has left us more room to describe the glories of Alaska in full detail, focusing on those destinations where cruise tours are most likely to take you.

Luxury vessels have been cruising regularly to Alaska since 1884, following on the heels of American naturalist and travel writer John Muir, whose summing-up of the Inside Passage voyage to Skagway still stands as an accurate description of the Alaskan cruise experience today: "No other excursion that I know of can be made into any of the wild portions of America where so much fine and grand and novel scenery is brought to view at so cheap and easy a price."

AND NOW, THE WEATHER

There's a strange, if extremely rare weather phenomenon in Alaska called the *fata morgana*. Named for the legendary half-sister of King Arthur who made her submerged crystal castle appear as a mirage above the waves, the Alaskan version can happen during temperature inversions when several layers of warm and cold air project images in the air of objects that may be well below the horizon. The most celebrated mirage, in the late 1800s, was the recurring vision of a populated city of gardens and tall spires that appeared in Glacier Bay.

As a cruise-ship passenger, you're not likely to experience the *fata morgana*, though it might be fun to see the Silent City hovering above Muir Glacier. The truth is, Alaska can be a most pleasant place to visit during the regular tourist season. The state remains green half the year, with virtually no snow in summer except on the hills and mountains; summer days are exceedingly long (on June 20–21, daylight hours in Ketchikan, Juneau, and Anchorage range from 17 1/2 to nearly 19 1/2); and occasionally the usual temperatures in the 50s and 60s leap into the 80s and 90s. Anchorage has a climate similar to the Great Lakes region; Ketchikan, lying at the same latitude as Glasgow, Scotland, has relatively mild weather distinguished mostly by the rain that makes it one of the wettest places on earth (though the rain and sun may alternate throughout the day).

Generally, May and June are the driest months in Alaska. July and August can be shirt-sleeve weather. The leaves of willows and birches begin yellowing in August. Fall may be the best of all, when the days are crisp and cold.

So what should you wear on a cruise to Alaska? Aside from the attire you take for shipboard life (travel agents and cruise brochures will guide you there), plan on casual, comfortable clothing that you can easily shed or layer back on as the weather fluctuates. The basics are good walking shoes (but probably not sandals or other open-toes), sweaters, medium-weight pants, and a lightweight, water-repellant coat. Bring an umbrella, but skip the mukluks and sealskin parka.

March 30th 1916.

The 49th Anniversary of the sign[ing]
of the Treaty of the Purchase of A[laska]
from Russia.

I introduced the first Al[aska]
Statehood Bill today.

H.R. 13987

I assume that L.P. Shackl[eford],
his friends are reporting —
that I have entered into [...]

A LITTLE ALASKAN HISTORY

The events that formed Alaska as a modern political and economic entity took place in the lifetime of most of today's cruise-ship passengers. We remember when Alaska joined the United States of America, when the Alcan Highway was built, when oil was discovered in the north. Fundamental steps accomplished long ago by other states, such as the disposition of land, continue to be taken in Alaska. The 49th state of the Union is creating itself before our very eyes.

THE FIRST PEOPLE

Today, crossing the Bering Strait has become something of a fad. In 1987, an Englishwoman swam the 56 miles of icy water that separate Asia and North America. In 1992, a Russian crew sailed from Cape Dezhneva, the easternmost point of Siberia, in a replica of the tiny 17th-century wooden schooners that brought Russian fur hunters to America. And in 1993, the members of an Alaskan church expedition were airlifted from the port of Wales to Little Diomede Island, an American possession in the middle of the Strait. They snowmobiled across three miles of ice to Russian-owned Big Diomede Island, and then were flown to Chukchi Peninsula in Siberia where they distributed gifts and clothing to Eskimos in several villages.

In Russia, the Alaskan missionaries met a group of Japanese adventurers who were planning to cross the Strait on foot, in imitation of the prehistoric people who entered North America from Asia eons ago. The ancient ancestors of the Native peoples of

Pages from the diary of James Wickersham—judge, politician, mountaineer—bring Alaska's history to life.

North America would not have got their feet wet when they made the crossing. The theory is that they followed the animals they hunted onto a dry, broad plain—the Bering Land Bridge. Exposed because ocean water had been absorbed by the growing continental glaciers, the so-called bridge was 1,200 miles wide from north to south. It remained passable until 10,000 years ago.

Beringia, as this land mass is known today, was most likely the route prehistoric peoples took to get to Alaska. Some of them drifted south as the ice sheets melted. Others stayed. The ancestors of the Athabaskan Indians spread into the Interior of Alaska and across northwest Canada; the ancestors of the Eskimo-Aleut occupied the coastal regions of Alaska and migrated through the Arctic to Greenland.

When these peoples first arrived is harder to pin down. Archeologists have found artifacts indicating that Eskimo hunters were on St. Lawrence Island in the Bering Sea 40,000 years ago. A Canadian archeologist has dated a bone-flake tool from a cave above the Bluefish River in the Canadian Yukon at 25,000 years. And in 1993, an American archeologist announced that while surveying on the northern slopes of Alaska's Brooks Range south of Point Barrow, he found paleo-Indian stone lance points that have been precisely carbon-dated at 11,700 years. The imagination is stirred by this discovery—that in a distant time hunters stood on a 200-foot-high mesa surveying the Alaskan plains for herds of bison and mammoth, and that their finely carved tools have endured many thousands of years longer than our own cultures.

THE RUSSIANS ARRIVE

Traditional history awards the first Alaska sighting in historic times to Vitus Bering, the persevering Dane, who undertook two monumental expeditions on behalf of Russia. Instructed by Peter the Great to locate the place where Russia joins North America, Bering set off from St. Petersburg in 1725, travelling arduously overland for three years before reaching the Pacific. In the summer of 1728, having built a small boat he named *Saint Gabriel,* he sailed north passing through a strait that would bear his name. Had it been a clear day, he might have seen Alaska. As it was, he continued north until he was certain the continents were separate. Sailing east the following spring, he again failed to find the American continent when he was blown off course in a gale.

Back in Saint Petersburg in 1730, Bering convinced the Admiralty College that America lay close to Kamchatka and that a second expedition should be financed. In 1733 he was appointed head of an overly ambitious endeavor that was mandated to explore and chart the Arctic and Siberian coasts, discover America and explore its coast to Mexico, establish trade relations with Japan, study natural history and ethnography, build lighthouses, Christianize the Natives of Siberia, and establish a postal system east of the Urals so that he could mail reports every couple of days.

Once again he trekked across the country, this time burdened by tons of equipment and 900 people, including scores of quarrelsome scientists. At last, on June 4, 1741, the 60-year-old Bering sailed from Avacha Bay. His two ships, which he had had to build, were soon separated. On July 15, Aleksey Tchirikoff, who was in charge of the *Saint Paul,* sighted what is believed to be Prince of Wales Island (west of Ketchikan). The following day, those aboard the *Saint Peter* saw a vast mountain range extending inland. Georg Wilhelm Steller, the German naturalist who was part of the expedition, reports that in this historical moment of discovery, Bering gazed at the land and shrugged his shoulders.

On July 20, Bering anchored off present-day Kayak Island (southeast of Cordova) and bestowed the name Cape St. Elias in honor of the prophet whose day it was. Steller had to plead with his incurious commander to be allowed to go ashore, and in ten hours he accomplished what he could, gathering specimens of plants and animals, and taking souvenirs from a dugout cellar stocked with arrows, seaweed straps, grass rope, and containers filled with smoked fish, which he said tasted better than the Kamchatkan version.

In quick order, Bering had the ship's casks filled with fresh water and headed home. It looked to Steller as though the sole result of the great expedition would be to carry water from America to Asia, but he was wrong. About 150 miles off the Russian mainland, Bering sought shelter from a storm on an island now named for him. The *Saint Peter* was wrecked, and the scurvy-weakened explorer and several of his crew died. The other men, having survived the winter on the meat of the abundant seals and otters, reached Russia in a makeshift boat bearing an unexpected cargo of furs.

Although official Russia showed no initial interest, individuals were quick to see the potential for profit, particularly in trade with China where one sea-otter fur was worth a Russian clerk's annual income. Within a year, the first merchant had built a *shitik*, a bargelike boat held together with leather thongs, and sent 30 hunters to Bering Island. On their second voyage, these *promyshlenniki* brought back the skins of 1,600 otter, 2,000 fur seal, and 2,000 blue fox, worth 200,000 rubles—a figure equal to the entire cost of the Bering expedition.

These lawless men hunted unhindered and unrestrained for several decades. They worked for shares of a voyage's profits, which in the early years were enough to make them rich had they not generally spent the winter back in Okhotsk, drinking and gambling and acquiring debts that forced them to hunt again. Unscientific as well as illiterate, they sailed into stormy and unpredictable waters, knowing nothing of marine navigation, a shortcoming shared by their navigators, who relied on acquired knowledge. One of these hapless men has given his name to a group of Alaskan islands—the Pribilofs—which he discovered while steering a drunken course. In 1745, the *promyshlenniki* found the outermost of the Aleutian Islands. They enslaved the Aleuts, forcing them to work until they dropped of exhaustion. As they depleted the animal stocks on each island, they moved eastward, within 20 years reaching the Gulf of Alaska.

For 30 years after Bering's discovery, Russians dominated these northern waters. But three European countries had been taking notice. In 1773 and several times thereafter, Spain sent expeditions to Alaska to check out the Russians' activities, possess land, and search for a passage through the continent. Although it had a strong claim to north Pacific territories, Spain withdrew from the region in 1795 when it surrendered a plot of land at Nootka Sound on Vancouver Island to the British. Alaskan place-names such as Valdez, Cordova, Revillagigedo, and Malaspina testify to the Spanish presence.

It was the English who were to leave an indelible mark on the north Pacific coast. They, too, believed in a northern passage through the continent and had offered a prize of 10,000 English pounds to the person who found it. On his third voyage in 1778, navigator James Cook, sailing north along the North American coast, sighted and named Capes Perpetua and Foulweather in Oregon, and Cape Flattery at the entrance to the Strait of Juan de Fuca. After spending a month in Nootka Sound on Vancouver Island, he sailed on through the Gulf of Alaska to Prince William Sound, where he went ashore on Kayak, the same island Bering had first sighted. Here, he left a bottle and two silver tu'penny pieces, evidence of his presence that has never been recovered. After sailing partway up Cook Inlet and concluding that it was a river, he followed the south shore of the Aleutians, passing into the Bering Sea and through Bering Strait. At 70°44' north, he was turned back by ice.

With him on that voyage, and a witness to his death in Hawaii later that year, was a young midshipman, George Vancouver. In the summers of 1792, 1793, and 1794 as captain of his own ship, Vancouver would complete a meticulous and arduous survey of the north Pacific coast, a survey that laid to rest the pipe dream of an easy passage through the continent, peppered the Canadian and Alaskan coasts with English names, and opened the area to commercial ventures. *(See* The Pacific Coast of George Vancouver, *page 54.)*

THE BARANOV ERA

By the 1790s, the cost of outfitting longer and longer voyages was putting many Russian fur merchants out of business. Among the surviving larger companies, one established the first permanent Russian settlement in Alaska, at Three Saints Bay on Kodiak Island. Grigory Shelikhov, a partner in the venture, lived there from 1784 to 1786 with his wife, Natalya, the first white woman in Alaska. Returning to Russia, Shelikhov hired the man who was to dominate Russian America for the next 27 years.

Aleksandr Baranov came to Alaska in 1791 and stayed until 1818, managing the Russian-American Company from the time it was formed in 1798. As the chief employee of the company that by royal charter had a monopoly on Russian trade in America, Baranov was the virtual governor of Alaska. He disciplined and punished his ruffian laborers but gave them ample reason to party with the aid of a home-brewed fruit and berry beverage. He established trade arrangements with British and American ships, buying their goods and selling his furs through them in China. Reaching far afield in an attempt to obtain secure supplies, he sent agents to King Kamehameha of Hawaii and established a fort in California sixty miles north of San Francisco Bay, which was to grow food for his ill-supplied colony. Fort Ross—from the old name Rossiia or Russia—remained in Russian hands until 1841 when it was bought by a Swiss rancher.

Baranov's dealings with the Natives were contradictory. He learned their languages, made his men treat their Native wives fairly, and took as his own wife the daughter of an Indian chief whom he described as a "Prince of Kenai." Even though he regarded the Aleuts with affection, he forced them to go on long hunting trips. He feared the Tlingits, who sometimes blocked the fur hunt and who destroyed the settlement of Mikhailovsk (Fort St. Michael), north of Sitka. In retaliation, he waged war on a Tlingit tribe, Kiks Adis, in 1804, pounding their sapling fort with fire from

Sitka's New Archangel Dancers
are a legacy of Alaska's Russian past.

the Russian ship *Neva*. Tlingit history says the battle reached a standoff, and the Russians displayed a white flag. A Kiks Adi woman, who was acting as mediator, told her people that the flag meant they would be wiped out clean as snow. And so they fled. (The site of that battle can be visited in Sitka National Historic Park.)

With Baranov Island cleared of Tlingits, Baranov began to build New Archangel on the site of present-day Sitka. When it was finished, the settlement had solid fortifications with 60 guns, streets with wooden sidewalks, cabins with flower gardens, a ship-yard managed by an American named Lincoln, an orchestra, and on a prominent height a two-story wooden kremlin. "Baranov's Castle" was residence and administrative center. Here Baranov maintained a 1,200-book library hung with paintings, and a ban-quet hall where amazed travellers, whose ships had been wel-comed in the harbor with gun salutes, attended brilliant balls.

Baranov had agreed to come to Alaska for only five years and frequently asked to be relieved of his duties. Two of the men who were to replace him died on the journey out. Finally, after surviv-ing an assassination attempt and periods of drunken despair, the 72-year-old ruler of Russian America was retired. He died in the Dutch East Indies in 1819 without seeing Russia again.

THE SALE

Under its second and third charters, the Company was governed by naval officers who were good at creating a bureaucracy but not as skilled at business as the encroaching Americans and British. They began their rule hampered by a czarist decree that kept for-eign ships from coming within 100 miles of the Russian coast in America. Intended to curtail foreign trading in Alaska, the ukase starved the colony of provisions. Clearly unable to maintain this isolationist stance, Russia signed treaties with the United States and Britain that reopened trade and defined the Russian territory. In 1824, an agreement with the U.S. set 54°40' as the southern Russian boundary. The next year, Britain and Russia signed the treaty that would later define the border between the U.S. and Canada.

Although official relations between Russia and the United States were extremely friendly, in Alaska itself the two nations were in conflict. In the mid-1850s, the Russian-American Company continued to ban foreigners from Alaskan ports, an unenforceable law, which American ships challenged by smuggling guns and liquor to trade for Native furs. The Czar's advisors wanted to sell the territory for a number of reasons. It would end the threat to the two countries' relations posed by these trade conflicts. It would avert a takeover of the territory by the United States, which seemed the likely consequence of American expansionism. And it would free Russia to deal with its Crimean War debts, its internal disorder, and its newly acquired territory in the Amur Valley in Siberia. The U.S. was eager to forestall a British takeover and to acquire a huge territory that Smithsonian scientists said held great natural resources.

The sale was negotiated in March 1867 by U.S. Secretary of State William H. Seward, an ardent proponent of Manifest Destiny, and the Russian ambassador Edouard de Stoeckel, who had helped convince the Czar to sell. Seward offered $5 million, but Stoeckel got the price up to $7.2 million. Although some newspapers blew frigid wind on the deal—coining labels such as Seward's Ice Box and Icebergia or Seward's Folly—most public comment approved the acquisition. The Senate ratified the treaty in 1867, but the House of Representatives had to be enticed by Seward to agree to pay the bill, which was done in July 1868.

The Russians handed over their well-organized territory to the American army on October 18, 1867, in a ceremony on the windy knoll in front of Baranov's Castle in New Archangel. With poignant stubbornness, the Russian flag entangled itself in its ropes and had to be cut down—causing Princess Maksutova, the wife of the chief manager of the Russian-American Company, to faint.

The event presaged 17 years of military misrule and neglect, which drove away the Russian families, who had been invited to remain. American settlers and speculators, who had hurried north, departed as quickly, discouraged by their inability to obtain title to land and by the rowdiness of the soldiers. These men contributed to the lawlessness of the period by teaching Hoochenoo Indians to distil a mind-blowing liquor, the kind we continue to call *hootch*.

The army ruled for a decade. When it left in 1877, the pretty little town of New Archangel—with its teahouses, theater, public library, two scientific institutes, and hospitals—had become Sitka, a ghost town, inhabited by only 20 families and stripped of public services. For the next two years, the law was a customs collector and a few deputies, who were unable to patrol hundreds of miles of coast. They watched helplessly as smugglers' boats brought in liquor, guns and opium. In 1879, as violence between whites and Natives increased, Sitkans petitioned the British Navy in Victoria, British Columbia: "We, the citizens of Sitka, Alaska, are now threatened with Massacre by Indians of this place." With the approval of Washington, Britain's Royal Navy sent a ship, and the predicted "entire demolition" of Sitka was averted. The U.S. Navy took over

The Russian Orthodox Bishop's House in Sitka: Father Ivan Veniaminov ministered to Natives during his 16 years here.

then, ruling with only slightly more approbation than the Army.

Years after the sale, Russian influence continued among those Natives who had been converted to the Orthodox faith. Early Russian priests had been chided for their neglect of missionary work, but those who came later Christianized the Natives and tried to improve their lives. One—Father Ivan Veniaminov— learned the Fox Aleut dialect, devised an alphabet, wrote an Aleut grammar, and translated religious books. In his Sitka seminar, he trained Natives for the priesthood. Back in Russia, he raised more money to support schools in Alaska than came from the American government.

Alaska was largely unexplored territory when it became an American possession. Private enterprise had instigated some exploration before the U.S. purchase: Western Union attempted and failed to connect America and Russia by telegraph cable in 1865–66, but the expedition mapped the entire 2,000 miles of the Yukon River and brought William Healy Dall to Alaska, where he stayed, chief among its naturalists. In the last decades of the 19th century, the exploration of Alaska was undertaken largely by federal government agencies—the Army, the Navy, the Revenue Marine (predecessor of the Coast Guard) and, in the final years, the United States Geological Survey. In the 1880s, the Army sent expeditions to the Yukon and Copper rivers. The most successful was Lt. Henry Trueman Allen's remarkable exploration of the Copper, Chitina, Tanana, and Koyukon rivers. In five months in 1885, this 26-year-old accurately mapped 1,500 miles of wilderness between the 61st parallel and the Arctic Circle. At the same time, the Navy and Revenue Marine competed in exploring rivers in the northwest, following the Kobuk from its mouth near Kotzebue, linking with the Colville, and ultimately reaching the Arctic Ocean.

The 1880 census found 430 white men in Alaska. Some fished for salmon, the first canneries having been built in 1878. Some worked for the San Franciscan-owned Alaska Commercial Company, which had a monopoly on the seal hunt in the Pribilof Islands and extended its influence to the Aleutians, Kodiak Island, and the Yukon River valley. And some were miners drawn by discoveries of gold as early as 1869. Then in 1880, two prospectors found placer gold in a stream near Juneau. This was followed by the discovery of a lode on Douglas Island, across the Gastineau Channel from Juneau, and the opening of the Treadwell Mine, which attracted hundreds of newcomers who found employment as shift-workers.

This growing white population created a demand for self-government. In 1881, Juneau miners sent a representative to lobby in Washington, and although there was opposition to territorial government, Congress agreed to end military rule and patched together the Organic Act of 1884, which made Alaska a district operating under the legal code of Oregon. The advance was minimal: Alaskans were denied a legislature, were governed by appointed officials, and still could not own land. In 1890, Juneau residents again sent a representative to Washington. This time he demonstrated Alaskan disaffection by offering to buy the territory back for twice what it had cost.

In April 1917, Juneau's Treadwell Mine was virtually destroyed when seawater swamped it during a cave-in.

THE GOLD RUSHES

The discovery of gold in Canada in 1896 played a significant role in Alaska's development. Ignoring newspaper warnings about hunger, hardship, and disappointment, 40,000 prospectors rushed to the Klondike in 1897 and 1898, many of them passing through Skagway or Dyea and dropping money in these lawless boom towns, before climbing over the White or Chilkoot passes into Canada. Finding the best stakes claimed, some of these stampeders returned to Alaska to prospect and joined the rushes that followed strikes in Nome in 1899 and Fairbanks in 1902.

With all this human traffic into its territory, Canada sought control of the heads of some fjords, such as the Lynn Canal where Skagway and Dyea sat. The Canadians cited ambiguities in the 1825 treaty between Russia and Britain that had defined the border the U.S. inherited in 1867. The Alaska-Canada Boundary Dispute was settled by an American-Canadian-British tribunal, which voted four to two in favor of the American position, the deciding vote being cast by the Briton.

Because the influx of argonauts doubled the Alaskan population in ten years, Congress saw the need in the last four years of the century to enact laws dealing with the economy and leading to self-government. The criminal code was altered to suit Alaskan needs. Settlers were allowed to have title to land, and railway companies could obtain a right-of-way to build. Nome and Fairbanks became the seats of new judicial districts, and the capital was moved from Sitka to Juneau. Towns were allowed to incorporate and elect councils. Business taxes were collected to pay the cost of governing the district, and business-licence fees were either turned over to the new towns or used to build roads, pay for education, and care for the insane. By 1906 the district had elected a non-voting delegate to the U.S. House of Representatives.

ELIZA, ALASKA'S
INTREPID TOURIST

Today, 700,000 visitors come to Alaska in a year, helping to make the tourist industry the second-largest primary employer. But the state's most ardent tourist may well have been one of its first.

Writer Eliza Ruhamah Scidmore was a passenger on the Pacific Coast Steamship Company vessel *Idaho* on its maiden glacier-seeking voyage in July, 1883. Only four years earlier, naturalist John Muir found and explored a bay of glaciers that Native seal hunters had described to him. Capt. James Carroll, following Muir's verbal instructions, eased the *Idaho* up the eastern shores of this bay looking for a large inlet. There, Muir assured him, he could safely anchor and see bergs breaking away from one of the largest glaciers. So it was, writes Scidmore, that Alaska's first cruise-ship passengers sailed into an unnamed and uncharted inlet and viewed for the first time the massive glacier at its head.

The next year, 1,650 people cruised the Inside Passage and Glacier Bay. Within a few years, Muir Glacier was world-famous and by 1890, the number of visitors had reached 25,000. Eliza was frequently among them. She spent four summers in Alaska, once camping for several weeks in a cabin at the side of Muir Glacier.

In a *National Geographic* article, she described 19th-century cruising in the bay. Because of the floating ice, boats had to stop, back up and proceed at half speed. There was the uncomfortable sound of paddle wheels crunching the ice.

In a more positive vein, in her 1896 *Appleton's Guide to Alaska,* she writes that the shipboard accommodations of the two major lines "are first class . . . catering to an expensive style of pleasure travel, offering most luxuries and comforts." Tourists could choose between mail steamers that took 14 to 18 days and called at many ports, canneries, and "out of the way places," or they could book on a passenger steamer, offering twice-a-month summer excursions arranged, like today's cruises, "to reach the places of interest at most convenient hours." The fare for a 12-day round trip from Tacoma, Washington, was $100.

Tourists of the 1880s and 1890s experienced Glacier Bay's marvels firsthand and at some risk. Steamers anchored about a quarter-mile below the east end of Muir Glacier and remained for six to eight hours. Once ashore, passengers followed a trail and boardwalk onto the surface of the ice, which they freely explored with the help of rented alpenstocks. Scidmore tells her readers of an easy walk up the east beach to the base of the ice-cliffs, but warns of the danger of being swept away at high tide when falling bergs could send great waves across the inlet. She confidently advises that it was also easy to climb to an 1,855-foot viewpoint known as the "Rat," which was "on the opposite bank of the raging ice torrent," and further on she describes a two-and-a-half hour hike to an elevation of 3,000 feet where one could look over the front wall of the glacier. It is an excellent spot for photographs, she says, while asking that people interested in contributing to a study of the glacier's retreat send their photos to the National Geographic Society in Washington.

Only a few years after the publication of Eliza's book, the situation in Muir Inlet had changed dramatically. On September 10, 1899, an earthquake devastated the glacier's terminus and clogged Glacier Bay with ice. For several years, ships could not get within five miles of the ice wall that Eliza had explored. Now, a century later, no tourist will ever see what Eliza so carefully described: the treacherous Dirt Glacier, with it sinkholes and quicksands; the splendid White Glacier, "with a black serpent of a medial moraine curving down its dazzling slope." These and other minor glaciers have melted away, and the great Muir Glacier, having retreated 25 miles, can no longer be seen from the cabin where Eliza once camped.

ALASKA FOR ALASKANS

Although Alaskans were infuriated by federal government interference in their affairs—notably the creation of the Tongass and Chugach national forests in southeastern Alaska, and President Theodore Roosevelt's closing of public lands to coal mining—they were by no means united in their desire for self-government. Conservationists feared the power it would give businessmen, and businessmen, notably the salmon packers, feared higher taxes.

James Wickersham—judge, politician, mountaineer—led the campaign for self-government. He had been appointed U.S. District Judge for Alaska in 1900; in 1908, he left the bench and became the unenfranchised delegate to Congress during the presidency of William H. Taft, who thought Alaska should be administered by the Department of War. Coincidentally, Taft lost the next election over an Alaskan issue—the Ballinger-Pinchot incident. (Secretary of the Interior Richard Ballinger was accused of having halted an investigation into the legality of some private coal-land claims in Alaska. Gifford Pinchot, Chief U.S. Forester, led a group of conservationists in demanding an investigation. Ballinger was exonerated, but Taft's support of Ballinger turned the 1912 election against him.)

In this climate, Wickersham succeeded in getting a territorial legislature approved by Congress. The Second Organic Act (1912) made the district of Alaska into a territory with a presidential appointee as governor and a legislature with limited powers. Its acts were subject to Congressional review, and it could not change existing laws on fish and game, which gave outsiders control of Alaska's natural resources. The first act of Alaskan legislators was to enfranchise women—six years before the other states did. Another early law allowed wives to dispose of property without their husband's permission.

During World War I, as men entered the military or left to work in southern armaments factories, Alaska's population declined. (By 1930, it had not returned to the 1910 level.) In the 1920s, the economy fed on the territory's natural resources, such as copper, gold, and timber. Salmon fishing was the uncertain mainstay. With the U.S. military as a major purchaser during the war, the industry had expanded but stocks had been depleted. Attempts by the Bureau of Fisheries to regulate the industry after the war were blocked by the outside-owned corporations that operated 143 canneries in Alaska. The many Alaskans who earned their living as independent fishermen resented federal control of their livelihood. Federal government conservationists prevailed in 1924 with the passing of the White Act, which required the industry to allow half the fish in most streams to escape.

The widely promoted potential for farming and ranching in Alaska's many fertile valleys brought only a few farmers to the territory. By 1929 there were about 4,000 acres under cultivation. Part of President Franklin D. Roosevelt's New Deal was a settlement program for the Matanuska Valley, which installed about 200 farming families in this beautiful area north of Anchorage. In the end, the hard work of farming in the valley's unpredictable climate and

Anchorage was born in 1915 with
the U.S. government land auction.

the high cost of shipping to an outside market defeated the colonists. Cattle and sheep ranching also failed, but a reindeer industry, operated by white people and employing Natives, succeeded for a time. The small number of animals introduced in 1891 increased to 700,000 in 40 years. Exports began in 1915, and in 1930 Seattle suppliers were buying the meat of 30,000 animals a year.

Transportation was the key to Alaskan development. A road-building program, begun in 1905, required every man to contribute two days' labor a year. Nearly 5,000 miles of roads and trails were built. There were privately owned railways, such as the Copper River and Northwestern Railroad, and a federal government-financed railroad from Seward to Fairbanks, finished in 1923. The truly effective means of linking the vast territory came with the arrival of the airplane in the 1920s. By 1937, Alaska had 97 civilian airports and a regular airmail service, and distant communities could finally be reached year-round.

WORLD WAR II

As Europe edged toward war in 1939, Alaska's vulnerability to Japanese attack was apparent. Thousands of troops and construction workers were brought north. They built bases at Sitka, Fairbanks, Anchorage, Kodiak, and Unalaska, and in eight remarkable months in 1942 constructed the 1,422-mile-long Alaska-Canada Military Highway from Dawson Creek, B.C., to Delta Junction, 100 miles east of Fairbanks. *(See* The Alcan—or the Canal?—Highway, *page 42.)* In June 1942, the Japanese bombed Dutch Harbor and occupied two of the outer Aleutian islands. A year later, American troops retook Attu Island—an exercise that cost 6,000 American and Japanese lives—and reoccupied Kiska, which the Japanese had evacuated.

The war transformed Alaska. A billion dollars had been spent on roads, airfields, docks, wharves, and breakwaters. With the recognition of Alaska's strategic importance in the Cold War, military spending continued on projects such as the Distant Early Warning

System. To accommodate a growing population, construction in the civilian sector kept pace. Soldiers who had served in Alaska during the war returned to settle, as did professional people. By 1960, the population was triple what it had been at the beginning of the war.

STATEHOOD

With patience and not a little ingenuity, Alaskans worked their way through the long process of achieving statehood. Early ill-fated bills had been presented to the U.S. Congress by James Wickersham in 1916 and by territorial senator Anthony J. Dimond in 1943. Fifty-eight per cent of Alaskans voted for statehood in a 1946 referendum, and President Harry S. Truman gave his support in his State of the Union address that year and in a long message to Congress two years later. Nevertheless, a 1950 bill died, after passing in the House and being revised in the Senate.

The statehood movement faced powerful opponents: the Seattle-based fish canning industry, which was making millions out of Alaska; Southern politicians, who feared that an Alaskan delegation to Congress would vote for civil-rights legislation; and President Dwight D. Eisenhower, who thought Alaskans would elect Democrats and wanted to protect the small Republican majority in the House. In 1954, a 14-member delegation from "Operation Statehood" chartered a plane and flew to Washington where they met with the President and convinced him of their determination.

To further show their readiness to govern themselves, Alaskans chose delegates for a convention, which in 75 days in 1955 and 1956 drew up a state constitution. The Convention also followed the example of Tennessee in choosing an unofficial congressional delegation—which for the next two years effectively lobbied in Washington. Finally, with Eisenhower's request that Congress admit both Hawaii and Alaska, a bill passed the House in May 1958, and the Senate in June. Alaska formally entered the Union on January 3, 1959.

OIL AND TROUBLED WATERS

Two cataclysmic events marked the new state's first decade. On Good Friday, March 27, 1964, the largest earthquake ever recorded in North America hit southcentral Alaska, killing 115 Alaskans and generating tidal waves that claimed the lives of 16 people in California and Oregon. The quake devasted Anchorage, Whittier, Valdez, Cordova, Seward and Kodiak, and caused damage amounting to nearly $300 million. *(See* The Bad Friday Quake, *page 139.)*

The second cataclysm was of an entirely different and more long-lasting nature: the discovery of a vast oil deposit at Prudhoe Bay on the Arctic coast by Atlantic Richfield in 1968. The following year, in one dramatic day, the state auctioned leases on 450,000 acres on the North Slope. Suddenly, Alaska had $900 million in the bank and could anticipate annual royalties on an estimated 9.6 billion barrels of oil under the ground at Prudhoe Bay. But it soon became apparent that the oil would remain in the north until an economical way could be found to transport it south. Three oil companies formed the Trans-Alaska Pipeline System (TAPS) and began the long process of overcoming objections and obstacles to a pipeline transecting the state. Chief among these obstacles were Native land claims.

Land disputes had been virtually guaranteed by the statehood act, which had given Alaska the right to select 103.3 million acres from vacant, unreserved, and unappropriated lands. At the same time, the act protected the rights or title to lands held by Eskimos, Indians, or Aleuts. As the state Department of Natural Resources made its land choices, the Natives, perceiving the threat to their way of life, protested the selections and filed their own claims. In 1966, the indigenous peoples founded the Alaska Federation of Natives to pursue their collective interests. In 1967, Secretary of the Interior Stewart Udall put a freeze on the transfer of land claimed by Natives.

Helping celebrate 50 years of the Alaska Highway:
Fred and Sandra Tremblay's 1915 Cadillac ➤

Realizing that Native claims would block their project, various oil companies lobbied for the Alaska Native Claims Settlement Act (ANCSA), which was passed in 1971. By 1973, the year of the Arab oil embargo, Alyeska Pipeline Service Company (which had originated as TAPS) received permission to build an 800-mile-long pipeline from Prudhoe Bay to Valdez. Opened in 1977, the line zigzags south over three mountain ranges and under hundreds of rivers and streams. Oil first flowed into the line on June 20, 1977, and took 38 days to reach its seaport destination. *(See* Prudhoe Bay, *page 183.)*

Two decades ago, the Alaska Native Claims Settlement Act was regarded as a model. ANCSA abolished aboriginal rights, including the rights of hunting, fishing, and trapping. In compensation for the loss of their vast hunting grounds, Alaska Natives received $962.5 million and title to one-ninth of the state—44 million acres of land. Natives living in Alaska were enrolled as stockholders in one of 12 regional corporations and, if they were villagers, in one of 200 village corporations. A thirteenth regional corporation was created for Alaskan Natives living outside the state. The corporations received a share of the compensation payment to capitalize business ventures.

ANCSA was an attempt to give Alaskan Natives the means and the expertise to survive in the modern world, and to an extent it has done that. Some regional corporations have been successful in market terms; some have chosen to earn less money in order to employ a higher percentage of their shareholders. The University of Anchorage's Institute of Social and Economic Research reports that "the real accrued wealth of the regional corporations in 1990 was about 10 per cent more than their initial capital." *(See* The Native Way, *page 111.)*

ANCSA contained the source of another battle over land use. The d-2 controversy, as it is known, arose from a paragraph in the act that allowed the Secretary of the Interior to hold up to 80 million acres of federal lands as possible wilderness. Alaskans were infuriated by Washington's interference, but they were also divided among themselves about land use, with environmentalists pitted against developers. The issue was complicated by the ambitions of four federal agencies: the National Park Service, the Fish and Wildlife Service, the Forest Service, and the Bureau of Land Management. The upshot was the Alaska National Interest Lands Conservation Act of 1980, which increased the national conservation areas by 106 million acres. In 1990, the Tongass Timber Reform Act added five more wilderness areas and expanded the Kootznoowoo Wilderness. Although 150 million acres of federal lands in Alaska are now national conservation areas, only about 15 per cent of the state is designated wilderness. The Bureau of Land Management presides over the continuing distribution of land to the Native corporations, the state, and private citizens.

For the moment, Alaskans find that their fortunes depend primarily upon the world price of oil. If the price drops, so do state revenues, 85 per cent of which come from royalties and taxes on North Slope crude. When prices were high, legislators abolished personal income tax. Seeing the state strapped for cash in 1993, a former governor commented, "Eliminating the income tax entirely was probably the dumbest thing we ever did."

Alaskans have attempted to preserve their oil income by establishing a trust fund. The Alaska Permanent Fund, built up from mineral-lease rentals and royalties, had assets of $14 billion in 1993, making it the largest pool of money in the nation. Residents receive an annual remittance from the fund.

Boom or bust has been the story of Alaska's economy ever since the days of the Russian fur hunters. But like them, Alaskans have always believed that the prize was worth the pain, the paydirt repaid the drudgery. The reality of the 49th state has more than matched its promise.

THE ALCAN—OR THE CANAL?—HIGHWAY

When Fred and Sandra Tremblay of Vancouver, British Columbia, drove the Alaska Highway in 1992, they had a rougher ride than most people do these days. The highway's 50th anniversary was celebrated that year with more than 200 events, including the car rally in which the Tremblays participated. They found the road to be surprisingly smooth, now asphalt-surfaced from Mile 0 in British Columbia through Mile 1,520 at Fairbanks. Their problem was that shock absorbers were not standard equipment on 1915 Cadillacs. By far the oldest entrant in the rally, the sturdy Caddy made the one-way trip in a week at a dignified, if bone-shaking, pace of 45 miles an hour.

The $150-million Alaska-Canada Military Highway has been called the major engineering feat of the 20th century. In eight months and a dozen days, 11,000 U.S. soldiers and 16,000 U.S. and Canadian civilians punched a 1,422-mile road from Dawson Creek in B.C. to Delta Junction, the official terminus. There the road joined the Richardson Highway for a final 100-mile run to Fairbanks.

The myth is that the highway was needed as a supply route in case the Japanese invaded the Alaskan mainland. The reality, according to Canadian historian M. V. Bezeau: the U.S. War Department and the Canadian–American Permanent Joint Board on Defense had taken the position that such a road would be of little defensive value. After Pearl Harbor, however, the War Department decided that the pressure of war could be used to get Canada to provide the right-of-way for a road that the U.S. wanted to build eventually anyway.

President Franklin D. Roosevelt gave the go-ahead on February 11, 1942, and Canada acquiesced two days later. Before the end of the month, the first soldiers from seven Army regiments, three of them segregated black units commanded by white officers, invaded Dawson Creek—with its one movie theatre, one liquor store, and 600 residents, some of whom had never seen a black person. Many soldiers, having never known snow, suffered terribly in the cold.

Considering that 80 per cent of the road is in Canada, it might more accurately have been called the Canada-Alaska Military Highway. Then, instead of the Alcan, its nickname would have been "the Canal"—a not-too-farfetched description of what its builders created in 1942. Working from both the Alaskan and Canadian ends, army engineers sought the easiest path through unbroken wilderness and five mountain ranges and over more than a hundred streams. Wherever possible, they detoured around the dreaded muskeg (which accounts for the road's still meandering route). This boggy material insulates permanently frozen subsoil. To get to a firmer footing, the roadbuilders tried scraping the muskeg off or covering it with gravel. Either way, the permafrost melted, and the roadway became a truck-swallowing canal. The solution, which required thousands of trees cut from nearby forests, was to place logs on the muskeg and build a gravel roadbed over this corduroy surface.

On September 24, the north-going crew met the south-going crew at a place now known as Contact Creek. The road was officially opened on November 20, but needed another 11 months of work to make it passable and to repair the 150 bridges washed out the first spring. In 1947, the road opened to unrestricted travel. As late as 1982 only a quarter of it was paved, and the Alcan became famous for destroying windshields, tires, and axles.

The Alcan's attractions are legendary: in Alaska, the town of North Pole, with its Santa Claus House and unbeatable postmark; in Canada, Watson Lake, where travellers have mounted 13,000 signs pointing to their hometowns; and Liard River with its hot-springs baths in the woods. Still, for Sandra Tremblay, simply looking out the window was the best. Wrapped in a quilt to keep warm, she admired the autumnal reds and golds in hoar-frosted forests beneath snow-tipped mountains. A bear approached the car; salmon leapt out of streams; eagles hovered overhead. "The scenery was unreal," she says.

THE LURE AND LORE OF THE INSIDE PASSAGE

It is the longest sheltered inland waterway in the world, 1,000 miles of protected Pacific Ocean from Puget Sound in Washington State to Skagway in southeastern Alaska. The longest, and one of the most seductive such channels in the magnitude and magnificence of its land and water scapes, its 50,000 square miles of mountain, sea, and ice. Carved by glaciers between the Coast Range peaks of mainland British Columbia and the umpteen offshore islands to the west, the Inside Passage is so extraordinary that the usual superlatives sputter out. Even someone as eloquent as the pioneering American naturalist John Muir seemed at a loss for words reporting his trip through the Passage in 1879: "Day after day, we seemed to float in a true fairyland, each succeeding view seeming more and more beautiful. . . . Never before this had I been embosomed in scenery so hopelessly beyond description."

In the day and a half it takes most large cruise ships to ply this passage serenely northward, through straits and narrows to Ketchikan, you will have been gradually introduced to the grandeur of the Pacific Northwest coast that reaches its crescendo in Alaska—the inconstant sea in all her humors, the endless armada of uninhabited islets, the rain-forested flanks of sky-poking mountains, the slow-moving fields of ice, and the fretwork of steep-sided fjords indenting the coast which, if straightened, would stretch about 17,000 miles. You will soon begin to pick out wildlife from this distracting backdrop: posses of sunbathing sea lions; pods of whales, humpbacks breaching and killer whales hunting; and loons and herons and a lone bald eagle circling the salmon'd sea.

"A true fairyland": the seductive
channel of the Inside Passage

Beyond Vancouver, the signs of human life will be scant—in only two spots along the Passage, the central Coast Salish village of Bella Coola and the northern port city of Prince Rupert are there roads that link with the rest of civilization. You'll spot some fishing and logging towns, a few isolated Native hamlets and abandoned fish camps, unmanned lighthouses, and the broken bones of long-ago boats.

There will be the occasional lonely vessels threading through what is really not one marine highway but an unknowable labyrinth of large and small channels. Most frequently visible might be fish boats seeking crab, herring, halibut, cod, sole, red snapper, and five species of salmon. Crab boats of about 120 feet setting their traps for Dungeness and Alaska Kings. Halibut schooners two-thirds that size paying out miles of lines studded with hooks. Forty- and 50-foot seiners spreading their saucer-shaped nets to enclose a school of salmon like a massive purse. Smaller trollers long-lining like the halibut boats. Other workhorses navigate these waters: tugboats towing rafts of logs or barges topped by loading cranes; local ferries scooting across the channels; large B.C. and Alaskan government ferry vessels carrying cars and passengers. And sometimes canoes and kayaks, sailboats and other pleasure craft braving the Passage, little cousins to the 18 or more cruise ships that make at least 236 sailings between Vancouver and Alaska each summer.

CENTURIES-OLD HISTORY

This sparse if constant stream of human traffic evokes the history of this place. Imagine the dugouts and sailing ships, the steamboats and fishing schooners. For centuries, the Inside Passage was an Indian pathway—in particular, the Route of the Haidas, whose warriors raided and traded its length and who still traverse the worst of its waters from their northerly home in B.C.'s Queen Charlotte Islands. The white man came from opposite directions. First, the Greek explorer who gave his Spanish name to the southern

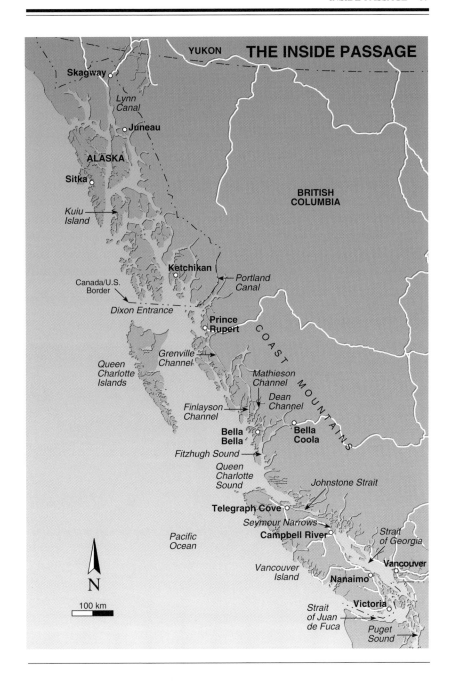

THE INSIDE PASSAGE

YUKON

Skagway

Lynn
Canal

Juneau

ALASKA

Sitka

Kuiu
Island

BRITISH
COLUMBIA

Ketchikan

Portland
Canal

Canada/U.S.
Border

Dixon Entrance

Prince
Rupert

COAST MOUNTAINS

Grenville
Channel

Queen
Charlotte
Islands

Mathieson
Channel

Dean
Channel

Finlayson
Channel

Bella
Bella

Bella
Coola

Fitzhugh Sound

Queen
Charlotte
Sound

Johnstone Strait

Telegraph Cove

Seymour Narrows

Campbell River

Strait
of Georgia

Pacific
Ocean

Vancouver
Island

Vancouver

Nanaimo

N

100 km

Victoria

Strait
of Juan
de Fuca

Puget
Sound

Strait of Juan de Fuca, a century after Columbus arrived in America. Then the Russian fur traders from Siberia who reached the northern end of the Passage in what is now Alaska. Next, Spanish ships sailing north, seeking a way through the continent, though Spain would cede its claims in 1795 to ever-venturing Britain, personified by Captains Cook and Vancouver. (*See* The Pacific Coast of George Vancouver, *page 54.*)

The first steamship to run the Passage continuously was the S.S. *Beaver,* launched in England by the Hudson's Bay Company in 1835. The elm-keeled paddle wheeler, 100 feet long, had several lives: for 26 years, trading for the fur company, with a cannon and large crew to keep the peace; for another 8, surveying the coastline for the Royal Navy; and for her final 20 years in private service, towing lumber and coal ships, supplying lumber camps, and

For half a century, the S.S. *Beaver* ran the Passage in many guises.

toting passengers. Refitted with fresh boilers at least five times, grounded and holed more than once, the *Beaver* ran aground finally in 1888 at Prospect Point off Vancouver's Stanley Park, where cruise ships now pass as they enter and leave Burrard Inlet.

The Inside Passage had increasing traffic after 1867, as seal hunters and some settlers headed for the new U.S. territory of Alaska. The first cruise ships to carry sight-seeing passengers as well as cargo for the villages and canneries along the waterway were lavishly fitted Pacific Coast Steamship vessels. The *Idaho* took the initial batch of tourists to view Glacier Bay in 1883 *(see* Eliza, Alaska's Intrepid Tourist, *page 32)*, and other paddle wheelers like the S.S. *Ancon* followed in her wake; within a year, there were 1,650 people cruising up here. A decade and a half later, the coast was awash in mostly American stampeders lusting after the gold in Canada's Yukon Territory. The Trail of '98 began in the Lower 48, usually in San Francisco and Seattle. By early that year, 40 ships were running regularly to Alaska from San Francisco— "greater in point of numbers, efficiency and carrying capacity than any fleet ever collected in any harbor in the world to engage in a specific enterprise," the local *Examiner* said. The enterprise: to carry six million tons of freight and 100,000 gold-seekers in a mad rush to the Klondike via Skagway, Alaska, the opportunistic settlement newly born at the end of the Passage. Typical of the fleet was the tiny steamer *Al-ki*, the first to leave after taking aboard 900 sheep, 65 cattle, 30 horses, 350 tons of supplies, and 110 people. Not all the ships arrived—many crashed, a few exploded—and those that did succeed often disgorged a cargo of ill, starving, miserable men, women, and animals.

The gold rush ebbed within a couple of years. And it was well into the new century when entrepreneurs voyaged up the Passage in search of other resources which it was (and remains) rich in: fish and lumber. Some of them stayed on this coast, living isolated lives on the islands, the mainland, or even on the water in floating camps.

You'll catch intriguing glimpses of them along the way. Cruising north from Vancouver—past the urban oasis of Stanley Park and beneath the graceful span of Lions Gate Bridge, named for the leonine peaks behind it—your ship enters the Strait of Georgia. Twenty miles wide, the strait begins in northern Washington and extends 100 miles and more until dissolving into a confusion of channels off the city of Campbell River (pop.: 21,200), halfway up Vancouver Island. Your route is through Discovery Passage, where ships must always be cautious. Here, between the big island and Quadra and Maud islands, tides of up to 17 miles an hour rush through Discovery's skinniest, trickiest stretch: Seymour Narrows. Beset with shifting currents and whirlpools, it's only 800 yards wide and makes a turn of almost 90 degrees.

THE BLASTING OF RIPPLE ROCK

Until the late 1950s, the narrows were perilous because of the submerged mini-mountain at their center. That year, in one of the most extraordinary feats in Canadian engineering history, the largest man-made, non-atomic explosion of its time blew Ripple Rock apart. Old Rip had two pinnacles—one 160 by 300 feet, the other 150 by 200—lurking at most only 19 feet below the water at low tide. Conflicting records reveal that at least 114 people had died here when an equal number of vessels, including 14 large ships, were sunk or damaged. The first known victim was the American gunboat U.S.S. *Saranac*, in 1875. Surprisingly, the city of Victoria wanted the rock to stay as a natural base for a potential bridge between Vancouver Island and the mainland. Mariners' demands to blast it away proved more persuasive. The idea was to drill a half-mile-long tunnel from Maud Island under the narrows and up into Old Rip, and there plant a special new high explosive so carefully that the resulting shower of shattered rocks would land in deep underwater holes—to avoid later dredging. The $3.1-million project used 1,375 tons of Nitramex 2H, enough to lift the Empire State Building a mile high. On April 5, 1958, as the world watched on television, engineers lit the 5.3 miles of fuse. Within moments, an estimated 350,000 tons of rock shards and 370,000 tons of water erupted a thousand feet into the sky. The explosion sheared at least 40 feet from Ripple Rock's peaks. Seymour Narrows was suddenly much safer.

Eventually every ship and boat voyaging up the Passage has to contend with Johnstone Strait. About 60 miles long, it lies just above Discovery Passage, off Vancouver Island, roughly between the port communities of Rock Bay and Telegraph Cove. It's a wide, windswept, choppy channel in a glorious mountain setting. The loftiest summit to the northeast, near the head of Knight Inlet, is Mount Waddington, second-highest peak in British Columbia. Where Vancouver Island's Tsitika River emerges, a dozen miles below Telegraph Cove, the recess of Robson Bight is an ecological reserve where killer whales gather and rub themselves against the

The 1958 explosion of Ripple Rock to make
passage through Seymour Narrows safer.

cliffs—the world's premier place to view orcas. Just north of Telegraph Cove, on Cormorant Island, the Kwakiutl Indian community of Alert Bay still has some of the world's tallest totem poles.

From here you cruise through Queen Charlotte Strait, passing the town of Port Hardy near the top of Vancouver Island, and enter the lone unsheltered patch of the Passage, open wide to the Pacific—Queen Charlotte Sound. The names on the map are expressive: Storm Islands, Cape Caution, Safety Cove. Vessels have to traverse Queen Charlotte's unruly 40 miles to reach Fitzhugh Sound and dart between Hunter and Denny islands and up past Campbell Island to Bella Bella. This fishing village, at the mouth of Dean Channel, is named for its local band of 1,400 Natives who call themselves Heiltsuk. An ingenious people, their ancestors built a

When Captain Vancouver's expedition sailed by in the late 18th century, present-day Glacier Bay was sealed by ice.

boat in the 19th century modelled after the S.S. *Beaver,* scooping out a tree trunk 30 feet long and carving and painting it to resemble the Inside Passage steamship. Today their houses, which you can easily see on the port side travelling north, ascend a hillside community that has revitalized itself in recent years, building new homes and apartments and developing businesses that include fishing for herring roe on kelp, a delicacy in Japan.

BIG LYNN

You then wind through Seaforth Channel, and the Passage's deepest waters, Finlayson Channel, which descends nearly a half-mile; cruise up Graham Reach and the steep, treed cliffs of Grenville Channel, only a quarter-mile wide; and perhaps catch a nighttime glimpse of Prince Rupert, the biggest city on the B.C. mainland coast above Vancouver. Founded by an American, Charles Hayes, this major fishing port of 17,000, only 90 miles south of Ketchikan, is the northern terminus of the B.C. Ferries system and a launch pad for the region's big-game hunting and sportfishing for salmon and halibut.

Soon you're into the broad reaches of Dixon Entrance, passing Dundas Island and crossing the unmarked Canada-U.S. boundary into Alaska. The next morning, along Tongass Narrows, you'll disembark at your first stop, Ketchikan. From here, cruise ships of various sizes travel individual routes and berth at different ports along the Inside Passage as far north as Skagway. If you reach this terminus of the inland waterway, you'll have gone up the 90-mile straightaway of the Lynn Canal, a wide cleft gouged by glaciers during an early Ice Age. One of Alaska's most scenic fjords, it's lined with tall mountains streaked with glaciers and waterfalls. In a modern vessel during the cruise season, when the still blue water reflects like a looking glass, you won't taste the canal's reputation for trouble. But give a thought to those who came before you who had to face the Big Lynn's worst conditions in lesser craft.

THE PACIFIC COAST OF GEORGE VANCOUVER

Had you sought Capt. George Vancouver's advice about cruising to Alaska, you might have stayed home. He found the Pacific Northwest coast a "dreary and uninteresting" place, but he was focused less on scenery than on the intricate task of mapping every foot of its convoluted indentations. Anytime you go out on deck, you will likely be seeing what he saw 200 years ago—and chances are you'll be looking at one of the 400 bodies of water or points of land he named.

It's tempting to imagine Vancouver taking compass bearings and soundings from the comfort of the *Discovery* or the *Chatham*. Indeed, he made this sort of running survey until he reached the Strait of Juan de Fuca, where he realized that his ships couldn't get close enough to shore. For the next three summers, he or his officers Joseph Whidbey and James Johnstone would leave their ships at a safe anchorage and set out in small boats, rowed by crewmen up inlets, into bays, and around islands. Charting around Portland Canal—the Alaska-British Columbia boundary—Vancouver kept his men out 23 days, during which they rowed more than 700 miles in order to move the survey north by only 60.

On his first voyage in 1792, after exploring Puget Sound and the site of present-day Seattle, he anchored in Birch Bay just south of the 49th parallel and rowed north into Boundary Bay, 'round Point Roberts and into Burrard Inlet—becoming the first European to see the site of what is now Vancouver, the starting point of today's northbound cruises. On your way out of or into Vancouver, you'll pass Point Grey on the north side of Burrard Inlet. It was here that Vancouver, much to his annoyance, found two Spanish vessels anchored. He had hoped to explore the area solo.

In 1792 and 1793, Vancouver worked from south to north. The first year, having charted between Vancouver Island and the mainland, he entered Queen Charlotte Sound, harboring at Calvert Island where he decided to return south for the winter. In the following year, he began where he'd left off. Just northeast of Bella Bella at the entrance to Echo Harbour in Dean Channel on June 4, he stood at the very spot where six weeks later the first European to cross North America would inscribe on a rock, "Alexander Mackenzie, from Canada, by land." A little farther north of Bella Bella, Johnstone's crew ate mussels for breakfast in a cove off Mathieson Channel, and immediately became sick. One of them died a few hours later, an unwitting victim of paralytic shellfish poisoning. That summer's work advanced the survey only 300 miles north, ending at Cape Decision on the southern tip of Kuiu Island, one of the islands of the Alaska Panhandle.

In the third year, Vancouver sailed directly to the Gulf of Alaska and proceeded southeast toward the Panhandle. Too sick to do the work himself, he sent out crews under Whidbey and Johnstone. The charting of Cook Inlet, which proved it was not the river Cook had assumed, took four weeks in April and May. Here, Vancouver ignored the repeated requests of the Russian-American Company's Aleksandr Baranov for a meeting, but stopped on the Kenai Peninsula to visit a Russian camp, the smell of which he described as "extremely offensive." In Prince William Sound, Whidbey's encampment just missed being buried by an avalanche, and his men first heard the thunderous sound of icebergs breaking off from glaciers.

In July, the expedition entered Cross Sound, north of Chicagof Island, and found it filled with huge chunks of ice. Whidbey reported a glacier at the entrance to present-day Glacier Bay. Now close to finishing, Whidbey and Johnstone charted Icy Strait, Lynn Canal (named for Vancouver's birthplace, King's Lynn, Norfolk), Stephens Passage, and Chatham Strait. When the two met in Frederick Sound south of Admiralty Island in August, they realized that the survey was complete and celebrated with a double portion of liquor. Vancouver returned to England and died four years later at the age of 40.

GLACIERS: THE POWER AND THE GLORY

For more than a century, Hubbard Glacier in Southeastern Alaska had been advancing gradually, but relentlessly. Then in 1986, icy tributaries of the longest valley glacier in North America began to accelerate into Disenchantment Bay. As this expansive stream of ice spread forward from its head in the St. Elias Mountains, the glacier blocked off Russell Fjord. The ragged ice dam trapped porpoises, harbor seals and otters in what became an instant lake, which grew with glacial meltwater and threatened to spill over into a prized salmon river that was the economic lifeline of a remote community. The international scientific excitement about this phenomenon focused less on the imaginative rescue efforts to free the sealife and more on the still-mysterious nature of glaciers themselves, especially on the mechanisms by which they move: advancing and retreating, and often inexplicably surging and galloping.

As wildlife rescuers guided seals across an earth bridge and lowered them on stretchers into salty water, glaciologists were intent on studying the factors that made the 95-mile-long glacier advance. At first they speculated that they were witnessing a true surge, when glaciers can extend themselves at a hundred times the normal pace in a process that is just starting to be understood. Only well after the dam broke in an hours-long deluge and the lake became a fjord again did the scientists declare that Hubbard had not surged. It was simply progressing normally along an inevitable path predicted a quarter-century before.

Yet it was another compelling reminder that Alaska's glaciers, like others around the world, are among nature's most destructive forces: flows of living ice which can ruthlessly crush and carve the

A helicopter ferries cruise-ship
passengers on to Mendenhall Glacier.

landscape and alter people's lives. In the words of an admiring 19th-century scientist, they are God's Great Plough. Glaciers contain within their frozen clutches 90 per cent of the globe's aboveground water; if they were to melt, most major ports would disappear, and the whole of Florida, for instance, would survive as only a few small islands. The world's glaciers are like immense icy currents caught in the freeze frame of a camera—and nowhere can they be better captured by eye and lens than in Alaska.

Glacial ice cloaks one-tenth of the earth's surface, but it is in Southeast Alaska, where geographical and meteorological conditions combine in ideal equilibrium, that glaciers can be seen most conveniently and at their most spectacular. Outside the polar regions, they and their handiwork loom largest here. Glacier Bay, a regular stop on most cruise voyages, may be the most magnificent example anywhere of a glacially sculpted complex of fjords, and its St. Elias and (misnamed) Fairweather ranges are the most elaborately glaciated mountains. And this is one of only three places in the world where tidewater glaciers exist. Their endless calving, or breaking off, creates instant icebergs which crash into the sea with a sound that the native Tlingit called white thunder.

A CENTURY OF VISITORS

In size, Alaska's estimated 100,000 glaciers range from leftover fragments of less than a square mile to tremendous sheets of ice that spread for hundreds of square miles. In accessibility, they can be as close at hand as the Mendenhall, just outside Juneau, which as America's most visited glacier can easily be reached by land and helicopter. Or they can be as remote as the glaciers in the high peaks of the Brooks Range north of the Arctic Circle. Perhaps the most approachable, in terms of sheer comfort, are the St. Elias' 16 tidewater glaciers in Glacier Bay National Park and Preserve, which visitors have been viewing from the decks of tour ships for more than a century. On July 7, 1890, the American naturalist John Muir noted with bemusement the arrival of the steamer *Queen* at the base of the glacier named for him: "She arrived about 2:30 P.M. with two hundred and thirty tourists. What a show they made with their ribbons and kodaks!"

John Muir, who had been visiting here since 1879, was the first to write extensively and eloquently about Glacier Bay and its rich lode of glaciers. His passion for them is expressed in this typically poetic passage from *Travels in Alaska*: "The whole front of the glacier is gashed and sculptured into a maze of shallow caves and crevasses, and a bewildering variety of novel architectural forms, clusters of glittering lance-tipped spires, gables, and obelisks, bold outstanding bastions and plain mural cliffs, adorned along the top with fretted cornice and battlement, while every gorge and crevasse, groove and hollow, was filled with light, shimmering and throbbing in pale-blue tones of ineffable tenderness and beauty. The day was warm, and back on the broad melting bosom of the glacier . . . many streams were rejoicing, gurgling, ringing, singing, in frictionless channels worn down through the white disintegrated ice of the surface into the quick and living blue, in which they flowed with a grace of motion and flashing of light to be found only on the crystal hillocks and ravines of a glacier."

Muir, the Scottish-born conservationist and crusader for national parks, was in Alaska to continue investigating the new theory of glacial erosion. In the continental United States, he had attributed the configuration of Yosemite Valley to such erosion, after painstakingly crawling around on all fours with a magnifying glass to document suggestive scratches in the bedrock. At Glacier Bay, he travelled by steamer, in canoes with Tlingit Indian guides, and on foot with his faithful dog, Stickeen (named for a local Indian tribe). One day, dog and master were alone on a glacier when they encountered a crevasse, which Muir could traverse only by chiselling foot- and finger-holds across a narrow bridge of ice. At one point this sliver of a span was a mere four inches wide, and Stickeen howled in panic at the thought of crossing it. Only at the

With the roar of "white thunder," the Columbia Glacier calves into Glacier Bay. ➤

last moment did he chance it—"with a nervous spring he whizzed up and passed me out on to the level ice, and ran and cried and barked and rolled about fairly hysterical in the sudden revulsion from the depth of despair to triumphant joy."

In risking his life, Muir was reaping the joy of chronicling a place that barely existed only a hundred years before, when Captains Cook and Vancouver, on separate voyages, had sailed right by a mammoth glacier then sealing the mouth of the bay. Cook, who had seen glaciers in the Antarctic, didn't even recognize this one. But Vancouver, while exploring College Fjord in Prince William Sound in 1794, did record the first account of an Alaskan glacier calving. The British explorers were preceded in the area not only by Russians but also by a Frenchman, the Count of La Pérouse, who precisely located five nearby glaciers and whose name now graces another ice stream on the coastline of Glacier Bay National Park. By 1879, the bay's ice sheet, at points 4,000 feet thick, had retreated 65 miles from the mouth—one example of a rate of glacial retreat that remains the fastest in the world. Today, only two of the glaciers are advancing; the rest remain stable or continue to withdraw.

"GOD'S GREAT PLOUGH"

At Glacier Bay, Muir was following in the scientific footsteps of French naturalist Louis Agassiz and his predecessors, who had only recently propounded the theory that moving sheets of ice, carrying outsized rocks along with them, had scarred and restructured vast surfaces of land throughout the world. It was Agassiz who described a glacier as God's Great Plough. This was heretical to early 19th-century scientists who still attributed the cause of most geological anomalies to the biblical Flood. Of course, nobody had yet seen the enormous ice sheets of the Antarctic. Agassiz's theory of an Ice Age—a "Siberian winter" in which glaciers from the North Pole grew to envelop much of the Northern Hemisphere—was scoffed at until the 1840s, when his scientific work in

A LITTLE GLACIER GLOSSARY

Ablation: The combined processes—including melting, calving, evaporation, erosion—in which a glacier loses ice and snow. The opposite of accumulation.

Bergy seltzer: Also known as ice sizzle, this is the simultaneous loud popping of the bubbles, under pressures of more than 750 pounds per square inch, that break when glaciers and icebergs melt.

Crevasse: Deep, steep-sloped open fracture in the upper ice, created by the stresses of a flowing glacier. In the illustration, a glacier is passing over a mound of bedrock, and the bending of the ice opens up crevasses in the brittle top layers to a maximum depth of about 100 feet—beyond which the pressure of the glacier keeps the lower ice more pliable.

Drift: All rocky debris, from mud to boulders, carried and deposited by a glacier.

Drumlin: A low, smooth mound of glacial drift deposited beneath a glacier.

Firn: Transitional ice grains, between snow and glacier ice.

Foliation: Layering within a glacier as its snow is transformed into glacier ice, with irregular bands usually alternating between fine- and coarse-grained ice or bubble-rich and clear ice; can be seen at a glacier's face.

Glacier flour: Bedrock ground to powderlike silt by the pressure of flowing ice; suspended in meltwater, it becomes a light-colored glacier milk.

Hanging glacier: Usually a small glacier that clings high on the wall of a U-shaped valley.

Icefall: Area where a glacier plunges over a steep slope, creating a heavily crevassed surface and a flow of ice triple the normal rate; the most hazardous part of a glacier.

Moraine: A ridge or group of ridges and mounds created from an accumulation of glacial drift. End moraine is a ridge or hill that can become several hundred feet high when the end of a glacier melts and its terminus stays in the same place for a long time; terminal moraine denotes a glacier's farthest advance.

Till: Stew of unsorted glacial drift deposited directly by a glacier and not reworked by water. Glacial till compressed into rock is tillite.

the mountains of Switzerland and the highlands of Britain secured his reputation. By mid-century, he was ensconced at Harvard University and would become one of the most popular American scientists of the era.

Louis Agassiz was not entirely correct. There had been not one but as many as ten periods of major glaciation around the globe over the past million years that define the Great Ice Age of the Pleistocene epoch. But eras of glaciation date back as long ago as 700 million years and as recently, in geological terms, as 150 years, when the Little Ice Age ebbed after five and a half centuries of glacial expansion.

Among the glaciers that had grown during this latest period were Alaska's. Then, when the world's mean temperature began to rise by about one degree Fahrenheit during the 19th century, they started to retreat. In the middle of the present century, as the Northern Hemisphere was re-cooling, seven per cent of them began to advance again—and today in total this minority holds more ice than all the rest of the state's glaciers.

Such movement is the very definition of a glacier, which is a flowing body of natural, land-borne ice—containing meltwater, algae, pollen, and the debris of rock torn from mountains and valleys, not to mention iceworms and snowfleas. *(See* Iceworms and Snowfleas, *page 67.)* Ice itself is a mineral, or monomineralic rock, created from soft snow which builds up in layers. Over the years, its massive weight and extreme pressure compacts snow crystals at a depth of about 200 feet into solid ice crystals, which can form up to one foot in length. Although much glacier ice looks white, some appears blue. The reason: As daylight passes through the dense ice, light waves at the red end of the color spectrum are absorbed, causing the human eye to perceive an enhancement of blue light.

Alaska offers textbook conditions for the growing of what scientists call temperate or warm glaciers (as opposed to the cold ones of Greenland and Antarctica). In the southeastern stretches of the state, the warm Japanese Current flowing through the Gulf of Alaska encourages precipitation, which at the 5,000-foot level becomes snow throughout the year. (The Juneau Icecap has an estimated annual snowfall of 100 feet.) In summer, the temperature of most of these glaciers remains just at freezing, 32°F, which enables meltwater to flow through the ice and form the spectacular ice caves characteristic of warm glaciers. The chilly summers allow snow to survive annual melting and become solid granules, known in their second year as firn.

Alaska's glaciers are born in alpine regions, valleys, and piedmonts—the flatlands at the foot of a mountain where one or more streams of ice spread out. A sheet of glacier ice, usually dome-shaped, with the flow radiating from the center, is called an ice cap. A large area of connecting valley glaciers is an ice field, such as the well-studied Juneau Icefield, where the Mendenhall flows. Islands of bedrock projecting through an ice field are called nunataks.

A MYSTERY BEING SOLVED

For most of the century and a half that science has been studying glaciers, their movement has been a mystery. Recent research has now identified two basic methods: internal deformation (alteration of form) and basal slip or sliding. Cold glaciers in the polar regions move because their ice acts like minerals and metals under stress which can deform and actually "flow." Most of the movement of warm glaciers, like Alaska's, depends on a base of meltwater that—although it may be only a mere fraction of an inch thick—acts like a lubricant to reduce friction as gravity and the weight of the ice send a glacier downhill. Crevasses are created when a descending glacier crosses bumps in its bedrock path, causing it to bend and open up long cracks in its upper layers to depths of up to 100 feet.

Along the way, a glacier manhandles everything in its path. It bends around, while roughing up, the largest rock barriers. It freezes onto smaller loose rock, dirt and other detritus that gathers along its sides, creating black borders called lateral moraines.

Sometimes glaciers merge, and the debris of each one produces a black stripe, which identifies the individual glaciers within the collective mass. As the glacier moves, the debris becomes its instrument of destruction and creation. Gravel frozen into the ice wears away the terrain, boulders gash the land and dredge up and drag along more rock.

The ice always moves downward, following the line of least resistance. When glaciologists talk of glaciers retreating, they aren't suggesting that the ice actually backs up a slope. But when the distance between the head of the glacier and its terminus begins to shrink—through melting and calving—it is said to be in retreat. Alaska has seen the world's most rapid retreats. In the 85 years between George Vancouver's and John Muir's visits, Glacier Bay had retreated 48 miles; between 1899 and 1916, Grand Pacific Glacier backed up the bay 65 miles and exposed the face of Johns Hopkins Glacier. Since then, Grand Pacific has been unpredictably to-ing and fro-ing across the adjacent Canadian border.

Advancing glaciers—those that grow longer—most often also move forward only a fraction of a yard a day, the glacial pace that has become a metaphor for slowness. Some, however, surge and gallop. In 1936 the retreating Black Rapids Glacier, amid the high Alaska Range in central Alaska, suddenly, inexplicably, began to surge forward with an ice face more than 330 feet high. Before it stopped—only a mile and a half from a lodge along the Richardson Highway—it had travelled four miles in three months. Alaska and neighboring northwest Canada have about 200 of these galloping glaciers between them. In 1982–83, an international scientific team studying the Variegated Glacier at Yakutat Bay on the southeastern Alaskan coast observed an 8,000-foot surge in progress, speeding along at 200 feet a day. They theorized that a buildup of meltwater increased hydraulic pressure, raising the glacier slightly off its bed and escalating the rate of basal sliding. And glaciologists camping atop it spoke of the noise of the surge, the cracking and thumping, and the rumble of a meltwater river deep inside.

ICEWORMS AND SNOWFLEAS

Wolves and bears have braved Alaska's glaciers. So have mice and shrews, and even bumblebees and hummingbirds. But perhaps the most intriguing creatures on these icy stretches are the minuscule and mysterious iceworms and snowfleas.

Although they were first recorded on a Canadian expedition to Greenland in 1872, and an American one on Muir Glacier five years later, iceworms were long thought to be a practical joke on newcomers to the north. (Alaskan shops sell postcards labelled "iceworms" showing strands of spaghetti curling on the snow.) In fact, they are a relative of the common earthworm, black, and usually no more than an inch long—about the length of a spruce needle and the diameter of a darning needle, says one scientist. They wriggle through crystals in partially thawed ice or through firn—transitional ice grains, between snow and glacier ice—and lay their eggs in sub-freezing weather. The colder it gets, the deeper they burrow into the glacier. It's assumed that they dine on pollen or red algae in the snow. And various birds dine on them.

Spotting the worms can be difficult. A member of the U.S. Geological Survey saw them early one morning in 1891 on Malaspina Glacier off Yakutat Bay: "These creatures were wiggling over the snow in thousands, but as soon as the sun rose and made its warmth felt, they disappeared beneath the surface." A few summers later on the same glacier, another observer watched them start moving sluggishly around 4 P.M. and stay on the surface until dawn.

If iceworms are hard to believe in, consider the snowflea, or glacier flea. A member of the order *Collembola*, it's a black bug that hops around warm firn and lives on a vegetarian diet of conifer pollen and red algae—and perhaps even dead iceworms.

Surging or snail-like, a glacier keeps moving, inexorably, until it reaches a point where the ice at its margin either melts or reaches tidewater. At its snout, a tidewater glacier can lie deep underwater where it deposits rock debris to create a protective shoal enabling it to advance in the water. Meanwhile, it will continually calve to form icebergs or ice sheets.

Bergs, composed of fresh water and floating seven-eighths submerged, come in all shapes and sizes. They range from an ugly black or brown from the stony debris called moraine, which the glacier has collected along the way, to the clear white and blue that John Muir described as ineffably beautiful, "in which the purest tones of light pulse and shimmer, lovely and untainted as anything on earth or in the sky." In size, icebergs in Alaska waters can be chunks just large enough to float a few seabirds, or huge flat-topped floating islands like the one spotted north of Point Barrow that was 18 miles long and 15 miles wide.

The immense power of glaciers has carved U-shaped valleys, islands, lakes and rivers, and the fjords of the Inside Passage, Glacier Bay and Prince William Sound. It has ground granite and limestone into a fertile mix that, borne by meltwater and blown by winds, has created what became the world's richest agricultural lands. And well beyond the Ice Ages, the influence of glaciers continues. The cold air above the major ice sheets affects global weather patterns. As efficient storehouses of water, glaciers power hydroelectric facilities, especially during the winter, in Scandinavia, Switzerland, and parts of the U.S. And they are effective outdoor laboratories for the arctic sciences as well as glaciology. The Juneau Icefield Research Program, which began in 1948, not only provides training for university and high-school students but also offers professional scientists—among them, climatologists, biologists, botanists, specialists in polar medicine—field experience and long-term research opportunities.

For the visitors to Alaska who view them from a cruise ship or on shore tours, glaciers can be appreciated simply as one of the most wondrous manifestations of the natural world.

WHERE TO SEE GLACIERS
IN ALASKA

Juneau Icefield

One of the most intensively studied ice fields in the world—site of
the Juneau Icefield Research Program—stretches for a thousand-
plus square miles along the crest of the Coast Range, from the Taku
River to just east of Skagway, and dips into British Columbia. It
comprises more than 30 valley glaciers, all of them retreating except for the aggressively advancing Taku. Alaska's most-visited—
and only drive-in—glacier is the *Mendenhall*, just north of Juneau.
Its 100-foot-high, 1.5-mile-wide terminus in deep Mendenhall Lake
is slowly retreating (at a pace of less than 100 feet a year) and fill-
ing the lake. Scientists have found the 12-mile-long glacier a supe-
rior source of big single-crystal ice samples. Visitors who come by
vehicle, or land by helicopter a mile or more onto the glacier's
face, find it a fascinating way to begin comprehending the size and
structure of glaciers.

Glacier Bay National Park and Preserve

Ringed by the superbly glaciated Fairweather Range to the west,
the Chilkat Range to the east, and the St. Elias, Alsek and
Takhinsha mountains to the north, the bay is 62 miles long and 10
miles at its widest. Located about 90 miles northwest of Juneau, it
became a national monument in 1925 and a national park and preserve in 1980.

The most dramatic modern event in the bay's history was the
1899 earthquake that shook the Alaskan coast, destroying the
front of Muir Glacier and sending others into fast retreat. The
Grand Pacific backed off 65 miles and exposed the face of Johns
Hopkins Glacier. All of this activity attracted scientists from
around the world, who have since turned the bay and its 16 tidewater glaciers into a natural laboratory.

Grand Pacific Glacier, along with neighboring Margerie, plugs
the extreme upper end of the bay. During John Muir's time, when

he camped on "the crystal bluffs of the vast glacier," the two ice flows were actually fused. Grand Pacific may be advancing now, but during the 1920s it had retreated across the adjacent Canadian border for more than a mile. Three decades later it had moved back again into Alaska, where it remains today—the longest glacier in the park, its face 260 feet tall and 3.75 miles across.

Margerie Glacier, which routinely calves for cruise-ship passengers in Tarr Inlet, is smaller but has the sharp features of a classic glacier. Its active calving and the resulting swells keep small boats and kayaks half a mile away from its 180-foot-high face.

Johns Hopkins Glacier, christened for the university whose glaciologists were pioneer researchers here, has been advancing for half a century out of the Fairweather Range. It chokes the inlet of the same name with ice that keeps most vessels four miles away.

Yakutat Bay

Northwest of Glacier Bay, at the top of the Panhandle, lie Yakutat Bay and, at its far end, Disenchantment Bay—into which *Hubbard Glacier* continued a century-long advance until it dammed Russell Fjord in 1986. (Scientists estimate that it had last advanced into the bay in the twelfth century.) Now, although the continent's biggest glacier is retreating to its source deep in the Wrangell–St. Elias National Park, its calving at mid-tide is a sensational event.

Prince William Sound

In the Gulf of Alaska, south of Valdez, Prince William Sound has more than 20 active tidewater glaciers amid 40 fjords, the most of any one area in Alaska. You can view abundant sealife here, from seals and sea otters to porpoises and whales.

College Fjord's six calving glaciers were named for eastern colleges by the 1899 Harriman Expedition of geologists affiliated with the institutions: Harvard (the most active) and Yale in two arms at the head of the fjord; Smith, Bryn Mawr, Vassar, and Wellesley on the western side. The inlet, 20 miles long, lies within the Chugach National Forest. Nearby *Harriman Fjord* has a dozen glaciers, including the advancing Harriman (the longest) and the stable Surprise, so-called because it was the first to be spotted by members of the expedition.

Columbia Glacier, the largest and most majestic in the Sound, spreads across 440 square miles from its head in Mount Einstein (elevation 11,522 feet). Its six-mile-wide terminus (only half-visible from the middle of the bay) is retreating from the tidewater of Columbia Bay near the port of Valdez, where the Trans-Alaska Pipeline fuels oil tankers. Scientists are studying the glacier's energetic calving—which can produce flat-topped icebergs 200 feet long—because of the long-shot possibility of a collision between berg and tanker. At some points, Columbia's ice front lies several thousand feet below sea level. As it retreats, the bottom of the bay is falling away under the glacier's snout. Eventually, glaciologists suggest, the water will become deep enough to virtually float the glacier, which will then disintegrate.

Harding Icefield

Amid the Kenai Mountains, in the Kenai Fjords National Park southwest of Seward, lies the largest of all icefields—the Harding. This remnant of the Pleistocene age, about 700 square miles, generates more than 40 sizable glaciers, 4 of them longer than 15 miles. Tours through this magnificent area of thickly treed slopes take in some of the most impressive of the icefield's progeny, including *Exit Glacier.*

Portage Glacier

The most popular attraction in the state lies within driving distance of Anchorage. *Portage Glacier* occupies what was once a low pass across the Kenai Mountains, which Alaskan natives and Russian explorers traversed before Vancouver's time. Even after the glacier filled it, the pass continued to be used as a highway by the U.S. Army at the turn of the century. As you approach the area, the jaw-dropping vista of Portage Glacier appears suddenly. Boat tours on iceberg-thick Portage Lake present a fine close-up view of the glacier's face, and in the visitor center you can wander through a simulated ice cave and even stroke a real iceberg.

WILD ALASKA

For a lover, or mere admirer, of the wild—of sealife, animals and birds, plants and flowers, the wild land itself—Alaska is America's most rewarding place. At least a half-dozen of its 38 kinds of sea mammals, including the most immense on the planet, are seen in Alaskan waters and nowhere else. Here too are some of the world's largest land mammals, in some of the largest groupings. There is one grizzly bear for every eight Alaskans; there are as many caribou as there are people. Golden and bald eagles, trumpeter swans, red-faced cormorants, all of which are rare or nonexistent in the Lower 48, flourish in this northernmost state among more than 400 species of birds. Wildflowers grow so prolifically in summer that they can be difficult to sidestep. And the plant life above and below the tundra is so diverse that one biologist compares it to the lushness of a tropical rain forest a few inches tall. What you will not find here, thankfully, are rattlesnakes and poison ivy.

LIFE IN THE SEA

Whales

An Alaska without whales would not be Alaska, says Dr. Victor Scheffer, the internationally renowned American zoologist. One of the most exciting events on a summer cruise in the state's southeastern coastal waters is the sighting of these leviathans—often the show-stopping leaps or the high-arched tail flips of that most acrobatic of whales, the HUMPBACK. This migrating species shares one characteristic with many of the cruise ships that enable so many of us to see them: most humpbacks spend their summers in Alaska and winters in Mexico and the Hawaiian Islands. Up to three-fifths of the world's 10,000 humpbacks summer here. Feed-

A killer whale in the Inside Passage
performs a sea-going ballet.

ing on herring and other fish close to the shore, they can be seen in Glacier Bay, Prince William Sound, and especially around Admiralty Island.

You can distinguish them by the telltale hump of their black-and-white bodies; their oversized flippers, the largest of any whales; and the wartlike bumps on their snouts, each holding a single hair, which scientists believe may be a sensor. Breaching, they fling their 35-ton, 45-foot bulk out of the sea in a series of twists and turns. In their dramatic descents, they flash the white flukes (or lobes) of their winglike tails, which bear markings so distinctive that they are as identifying as fingerprints.

Although humpbacks may be the whales most often spotted by cruise-ship passengers, they are only one of 15 species that make Alaska the best whale-watching state in America. They are members of the order *Cetacea*, which also includes dolphins and porpoises, all of them descendants of warm-blooded, lung-equipped land mammals who as far back as 100 million years ago adapted to the sea. (Some researchers see parallels between the mating habits of humpbacks and Rocky Mountain bighorn sheep.) Cetaceans are either toothed *(Odontoceti)*, with conical teeth adapted for seizing fish and other sizable prey, or baleen or moustached *(Mysticeti)*, so-called because of the flexible bonelike fibers of their enormous jaws, which filter water as they entrap much smaller sealife. Most baleen whales—the blue, fin, sei, minke, and humpback among them—have pleated throat grooves which extend as they feed. The humpback has another remarkable feeding technique: after using its blowhole to create a "net"of large bubbles that encircle and baffle its quarry, it plunges through the net—its massive mouth gaping as wide as 90 degrees—and gulps up its panicked prey.

The BLUE WHALE—blue-gray in coloring—is the largest animal on the planet. Larger than even the mightiest dinosaur was, it has been known to grow to 150 tons and 100 feet, though most today are 10 to 30 feet shorter. Its heart alone can weigh in at half a ton (an adult could squeeze through its arteries), and its belly can take in two tons of seafood. For all its size, it feeds in shallow waters on an exclusive diet of minuscule shrimplike crustaceans called krill. The blue is seen on occasion in Prince William Sound.

The slightly smaller FIN WHALE—less than 70 feet long—has a sleeker appearance, a more diverse diet, and travels even faster than its cousin. Its back is darkish gray or even black, its undersides white, and two chevrons of white stretch diagonally from behind the blowhole down the sides to its tail. The fin, which has been observed in the Aleutians and Prince William Sound, cruises up to 6 knots, with spurts of more than 20. Its food includes anchovies and squid as well as krill. More sociable than the blue whale, the fin swims in pods of from 10 to 100.

Among the more commonly sighted whales, from May through September, are the gray-backed SEI (pronounced *say*, named for a fish that migrates at the same time in Scandinavia), a bottom-feeder with a pointier snout than the fin whale and a speed fleeter than any of its kind—38 knots or more; the MINKE (pronounced *min-key*), not much bigger than a killer whale, with a gray-black back sometimes seen romping gregariously around ships and boats; and the equally friendly PACIFIC GRAY, christened for its mottled appearance, and known for migrating the longest distance of any mammal. During their 12,000-mile return trips from the lagoons of Mexico to the Bering Sea, increasing numbers of grays can be seen along the shoreline of the Pacific coast. (In 1988, the world watched via TV as the Alaska National Guard, oil industry personnel, and Eskimo hunters carved breathing holes in the ice near Barrow on the Arctic coast to help two of three trapped gray whales reach the open sea.)

Most whales have been hunted commercially, often near the point of extinction, but the BOWHEAD remains an important source of food and oil for Eskimo whale hunters. (Its horny baleen, or whalebone, was once prized for use in corsets). Eskimos fancy a delicacy called *muktuk*, made from the whale's outer layers of skin and blubber. The bowhead, growing to 60 feet long or more, has a stocky body and an upwardly bowed mouth in a head that extends one-third its length. It leaps high and lands on its side, and sometimes groups with a dozen others, in an efficient V-shaped pod like geese in flight, to hunt prey. Cruise passengers who take land tours to the Bering, Chukchi, or Beaufort seas are most likely to sight this endangered species, which now can be hunted only for subsistence by Arctic Eskimos. (In 1992, for example, Alaska's nine whaling villages were allowed a quota of 41 landed whales.)

KILLER WHALES, or orcas—which are technically members of the dolphin family—have been given a bad rap until recently, one that endowed these highly social creatures with their distasteful name. In fact, there has been no recorded case of these black-and-white wolves of the sea ever willfully attacking humans (as any visitor to an oceanarium show would guess). In the wild, however, hunting in packs and wielding their two-dozen conical teeth, they are savage and quick-witted predators of birds, fish, turtles, squid, seals, sea lions, porpoises, and even the big blue and gray whales. And they can turn on their own too: in the spring of 1993, two orca-literate biologists aboard a ferry in British Columbia's Inside Passage saw a pack of locals brawling with three transients in what they suspect is the first recorded killer-whale "rumble."

Marine experts consider orcas even more intelligent than dolphins, who earned such flattering reviews for *Flipper* and other TV appearances. Zoologists have watched two killer whales tilt an ice floe with their backs and dump a seal into the awaiting mouth of a third orca. Others routinely liberate blackcod from fishermen's longline hooks.

Mature males can grow up to 30 feet and 8 tons. The orcas' singular dorsal (back) fin, which may work like a keel, is triangular-shaped and can reach 6 feet in height. Orca water ballets have entertained hundreds of thousands at aquarium shows where their streamlined bodies, showing characteristic white bellies and flanks, take to the air and land with a calculated splashing of the audience. But they are never more gymnastic than when the male courts a female, leaping like a Barishnykov and churning the water to froth. The resulting families bond over long periods of time; orcas have the most stable society of any mammal. A B.C. ferry captain has described how a pair of killer whales kept a bloodied young orca calf afloat after it had been cut by the ship's propeller; 15 days later, they were still there trying to save the victim.

Dolphins and Porpoises

PACIFIC WHITE-SIDED DOLPHINS are the other stars of the world's oceanariums, vaulting well out of their pools, sometimes turning somersaults, and splashing down on their sides or backs. They perform the same hydrodynamic stunts in the open sea while travelling in herds of up to several thousand, from the Aleutians' Amchitka Island through the Gulf of Alaska and as far south as Baja California. Feeding near the shore on squid, anchovies, hake, and other fish, they can be identified by their tall black-and-white hooked fins. As jet black and snow white as killer whales, but with a pair of gray suspenders along the back, they are about a quarter the size of the orcas—whom they sometimes hang around with in the wild, hitching a ride in the wake of a killer-whale pod.

HARBOR PORPOISES are many times more bashful than their dolphin cousins. Although tending to congregate in the shallow waters of harbors, they are seldom seen for more than a moment in their Alaskan hangouts, which range as far north as Point Barrow, around Prince William Sound, but mostly along the coasts of the Gulf of Alaska. The smallest of the cetaceans, half a dozen feet long, these blunt-nosed porpoises with small back fins are also hard to spot because of their prosaic brown-and-gray coloring.

DALL'S PORPOISES (named for American zoologist William Dall) are among the speediest of cetaceans, jetting along in bursts of up to 30 knots. While some are all white or black, most of these small-headed animals are black with white flanks. No longer than the Pacific white-sided dolphin, but a lot bulkier in build, they streak through Prince William Sound, the Gulf of Alaska, the Pribilof Islands, and as far north as the Bering Strait. Occasionally, like dolphins, they ride the waves at the bow of a ship for several hundred yards.

Seals, Sea Lions and Walruses

These are all members of the fin-footed pinniped family, who share big eyes and snouts, spindle shapes tapering at both ends, and great diving ability. The shy PACIFIC HARBOR SEAL hides out from predators and humans by plunging up to 200 feet for more than 20 minutes at a time. Its heart rate can slow by three-quarters, to 15 or 20 beats a minute, and its blood vessels constrict to conserve oxygen. Harbor seals' keen vision is better undersea than ours is in the air. Living on land as much as in water, these relatively plentiful seals are common along the Pacific Coast from Baja California to Alaska, especially on the reefs and sandbars, the rivers and estuaries of the Inside Passage. They breed in the water, exuberantly; the female's nips on the male's neck and shoulders appear far more brutal than mere love bites. They give birth in summer on rocks and icebergs, sometimes near tidewater glaciers like those in upper Glacier Bay. About six feet long and weighing up to 250 pounds, they can be colored almost white or black but are usually a bluish gray, spotted with black and erratic white loops and rings. For more than two decades, they have been legally protected in both the United States and Canada. But because they go after the same food that fishing boats track—shrimp, squid, herring—they are often considered a nuisance and killed.

The calisthenic STELLER SEA LION is as surprisingly mobile on land as at sea. Waddling and lurching, it cavorts in rookeries on Benjamin Island in the Lynn Canal near Juneau and Forrester Island at the southwesternmost tip of the Panhandle. There, while the males can be triple the size of females—at ten feet and more than a ton—the females can be ten times more abundant. Males are tan or the color of cork, darker on the chest (though white-looking underwater); females are lighter but darken with age. The pups are silvery black. During the two months or more of summer breeding, male Stellers do not feed, but they may have more than a dozen biting, battering fights with other raging bulls, and mate with a harem of up to 30 females.

In recent years, sea lions have been declared a threatened species, their numbers having declined from 150,000 in the 1950s to an estimated 25,000, possibly because of a shortage in herring, capelin, and other preferred food.

The PACIFIC WALRUS, which is more plentiful than it was a century ago, inhabits the Bering and Chukchi seas. Eskimos in Nome

A lone seal basks on an iceberg
calved from the Columbia Glacier.

and other centers still hunt them for subsistence meat as well as the ivory of their tusks, which they carve. Every summer, as many as 15,000 walrus bulls, about two tons apiece, gather on the Bering's Round Island before going north to meet their mates and calves. There they swarm together like college kids trying to squeeze into a telephone booth.

The walrus' warty hide and impressive tusks (they can weigh as much as 12 pounds) make it unmistakable. After its fur molts, the bumpy, hairless skin looks white in the water but pink in the sun. Its scientific name, *Odobenus rosmarus*, comes from its habit of "tooth-walking": using its tusks to pull itself into position on an ice floe. On the sea bottom, those tusks, more than a yard long in the males, may be used like the runners of a sled as the walrus burrows in the mud to actually suck out from their shells the 150 pounds of mollusks an adult can dine on every day. And its sensitive whiskers help the walrus find and sort the food. Less evident in looking at a walrus are the twin air sacs in its neck, which add resonance to its mating and communication sounds as well as inflating to let the animal sleep with its head above water.

Otters

The Russians called them "sea beavers" and referred to their valuable velvety fur as "soft gold." In hunting down SEA OTTERS, the Russian, and later American, traders nearly annihilated them. Once almost as thick in the water as flocks of sea birds, these affable mammals are resurfacing in southeastern Alaska, where ship passengers occasionally spot them. Several hundred were brought there in the late 1960s because of the underground nuclear testing on Amchitka Island in their traditional Aleutian home. These members of the weasel family are the smallest marine mammals: the adult male weighs no more than 100 pounds and measures less than five feet long. Its dense dark-brown or black fur may have almost a billion fibers. Feeding on the bottom of shallow waters, the sea otter uses uniquely rounded teeth to crush the clams and snails it carries to the surface in pouches that stretch from its forelegs right across its chest.

THE RHYME OF THE ANCIENT HUMPBACKS

Dolphins send out sound waves for bouncing off any fish within their range to identify where and how far away and how big it is. Tests show that they can discriminate between objects about the size of B-B-gun shot or a corn kernel at 50 paces. Killer whales' screams—called pulsed calls—keep members of a pod in contact with one another at long distances; each pod has its own dialect as well as at least one distinctive scream of its own. But the most fascinating sea-mammal communication may be the songs of humpback whales—which intrigue musicians and mammalogists.

The trumpeting, low-frequency pulses of the humpbacks in Alaska differ from those in Hawaii, where as they mate and calve they sing complicated songs that can last half an hour and be repeated for nearly a day. Some researchers believe that the songs are one way a female humpback chooses the right sire; others suggest they're symbolic weapons as males fight one another for the attentions of the females.

We now know that though the songs can differ widely from year to year, each whale always sings all the verses of the same current song. Which leads to the most intriguing hypothesis: humpbacks may actually use a kind of rhyme as a key to remembering the verses. Biologists Linda Guinee of the Long Term Research Institute of Lincoln, Massachussetts, and Katharine Payne of Cornell University's Laboratory of Ornithology captured linear pictures of hundreds of the songs on a spectograph. Sorting them into themes with phrases and sub-phrases, they noticed that a certain sub-phrase would frequently appear in the same place in adjacent themes, just as a rhyming pattern links a poem. And they found these rhymes showing up most often in the more elaborate and harder-to-remember of these ever-changing songs— a discovery which Katharine Payne calls "one of the nicest examples of cultural evolution that has been gathered from any species in the animal kingdom, including man."

Sea otters are sometimes mistaken for their more detectable cousins, RIVER OTTERS, which also frequent salt water. Check the tail to identify which is which: the river otter's has a thick base and is more than half as long as its body—the sea otter's, which is flattened, is only a third of its length.

STALKING THE LAND

If there's one sight in the Alaskan wilderness that embodies all of the state's grandeur, it's the vision of a 7-foot-tall, 1,600-pound giant sauntering down a hillside to draw water from a glacier-fed stream, its 70-pound antlers bobbing as it drinks. Faced with the spectacle of a full-grown Alaskan moose, pioneering naturalist Charles Sheldon thought he had caught a glimpse of a dinosaur. Certainly, for him, "the sight of the moose among the spruces evokes a sensation of the creations of the long past." The antediluvean armature of the Alaskan moose is less a throwback to the Jurassic past and more an emblem of the way the state's mammals have adapted to its multifaceted terrain. When the earth began heating up 14,000 years ago, the mammoths, sabre-toothed tigers, and lions inhabiting Alaska disappeared. Moose—with long legs that let them graze above the snow line and impressive antlers to defend themselves—thrived. Meanwhile, in thick interior forests, Northern flying squirrels evolved a pouch, stretching from foot to foot, which allows them to swoop from tree limbs in search of prey. On the northern ice, polar bears set up dens whose inner chambers can be as warm as steam baths. The Barren Ground caribou survived by developing their endurance and mobility as they roam the northern plains in an incessant search for calving grounds and their lichen of choice, caribou moss.

Moose

While other mammals burrow or rely on camouflage as winter approaches, the MOOSE has taken the route of gluttony, giving it the sheer bulk to take on—or at least scare off—the grizzlies that often share its territory (the Kenai Peninsula, the Alaska Range, and Mount McKinley National Park). Throughout the summer, moose browse on aspen and birch, though they'd walk a mile for a willow, their favorite tree. As the first flakes of snow start to fall on the upper limbs, most moose have forgone sleeping and will spend 12-hour days eating up to 60 pounds of leaves. During the winter, bulls and cows are hard-pressed to find foliage, and often driven to burrow through packed snow for a handful of lowbrush cranberries. Their ceaseless browsing draws them toward towns, where the living is sometimes easier, but also across highways, where a frontal collision with a vehicle is often fatal to both man and beast. (An underpass was built beneath a six-lane highway leading to Anchorage to prevent such encounters.)

More than 160,000 moose are scattered throughout the state, showing their donkey ears and dangling noses almost everywhere except the southeastern Panhandle. They are shambling, affable creatures, except when in rut. Then the males, lean after a winter of avoiding the Alaska Railroad's cowcatchers, are ready to joust. Cows mingle around like half-amused courtiers, until two bulls square off, lowering the seven-foot spread of their antlers to charge. Antler tines often make their mark, causing serious or fatal gouges. All in all, it's a relatively chivalric affair—a browbeaten loser can step down, though there's no question of taking his pick of the onlookers.

Bears

Moose, like most of Alaska's herbivores, are no danger to visitors, whom they take care to avoid—especially when there are calves around. The opposite is true of the largest carnivorous land animals in the world, the bears. They are common sights in Southeast, whether waddling up mountainsides with their cubs, gorging on ten-pound salmon adroitly swiped out of streams, or lacerating tents with a casual brush of a paw. Black bears, which can actually be cinnamon, yellow, or even blue, thrive in the Panhandle, especially around Prince William Sound. Brown bears roam most of the state, especially their sanctuary, the Kodiak Island Wildlife Refuge.

On the northern ice, polar bears prowl in search of seals or the occasional stranded whale.

BLACK BEARS, relatively small (200-pound) roadside clowns in national parks from California's Sequoia to Virginia's Shenandoah, are the aggressors in hundreds of disquieting—and sometimes fatal—encounters in Alaska. In Juneau and Ketchikan, they have been known to saunter up and down streets, inviting caresses that become deadly embraces. In the wild, their unpredictable behavior is a given. They may seem oblivious to the existence of passersby, allow them to continue on their way, and then suddenly charge at 35 miles an hour, as fast as a horse, often because hikers have approached a hidden cache of food. A sow with her cubs is the most likely to attack. One 175-pound beast in a maternal rage dragged off a geologist, no doubt planning to bury her catch for later consumption—the ursine method of choice for protecting corpses from marauding birds. The geologist was saved, though badly injured, and the bear was shot by rangers, who spared her yearling cub.

Black bears look like pikers next to the BROWN or GRIZZLY BEARS, who outweigh them by more than a ton, attaining up to 1,600 pounds. Though Alaskans often call coastal bears "browns" and the bears of the Interior "grizzlies," there's no real biological difference, in spite of the grizzly's distinctive shoulder hump. Browns thrive on the Kodiak Island Wildlife Refuge (set aside by President Franklin D. Roosevelt 50 years ago) where they slash out at the abundant sockeye salmon with a seasoned harpoonist's precision. Having a 300-pound weight advantage over mainland bears, the 3,000 Kodiaks evoke the Alaska that Charles Sheldon described in 1912: "No sight in the American wilderness is so suggestive of its wild charm as that of the huge bear meandering on the mountainside, or walking on the river-bank, or threading the deep forest. He who still retains his love of wild nature . . . feels a lack in the wilderness—perhaps the loss of its very essence—when, tramping about in it, he knows that the bear, that former denizen of the depths, is there no more."

Sheldon's fears that the browns might one day be exterminated are so far unfounded. His biggest problem today would be keeping a safe distance from the 20,000 or so of these giants. Confronted with a grizzly on the same trail, experienced guides graciously step off the path. On the tundra, they walk away rather than run: browns consider anything that flees to be game, and a human being as delectable as a caribou.

One hundred thousand years ago, a group of grizzlies walked out on the arctic ice north of the Brooks Range and never returned. They became POLAR BEARS, white-coated behemoths, as at home swimming around ice floes as they are stalking seals on glaciers. They rove incessantly in search of fish, birds, walruses, and whales trapped in the ice. The only time they pause is beside the breathing hole of a ringed seal, where they'll wait hours for their favorite prey to surface for a lungful of air—then crush its skull with a single blow and haul it from the water.

Since the beginning of the 1970s, more than 600 polar bears have been tranquillized by scientists working with helicopter pilots, often Vietnam vets whose military experience helps them dart away from the lunge of a half-dazed bear. Their study has shown that the bears, tagged and tracked by satellite, respect no international boundaries; like the 4,400 other polar bears in Alaska, they'll set up a winter den in Canada or Siberia just as easily as in Prudhoe Bay.

They deserve a winter lodge: polar bears walk more than 1,000 miles a year, and wind-chill factors of -75°F call for a comfortable den. Sows with cubs rest in chambers of mounded snow for up to six months, from October to March, only leaving on brief forays to teach the infants to fend for themselves, including suchs tricks as covering their black noses with white paws in order to camouflage themselves from seals basking on the ice. The cubs, duly trained and dispatched at about two years, will become independent adults, some of the few remaining predators truly fearless of human beings—mostly because they almost never encounter them.

A mother grizzly looms
on guard, watchful for her cubs.➢

Elk

The ROOSEVELT ELK lives in more temperate climes, on the islands off the south coast of Alaska, which also means that it is closer to humans—and overhunting. In fact, the seven distinct herds of the deer's dark-throated cousin, with its distinctive yellow rump patch, are the ancestors of three young couples shipped from Seattle in 1928. Alaskans wanted to see the elk roam through the state, as they did before the last Ice Age, and now there are about 1,300 on Kodiak, Afognak, and Raspberry islands. This is not many compared to the herds in the lower western states, but elk in Alaska grow to an impressive size, rivalling the tonnage of moose. Since the end of the 1920s, the herds dropped in number and nearly disappeared before recently resurging—especially on Northwestern Afognak Island, where the abundance of spruce and the lack of clearcuts and logging roads prevent overhunting. So far, transition to the mainland has not taken place.

Deer

Though Alaska has no shortage of SITKA BLACK-TAILED DEER, a colony of this relative of the elk was transported to Afognak Island, and now abounds there. But Sitkas are far more common in the rainforests of southeastern Alaska and northcoastal British Columbia, where the climate is tempered by the Japanese Current. On mountainsides, their black-tufted tails can be seen darting from sedge to salmonberries in spring, gradually moving up the mountain as melting snow unveils new growth. By July they're feasting on deer cabbage, a protein-rich plant that sprouts at alpine heights. In winter, they descend with the snow, trying to get by on dogwood and skunk cabbage. Often, they'll spend all of their short lives—eight to ten years—around the same mountain.

Caribou

The real nomad of the north, the 20th-century equivalent of the buffalo that once furrowed western plains, is the BARREN-GROUND CARIBOU. A caribou is a readily distinguishable deer: both males and females are horned, and their striped flanks and white neck patches bleach silver in the Arctic sun. They eat on the fly, entering Mount McKinley National Park at the beginning of spring, heading south toward the Alaska Range. When the mothers have time for their knock-kneed calves—their maternal instinct is so weak that they have been known to let their offspring drown in a torrent without glancing back—they grant them the richest milk (containing 20 per cent fat) of any land mammal.

A caribou herd crossing the tundra is like a dam-break suddenly flooding a peaceful valley. The animals flow over plains by the tens of thousands, driving snowy owls and Peregrine falcons before them, trailed by wolves looking for laggards. Snipping at lichen and sedge, the bulls grunt and roar, relentlessly urging on the cows and calves as they test the wind for the odor of predators. Part of their agitation is caused by nose botflies, the beelike pests that spend most of their life cycle entrenched in the caribou's backs or nasal passages. A caribou's only respite from the

The northern light illumines the
antlers of a caribou in velvet.

sting of the flies is the cooling flow of water as it fords a river. To make matters worse, the female fly invades the nostrils of a caribou to store its larvae, which move on to the animal's throat where they overwinter—waiting until spring to emerge, often forced out by the caribou's frantic snuffling and sneezing.

What makes the caribou migration really urgent is the fact that plant life is so sparsely distributed over the tundra. Lichens grow only a sixteenth of an inch a year, and a willow branch might have taken two centuries to become finger-thick. In spring, when the plants of the northern plains start to flourish, the pressure to feed is lessened, but a new imperative takes its place: the search for calving grounds. The 150,000 animals in the Porcupine herd, the most important of the caribou groupings, make a beeline for the tundra north of the Brooks Range each spring, undeterred by rivers, railroads, or mountains. Congregating in the tens of thousands, the bulls watch over the cows, whose horns drop off as soon as they have given birth. The calves are active almost immediately, running rings around their mothers, as though eager to start their lives of perpetual wandering.

Musk-oxen

The calving grounds are shared by the horned MUSK-OX, one of the most astonishing mammals in Alaska. Biologists say that from a distance they resemble giant caterpillars: their skirt-length coats make it almost impossible to distinguish rumps from heads. For the Eskimos, the musk-ox was *oomingmak*, "the bearded one," a shoulder-humped source of fur and meat. Traders killed off the last musk-oxen native to Alaska in 1865, but in 1930 the legislature had 34 of the hoofed mammals brought from Greenland. Gradually, tame animals were released on the Seward Peninsula and Univak and Nelson islands. Their distinctive tendency to huddle in protective circles, horns outward, helped them thrive in spite of harassment by wolves, and restrictions on hunting prevented a recurrence of their 19th-century extermination.

Today, more than 1,000 musk-oxen live on the tundra and islands north of the Arctic Circle, grazing on cotton grass, willow and birch. Since 1986, the splay-footed animals have been raised on a farm in Palmer, north of Anchorage, where they graze as peacefully as cattle on a plain. At April's end, farm managers start combing the 900-pound bulls, a three-hour process that yields up to seven pounds of *qiviut*, their soft underwool. (A single pound of the wool can be woven into a strand over 25 miles long.) Eight times warmer than sheep's wool, shrink-proof and nonirritating to sensitive skin, *qiviut* is woven into elaborate garments and sold in boutiques throughout the state.

Dall Sheep

The coat of the DALL SHEEP, the only white, wild sheep in the world, is equally remarkable. Three inches thick in winter, its hollow hairs channel the warmth of the sunlight toward the sheep's body. Dall sheep can be seen jumping from cliffs to peaks on all the major mountain ranges of Alaska. Constantly on the lookout for wolves, they will graze nervously on low pastures and then make a sudden—and unexpected—dash for the safety of a jumble of

Musk-oxen gather in a
characteristic circle of defence.

craggy rocks. The rams have curling horns up to 50 inches long, which are more useful in establishing dominance during mating periods than in standing off a wolf pack. It's only through constant vigilance, keen eyesight, and a fleet-footed grasp on rocks inaccessible to predators that the 3,000 Dall sheep of Mount McKinley National Park manage to survive.

Mountain Goats

The only animals that can be mistaken for Dall sheep are the MOUNTAIN GOATS of Southeast. The goats' horns are much smaller, however, and black rather than golden brown. They are even more agile than the sheep, with cushioned, skid-proof pads on their black hooves. Hunters and hikers have tried to follow the goats up coastal mountains, only to find themselves inextricably trapped on a rocky face, unable to continue upward or descend, while the goats continue to jump from cliff to cliff.

Small Mammals

Alaska is host to colonies of smaller mammals, whose range and populations often fluctuate wildly. The periodic peak in the numbers of SNOWSHOE HARES is one of the more spectacular examples. In ten-year cycles, the population mounts until thousands can be seen on a single field, gnawing on power poles when they've stripped the bark from all the available trees. The hares that survive the summer competition for birch and willow turn all white in winter; they wildly search the snow for vegetation as they're pursued by their chief predator, the LYNX. This three-foot-long feline lies in wait as bands of famine-crazed hares pass by, flattening itself to the ground only to leap out at the last minute. The lynx's feast ends the spectacular explosion, and in turn the cats die off as the hare population crashes.

BROWN and COLLARED LEMMINGS—the five-inch-long rodents that range most of the state with the exception of southeastern Alaska—are even more astounding breeders. If food is abundant, the females can have 7 litters of up to 11 kits per year, who inevitably strip the surrounding grasses and sedges bare. After the typical four-year population rise and crash, only one lemming may remain per acre for every 50 that crowded underground nests the year before. If vegetation has been completely gnawed away, lemmings often move on in a mass exodus, snapped up by predators or dying of hunger or exhaustion along the way. The Eskimo word for the lemming is *kilangmiutak*, "the one that comes from the sky," a traditional way to account for the torrents of rodents that seem to have fallen from the clouds.

If there's one predator in Alaska willing to kill at the drop of a hat, it's the WEASEL. The agile, seven-ounce bundle of fur will attack hares that outweigh it several times over, gripping their throats until they bleed to death. It will pounce on fish in rivers, leap for birds on the fly, and even threaten humans who come too close. One biologist saw a weasel attack an eagle, relentlessly clinging to the bird's neck as it was borne aloft. The ERMINE, or short-tailed weasel, ranges through most of the state, turning brilliant white in the winter. It often moves into cabins, where it can mop up the entire mouse population in a couple of days.

Wolves

In contrast to weasels, Alaska's WOLVES hunt with moderation. Running in packs of 30, they'll take on Dall sheep, caribou, and even moose, but the sheep can outleap them, the caribou can outrun them, and a bull moose can drive them off with its antlers and sharp front hooves. The 7,000 wolves of Alaska (a wolf can weigh up to 75 pounds) are significantly larger than the endangered gray wolves down south. They can be found throughout the state, in dense rain forests, on northern tundra, or trotting along high ridges in Mount McKinley National Park. They have been a source of fear and controversy for generations, but scientists are coming to understand that wolves are hardly indiscriminate or rapacious killers.

Wolf packs are, in fact, highly complex groupings, led by a male and a female who control the breeding of other couples. If food is scarce, the dominant male will prevent others from mating, communicating his authority through growls, the baring of teeth, or a simple grim-eyed stare. Wolves rarely fight among themselves, and the whole pack participates in the feeding and rearing of pups, licking muzzles, and giving the newborn babies a share of the food. As the pups are weaned in summer dens, the pack shows that it really is an extended family: aunts, uncles, and grandparents all help nourish the young.

A group of wolves, bonded together by lines of authority and family ties, defends its territory from other packs, preventing intruders or lone wolves from crossing strictly marked boundaries. In Denali National Park, the packs control areas of up to 800 square miles, leave "scent posts" by urinating on rocks or trees to mark the limits of their land. During the hunt, an encounter with another pack might lead to a standoff and an angry dispute; more often than not, the outnumbered pack simply steps down.

Ranging forth from its den, the pack hunts for 12 hours at a stretch, usually encountering several groups of prey: mountain goats, caribou, Dall sheep, moose, or deer. In most cases, the hunted animals outrun or outmaneuver the wolves: a caribou can easily outdistance a wolf, even when it's trotting at 25 miles an hour. Moose stand their ground, and unless the animal is obviously weak, the pack usually withdraws—the kick from the front legs of a bull moose can send a wolf flying 15 feet. Because the animals that wolves succeed in bringing to the ground are usually sick or lame, their hunting only rarely interferes with the healthy population of herds. When wolves do manage to make a kill, they tend to gorge, and can bolt down as much as 20 pounds of meat at a time.

Returning from a successful hunt, wolves wag their tails, start to whine, and eventually one of the pack raises its muzzle and howls. The others join in gradually, shifting a note or two, creating chords. The mournful chorus is one of the most haunting sounds in the Alaskan wilderness. Its echoes delineate the contours of surrounding cliffs, valleys, and mountains, serving as a reminder of the vastness of the surrounding landscape.

MASTERS OF THE AIR

At Bella Bella, as the ship threads through the Inside Passage's narrowest channel, they wheel overhead like traffic helicopters. When the float plane lands on Rudyerd Bay in the wilderness of Misty Fjords National Monument, at least one of them is waiting, atop the tallest hemlock, its golf ball of a head lazily turning. And high in the woods of the national park in Sitka, looking like figures torn from the totem poles that line the pathways, they are there.

Bald eagles—10,000 to 15,000 of them in Southeast alone, more in this part of Alaska than in all the other states combined. America's national symbol, struggling back from a population of only 3,000 in the Lower 48 two decades ago, seems everywhere in Alaska. But while the state's biggest bird may be the most obvious master of the air to be seen here, it merely symbolizes a richness in bird populations. Among them are such permanent residents as the submersible American dipper; the state's official bird, the willow ptarmigan, which has an enlightened male spouse; and the smallest visitor to summer here, the pugnacious rufous hummingbird, whose female partner can be vicious.

For bird-watchers, Alaska is next to nirvana, as they begin to realize soon after their cruise ships dock in Ketchikan, the traditional first port of call. Here, during migration flights, are sleek green-black cormorants, seabirds with skinny bills and four webbed toes; and long-legged, long-necked sandhill cranes, a wading species, which ranks among the world's tallest birds. Many species are resident in the state (or in Siberia) and nowhere else, including the whiskered auklet and the red-legged kittiwake gull; and others from Asia make their only North American visits here, such as the eye-browed thrush and the great knot sandpiper. The summer visitors come in unimaginable waves of waterfowl followed by shore birds and finally land birds, all intent on mating and nesting in the bittersweet briefness of the season. In his brilliant book *Arctic Dreams*, Barry Lopez describes astonishing concentrations of birdlife in the southwest around the Bering Sea: 24 million migratory waterfowl and shorebirds summer on the delta of the Yukon and Kuskokwim rivers, including all of the continent's emperor geese and rapidly declining spectacled eider ducks. One day in May 1982, the people of Nome watched whole flocks of sandhill cranes en route to Russia as they flew over the town virtually nonstop for two hours.

"One of the most exciting aspects of watching birds in Alaska," writes University of Alaska zoology professor Brina Kessel in her foreword to Robert Armstrong's *A Guide to the Birds of Alaska*, "is that there is so much yet to be learned about them. We are still at the frontier of knowledge about so many aspects of Alaska's bird life that any observant bird watcher has a good chance of contributing new and valuable information about them. . . ."

Because there are at least 430 species in the state, we have confined our descriptions to a sampling of some of the most common and interesting birds likely to be seen by cruise passengers.

Birds of Prey

Anywhere else, the display in the Alaska State Museum in Juneau would be impressive: you walk up and around a life-sized eagle's nest, 8 feet wide and 12 feet deep, typical of the sticks-and-moss eyrie this bird of prey expands year after year atop old-growth spruce and hemlock. Then you visit the Forest Service building next door to watch a film about a fledgling eagle's first clumsy attempts to fly. Anywhere else, museums and movies as well-conceived as these would be satisfying of themselves; in Alaska, they are a mere adjunct to the reality of observing BALD EAGLES in the wild.

Come spring, a visitor to Alaska can see a pair locking talons as they cartwheel in aerial courtship, swooping as low as a couple of feet from the ground. In summer, ship passengers approaching Sitka through the narrows in Neva Strait may count nearly 100 eagles. Later in the year, the world's largest convention of the birds—more than 3,500—gather at the Chilkat Bald Eagle Preserve near Haines, where these noble raptors lose most of their dignity gorging on a late run of spawning chum salmon. Balds bond for keeps, generally occupying a single nest throughout their 38-year lifetime. Adults, with their white heads and tails and yellow talons and beaks, stand up to 43 inches tall and have wingspans as wide as 8 feet. They can fly 30 miles an hour, plunge at 100, and detect a trout a mile distant. They will eat small mammals and birds, but as lazy scavengers (some Alaskans call them dandified vultures) they prefer carrion and even garbage. Their predators are humans—who slaughtered 100,000 of them between 1917 and 1952—which is why the Bald Eagle Protection Act now makes it illegal to kill or possess any part of an eagle or disturb its nesting site.

GOLDEN EAGLES look like immature bald eagles (which also don't have white heads), but these smaller raptors have gold on the back of their neck and on the leg feathers that stretch to their feet. Common in central Alaska, they are celebrated in many native cultures as the Thunderbird or Great Spirit. And, unlike the balds, they generally eat live prey.

NORTHERN HARRIERS, the only hawks to nest on the ground, are sometimes confused with SHORT-EARED OWLS. Both wing their way through the wetlands and salt marshes of Southeast in spring and fall, hunting the ratlike voles by day. Both have similar facial disks and bodies shaped like an ice cream cone. But the gray-and-brown harrier, or marsh hawk, has a white patch on its rump and flies in a series of smaller flaps of its long wings, interspersed with a glide—whereas the buff-to-brown owl makes the more exaggerated flutters of a moth.

Seabirds

Of all birds, ARCTIC TERNS are *the* long-haul flyers. They are known to make an annual 22,000-mile round trip between the Antarctic coast and the western hemisphere's northernmost reaches. On their layovers in Alaska, they breed anywhere from beaches and tidal flats to rivers and marshes, and even on glacial moraine. They dive below the water to catch small fish with their sharp-pointed beaks. You can glimpse these tall birds—with their characteristic black cap, white body, and red bill and feet—throughout

A bald eagle delivers a Dolly Varden dinner to its mate and three-week-old offspring.➤

the south of the state anytime but winter. One hangout: Potter Marsh, at the Anchorage Coastal Wildlife Refuge, just south of the city.

Members of the auk family are the North American equivalent of penguins, standing as erect as their Antarctic cousins, but *they* can fly, though awkwardly. Black-and-white, bright-billed PUFFINS, the most prominent of auks, use their meagre wings and strong legs, set well back, to swim underwater and catch fish and squid. They come ashore only to breed on cliffsides. Tufted puffins, so-called from the yellow feathers that flourish behind their eyes in nesting season, can sometimes be seen in Glacier Bay (along with the odd horned puffin, its white-bellied brother) and on Saint Lazaria Island near Sitka, one of the region's islands within the National Wildlife Refuge system.

All eight of the North American species of stubby-bodied, short-necked SEA DUCKS spend time in Southeast, the most numerous of the million ducks that winter here. Two of the more eloquently named, which are also on show for the cruise season, are the harlequin, whose blue-and-white body and chestnut flanks are reminscent of the traditional clown's costume; and the very vocal old-squaw, which has a long, needle-pointed tail.

Shorebirds

OYSTERCATCHERS, SANDPIPERS, and PLOVERS are the major families of numerous species of shorebirds visiting and often nesting in Southeast. Many of them migrate here from the southern coast of the U.S. and South and Central America. The vociferous oyster-catchers are larger and more colorful than the others; they wield their long, blunt, flat red bills to shuck clams, mussels and oysters. Sandpipers, including the snipe and curlew, are wading birds with sewing-needle bills and stovepipe legs on which they walk slowly and relentlessly as they graze the beach. The chubbier, shorter-legged plovers tend to run a lot before stopping to feed with their pigeon-sized bills—and some of them are masters of misdirection, decoying interlopers away from their nests by feigned injuries and pathetic little cries.

Waterfowl

The world's largest waterfowl, the legend-inspiring TRUMPETER SWANS, summer in Alaska—80 per cent of North America's no-longer-endangered population of 12,000 flock to the south coast of the state. White as Arctic snow, they have sinuous necks and the buglelike cry that christened them. With wingspans the width of eagles', they soar to heights of nearly two miles on their migratory flights to the Pacific Northwest. Trumpeters are hard to distinguish from the smaller WHISTLING SWANS, which usually have a yellow spot on their black bill. Perhaps ten times as abundant, the whistlers frequent Southeast waters.

VANCOUVER CANADA GEESE live and breed throughout the year from northern Vancouver Island to Prince William Sound. And all summer long, they abound in the Mendenhall Wetlands; you can see them conveniently in these tideflats near the Juneau Airport. The monogamous adults leave in April to nest elsewhere, whereas their adolescents remain until late June, when they head to Glacier Bay to molt. By August the whole family is back honking on the tideflats, a togetherness pattern they'll continue all their lives. The most sizable of Canada geese, they have the typical black head, white cheeks, and long black necks, but can weigh 16 pounds. Unlike others of their species, they nest on the ground in thick woods and occasionally even in trees, rather than on water.

The noisiest of all waterfowl, SNOW GEESE—all white, with black wing-tips—are more frequent in south-coastal and central areas during spring and fall. In September they migrate from Siberia to the Seward Peninsula and then the Yukon River delta before heading to California and other southwestern states. (Huge flocks touch down near the international airport in Vancouver.)

Land Birds

The AMERICAN DIPPER'S name may be an anomaly under this heading: the lyrical songbird spends a lot of its time underwater, on the bottom of streams where it walks along looking for insects and little fish. The Eskimos call it *anaruk kiviruk*—sunken old woman. And these chunky, short-tailed, gray perching birds are well endowed for their aquatic actitivies, with glands that create oil to waterproof their feathers, valves in their noses to keep out the water, and ducklike down that insulates them to -40° weather.

STELLER'S JAYS are amusing regulars at bird feeders in Southeast, where they display their street smarts in foraging—often ganging up to bully other species, and aping the cries of predators such as eagles to scare away competitors for food. Permanent residents here, they are dark blue, even black, and have the high-peaked comb of the common blue jay.

RUFOUS HUMMINGBIRDS, relatively recent arrivals in Southeast Alaska, now journey up from Mexico every mid-April while the snow is still around, then head south by August. They feed first on nectar from blossoming blueberry and salmonberry bushes before the flowering of western columbine and Indian paintbrush, which partly rely on these bird-world midgets for pollination. The rufous, all 3.5 inches of them, have needlepoint bills to suck the nectar, and split-end tongues that fold it back into their throats. Male hummingbirds seem all show, with their shimmering burst of orangey-red at the throats and their lack of interest in raising the young—a job they leave to the greenish-hued females, who are ferocious in their nestlings' defense against any human or wildlife interloper.

PTARMIGAN, Alaska's most plentiful grouse species, are a close cousin to another famous game bird, Scotland's red grouse. Although rock ptarmigan are more common, local school children cast ballots and made the willow ptarmigan the state bird. Perhaps they were influenced by the fact that the male is a good family man, assailing predators as big as hawks, helping tend the chicks as they hatch by early July, and even assuming the maternal duties if the female should die. Both types—which can be told apart only in summer by the willow's redder hue—were named for the habitat they prefer.

THE RASCALLY, MYTH-MAKING RAVEN

High atop Mount McKinley, ravens are more than a nuisance. When mountain climbers hide caches of food below the snow, marking them with staked flags to locate them on the descent, they find the birds have often got there first, delving a yard or more to pillage the bags and boxes. On the other hand, the Athabaskan Indians in the Brooks Range of northern Alaska claim that ravens will help them find game by uttering a special call—*ggaagga, ggaagga*—and by folding a wing and tumbling in the sky to pinpoint an animal.

Ravens have been bedevilling and bewitching humans throughout history, throughout the world. But it is in the Great Land where the glistening-black, two-foot-plus raven *(Corvus corax)* still looms even larger in the mind than its presence does in real life. Native peoples here have endowed the raven with mystical powers, symbolized on their totem poles. Elsewhere, it is an evil presence (as Edgar Allen Poe pointed out), but Indians of the Pacific Northwest and Alaska long ago considered the raven the creator of earth and—to amuse itself—of people.

With a wingspan four feet wide, and a weight about quadruple the American crow's, the imposing raven can also be distinguished from its relative by pointed rather than blunt wings, a long wedge of a tail in place of a square one, and a mostly caw-less vocabulary of calls that may be second only to humans'. They sing musically in choirs and coo to their mates-for-life softly and tenderly.

In scavenging and hunting, they demonstrate their astonishing intelligence. They have been seen working in teams to kill newborn reindeer fawns, with one raven separating mother from infant. And other teams have been observed stalking young seals sunning by their holes in the ice. A raven might fly into such a hole, blocking the escape hatch, while its colleague drives the seal away from the hole and then kills it with a well-directed strike of its powerful bill to the fragile top of the mammal's skull.

TUNDRA, FIERCE AND FRAGILE

Strolling the summer rainforests of Southeast Alaska, plush with cloud-scraping spruce and hemlock, you may wonder about the barren Alaska of the storybooks. But head just north and west of there, on land excursions that take you to such destinations as Denali National Park, Nome, and Prudhoe Bay, and you will begin to appreciate the expanse and allure of the TUNDRA.

This vast, mostly treeless plain (tundra is derived from a Finnish word for land without trees) stretches across the northern verge of the continent. Swathed for most of the year in hostile snow and ice, each summer it becomes a crazy quilt of hues as vegetation—including more than 600 species of flowering plants—erupts with a sudden glory. The tundra is not homogenous in plant life nor, despite its winter bleakness, monotone in color. Microclimates and unexpectedly rich soil combine to create startling vegetation vistas, such as the lush meadows of cotton grass that flourish not far from the bare foothills of the Brooks Range.

The transition between the northern forest and the tundra is called the TAIGA—Russian for land of little sticks, which nicely describes the pipe-cleaner-thin white and black spruce in South Central and the Interior. North of the taiga, the shrubs and stunted trees of the tundra, in tints of flame and gold during autumn, make way for viridescent grassland, which then yields to a polar desert dotted with lichen and moss—and a handful of tenacious perennials with blooms that seem prettier here than the most spectacular displays in the Lower 48.

The newest land in the world, tundra emerged when the glaciers retreated as recently as 8,000 years ago. Below most of it lies PERMAFROST, the perenially frozen ground that makes up 82 per cent of Alaska. Sometimes only a foot below the soil, it can be 2,000 feet or more thick and often choked with ice. Given this impermeable base, water has nowhere to drain each spring so it advances across the land while forcing the earth to bubble up in boil-like ruptures. Common to all tundra are PINGOS, ice mounds carpeted in soil and plants, which can rear up like tiny volcanoes to 150 feet and spread thousands of feet in diameter through the expansion of freezing water trapped between permafrost and the surface. Prevalent too are POLYGONS, a series of ice-edged, interlocking landforms shaped like huge honeycombs, created by the endless action of freezing and thawing. Polygons fill with shallow pools of summer meltwater that often swell and spill their banks to become ponds and well-defined, elongated lakes. The land in summer is awash in water despite annual snow and rain of 20 inches or less.

Trees grow slowly and low to the ground here, to withstand brutal winds; a willow that stands only a foot tall can be 15 feet long and a century old. Arctic plants have developed different techniques to withstand the intensity of their environment. The woolly lousewort uses the insulating hairs on its stems and buds to contain heat. Virtually all of the tundra plants are perennials; they survive the long, bitter winters by reserving their food and energy in bulbs and roots reaching well underground. Primitive lichens combine funguses and algae in a synergistic bonding: the algae creates carbohydrates for the fungus, which then gives the algae the necessary minerals and moisture.

Animals too must adapt to the tundra's inflexible conditions. Arctic ground squirrels hibernate for nine months deep in snow burrows that never get colder than 10°F because the squirrels put their doorway below their sleep room, which prevents their body heat from escaping. And the snowy owl is so well adjusted to this land—the hostile yet life-enhancing tundra—that it even lays its eggs in the snow.

A splendid view of the tundra against the backdrop of the Alaska Range in Denali.➤

A WORLD OF WILDFLOWERS

"In whatever direction the eye might look, wild flowers were growing in greatest profusion. Dandelions as big as asters, buttercups
twice the usual size, and violets rivalling the products of cultivation were visible around. Berries and berry blossoms grew in a
profusion and variety which I have never seen equaled in lower
altitudes." That's Frederick Schwatka, a First Lieutenant in the U.S.
Army and a graduate in law and medicine, rhapsodizing in *Along
Alaska's Great River*, his account of an expedition along the Yukon
River in 1883. Today you can view about 1,500 species of plants in
Alaska, including trees, shrubs, ferns, grasses, and sedges—but of
them all, the brief-lived, gloriously painted flowering plants may
delight you most.

As in the south, Alaska's wildflowers thrive along lakes and
roadsides and across alpine meadows, and you can always find
them here in thick throngs on the tundra. The majority are delicate and, like their growing season, short. The official flower, for
instance: the fragile-looking forget-me-not *(Myosotis alpestris)* has
vivid blue petals around a yellow center; it grows no more than 18
inches while its arctic counterpart never tops 4 inches. But some
flowers take terrific advantage of the long days and explode like
fireworks. Blooming through the summer, throughout most of the
state, are easily identifiable stands of stately, violet-blue lupine,
up to 4 feet tall, and magenta fireweed, which can reach 10 feet
(and whose shoots helped feed the 18th-century Vitus Bering expedition). In meadows near the tides of the southern regions, you
can walk through fields of flowers as high as your hips: yellow and
red Indian paintbrush, white yarrow, purply blue flag (or wild iris).
Along with the blossoms you know from the south—violets and
buttercups and wild roses—look for such indigenous delights as
the delicate Arctic poppy and the chocolate lily, a purple-brown
flower growing 2 feet high in open grasslands, whose nickname Indian rice comes from the edible pellets that coat its bulbs.

The photographs on the facing page are a mere sampling of
the pleasure that awaits you.

Indian Rice or Chocolate Lily

Arctic Poppy

Fairy Slipper

Western Columbine

Cinquefoil or Tundra Rose

Chiming Bells or Languid Lady

THE NATIVE WAY

Their homes may be in Anchorage where 14,500 live, or far north in the Arctic National Wildlife Refuge, where the isolated village of Kaktovik has a few hundred permanent residents. Alaska's 86,000 Native peoples collectively own one-ninth of the state and are dispersed throughout it, most in rural areas, some in isolated villages with no road connections to the outside. Their lifestyles combine imported southern comfort and traditional northern toil. Satellite telephones link distant health clinics to a modern hospital; high schools have indoor swimming pools; planes fly in with pineapples and Pampers. While some men might earn $60,000 a year on the oil rigs, others with considerably lesser income hunt and fish to feed their families because store-bought food is so expensive. Though they travel to the open sea in snowmobiles and put outboard motors on their modern boats, they will work together in the old way to land a whale. Not long ago, 150 Inupiats from Barrow spent five hours hauling a 50-ton bowhead out of the Chukchi Sea and another seven hours carving and sharing its meat and blubber. Alaska's Native Indians, Eskimos, and Aleuts continue to subsist on and care for the land that sustained their ancestors. As the Yup'ik Eskimos say, the sea is their bank, the land is their life.

Alaska's First Peoples have long been political activists. To promote their rights, they formed the Alaska Native Brotherhood in 1912 and the Sisterhood in 1915. Also in that year, Athabascan chiefs convinced Alaska's delegate to Congress that the state should not have a reservation system. Native peoples elected a representative to the state legislature as early as 1925. A decade later, they sued the federal government over lost timberlands. They stopped the proposed use of a nuclear device to excavate a harbor on the northwest coast. They tied up the entire state in land-claims litigation, and formed the Alaska Federation of Natives

Eskimos, though no longer dependent on
sled dogs, still cherish their hardiness.

to push their claims through Congress. Finally, they allied themselves with oil companies to achieve the Alaska Native Claims Settlement Act of 1971.

ANCSA plucked Native peoples from lives of communal subsistence and plunged them into the business world as stockholders in landholding, multimillion-dollar corporations. It may have taught them to function more like white people but it has paradoxically led to a cultural rebirth. University of California anthropologist Wendell H. Oswalt points out that ANCSA required Natives to examine their historical, biological, and geographical connections in order to claim the right to be enrolled in a regional and village corporation and to share in the corporations' money-making ventures. As a result, he writes, "a personal identity as a Native Alaskan became a favorable status for the first time in this century."

While Native corporations made and lost millions of dollars in the 1970s and 1980s, some members became increasingly nervous about losing their land, which the corporations owned. If individuals sold their stocks, the corporations would be vulnerable to non-Native takeover. A 1987 amendment to ANCSA prevented the sale of stocks unless a corporation voted to lift the ban. (By 1993, no corporation had taken that step.) Coincidentally, in western Alaska one village began a movement to dissolve village corporations in favor of tribal councils, which are protected from takeover under the Indian Reorganization Act of 1934.

In the 1990s, the right of villages to govern themselves is likely to be a prominent issue. This movement toward sovereignty offers hope for control and revitalization among people who have been particularly afflicted by modern social ills. Life expectancy among Alaskan Natives is astonishingly low: a 50-year-old Eskimo comments with sadness that in the Yukon-Kuskokwim area he is one of the older people. The suicide rate among young native men is ten times the national average; the occurrence of fetal alcohol syndrome in native infants is twice the national rate. Murder, rape, arrest, and psychiatric-admission rates for native Alaskans are all multiples of those for non-Natives.

On the other hand, there are villages that have banned alcohol, high schools that invite elders to teach traditional skills, communities that keep alive ancient ceremonies. In some cases, tribal councils have stimulated an examination of cultural values. Anthropologist Ann Fienup-Riordan studied one example in western Alaska. In the 1980s, several villages dissolved their corporations and formed the Yupiit Nation. Trying to find a culturally appropriate way to govern themselves, its members have researched traditional forms of government and resurrected a respect for their ancestors' ways. Participants in their meetings use the Yup'ik language; elders are allowed to speak first and are rarely interrupted; everyone who wants to speak is given a chance. While the Yupiit Nation has not realized its goal of dealing directly with the U.S. government, it has given its members a forum where, in a traditional way, they can discuss the issues that concern all Native Alaskans today: control of land and local affairs, economic conditions, and the survival of their languages and values.

THE COMPLEX ESKIMO CULTURE

The Eskimos we know from movies and schoolbooks lived in igloos, hunted polar bears, ate raw seal meat, and struggled to survive in a punishing environment. This stereotype, drawn from the peoples of the high Canadian Arctic, never applied to Alaskan Eskimos.

The people anthropologists call Eskimo extend from Siberia through Alaska and Canada to Greenland, but Eskimo isn't what they call themselves. Even the widely accepted source of the name—from the Algonquian for "eaters of raw flesh"—is being challenged by authorities who say it is a Chipeweyan word meaning "snowshoe-netter." In Canada, Eskimos are known as Inuit; in Alaska, two broad designations are used: Inupiat for the Eskimos north of Norton Sound and Yup'ik for those south of the Sound. Both mean "a real or genuine person."

Early anthropologists found a rich complexity and diversity among Alaskan Eskimos, so much so that it was impossible to define an Eskimo culture. Grouped in 21 tribes, they lived, and still live, in a variety of climates from the relatively warm and abundant islands and shores of the Gulf of Alaska to the frigid desert of the Arctic slopes. Some never saw polar bears. Some hunted great whales, others only caribou. Some scooped salmon out of rivers and were more like their Indian neighbors. But none lived permanently in igloos, nor ate raw meat. And for most, their environment, rather than being impoverished, was an ample provider. Even though we picture Eskimos busily gathering enough food to last through a winter, Wendell Oswalt found that many tribes had a more relaxed attitude and would let fish go uncaught while they feasted on their dried stores. There was, he says, "no Protestant ethic among Alaskan Eskimos."

While most now communicate in English, language once created a major distinction. From the north shores of Norton Sound around to the Canadian border, the Inupiat spoke Inupiak. Central,

Late 1800s: a baby wearing a Tlingit-type cap but asleep in an Athabascan-style sling.

Pacific Gulf, and St. Lawrence Island Eskimos spoke Yup'ik, a language with many dialects. The two tongues are as different as English and French, and it is easier for an Inupiak speaker to communicate with an Eskimo far away in Greenland than with a Yup'ik neighbor.

If the Inupiat and Yup'ik didn't build igloos, where did they live? Some inland tribes close to the Athabaskan Indians fashioned dome-shaped houses with pole frames, but usually Alaskan Eskimos established villages of permanent semi-subterranean houses of driftwood, whalebone, and sod, sometimes heated with a fireplace or seal-oil lamp. The inhabitants entered their homes by way of a cold-trapping tunnel, set deeper the farther north they lived. Most houses were equipped with raised sleeping platforms, and some were finished inside with driftwood-plank floors and cupboards. In summer when families were more mobile, they used portable tepees or campsite shelters.

Studies of the traditional lives of the Yup'ik contradict the common conception of a peace-loving people living in nuclear families. Men, and boys after the age of five, occupied a communal residence—a *qasgiq*, or kashgee. Wives brought meals to their husbands in the qasgiq, and husbands visited their wives who lived with their young children and other female relatives in a smaller house called an *enet*. So important were children that both parents dropped their own names and were known by the name of their firstborn. Feasts marked a child's achievements: the first time a boy killed anything, even an insect, and the first time a girl picked a berry or provided something the family could eat.

Divorce was common. A woman with a lazy husband ended the marriage by refusing to cook for him; a man divorced a wife who hoarded food, perhaps by abandoning her without supplies. Though wars between tribes had ceased by the 1830s, before then bloody battles were commonly waged. Long-standing grievances led to surprise attacks in which the goal was to exterminate the enemy, leaving one survivor to tell the unhappy tale. Warriors tattooed their faces and chests to indicate the number of enemies they had killed.

ALEUTS: A RETURN FROM TRAGEDY

The Aleuts have had a tragic history. It is no exaggeration to say that in the past 250 years their numbers have been decimated by contacts with outsiders. When the Russian fur traders invaded their windblown homeland, there may have been as many as 25,000 individuals throughout the 279 Aleutian Islands. By the end of the 18th century, there were perhaps 3,000 left. As American citizens, the Aleuts were unceremoniously herded from their homes in 1942, after the Japanese bombed Dutch Harbor. They were moved to a cannery in Southeast for two miserable years during which a fifth of them died. Today, there may be 1,000 full-blooded Aleuts on a handful of the islands or in the Pribilofs. Their fortunes have taken on optimistic overtones in recent years: the Aleut Corporation, with more than 3,000 shareholders, has surface rights to 52,000 acres and sub-surface rights to 1.25 million acres. Commercial fishing and eco-tourism are rejuvenating the islands of St. Paul and St. George in the Pribilofs, where most of Alaska's Aleuts live.

Anthropologists believe that at some time after their arrival in North America, the Eskimoan people subdivided into Eskimo and Aleut. The Aleuts occupied the 1,200-mile arc of islands—the longest archipelago in the world—that separates the Pacific Ocean and the Bering Sea. In spite of moderate temperatures, the islands are frequently enshrouded in fog or whipped by high-velocity winds, known as williwaws. Bushes, grasses, and sedges grow luxuriantly on the almost treeless land. The oldest known settlement in the Aleutians dates back 8,750 years.

The precontact Aleuts had a high standard of living. They practised medicine and surgery. They developed art and music, and mounted elaborate masked ceremonies (the conclusion of which, unfortunately for art history, sometimes meant the destruction of the masks). They lived in semi-subterranean sod houses, which were earthquake-proof and sheltered from the capricious winds. A rich Aleut might have as many as 20 slaves, obtained as prisoners of war. The Aleuts were skilled hunters of sea

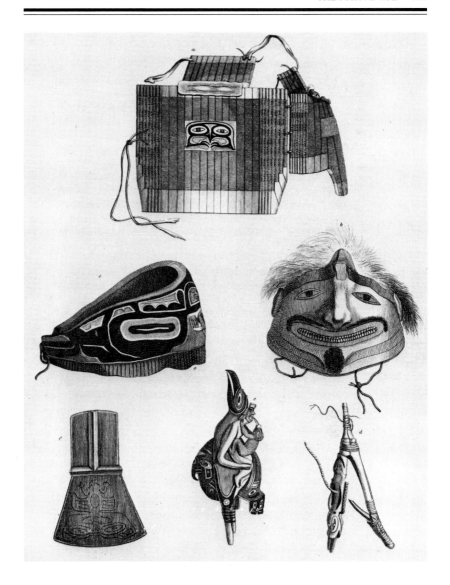

In 1805, Russians sketched this sampling of Tlingit artifacts, including the versatile *ulu* knife (bottom left).

mammals, and much of their art was created with the hope of ensuring successful hunting.

THE ART OF ALEUTS AND ESKIMOS

Three overlapping motivations categorize Eskimo and Aleut art. In the traditional period before outsiders arrived, spiritual beliefs inspired the crafting of ceremonial and utilitarian objects. Charms carved in the shape of a human face were attached to Aleut hunting weapons to guide them to the animals. Human figures, which seem to be searching the sea for prey, crouched atop Aleut hunters' hats. An Eskimo hunter might make a seal-shaped box to hold his lance points, believing that the tools would become accustomed to being inside a seal.

While this sort of artistic expression continued after contact with Europeans, Eskimos and Aleuts quickly learned to make objects for sale. (When Captain Vancouver visited the Kenai Peninsula in 1794, he was offered model kayaks that had been made as souvenirs.) Throughout the 19th century, the production of beautiful objects for personal use was accompanied by those offered for sale. In the 20th century, Eskimo and Aleut artists have continued to make art for the tourist and gallery markets, emerging from anonymity by signing their work. Only in recent times have they entered a third phase of artistic expression that steps outside their own culture—the making of art for art's sake.

Throughout Alaska in traditional times, Eskimos and Aleuts used ivory, stone, wood, bone, grasses, hides, furs, and animal intestines to make a dazzling variety of art objects. A visit to one of Alaska's museums might be enhanced by the selective viewing of a few outstanding items.

Prehistoric stone lamps: Found in archeological sites, especially in the Kodiak Island area, these oval containers were decorated on their outside rims with sculptured animals, whales, or humans.

Carved ivory weapons: The Eskimo believed that an animal should be hunted with beautiful implements because the animal's spirit—its *inua*—would be reborn in another animal and would remember that it had been treated with respect. Their fish spears, toggle-headed harpoons, and harpoon darts, as well as being technically ingenious, were works of art.

The Nunivak tusk: In the 1920s, the Eskimo men on Nunivak Island began carving walrus tusks in a unique way, with animals and birds linked in one long, deeply carved chain.

The Nunivak eye: Many ivory objects are decorated with this dot-within-a-circle motif, which is called "the eye of awareness." It has been explained as a symbol of the ability of a shaman—the spiritual leader who may cure people and tell the future—to journey into another world (through the hole in the circle) or to see into other worlds.

Amulets and charms: Made by both Aleuts and Eskimos, they provided supernatural protection or help. Aleuts most often carved ivory sea otters as charms. An Eskimo might have two dozen amulets, each representing a spiritual helper. Charms were attached to boats or houses.

Ivory drill bow handles: In the historic period, these drilling devices, which resemble a bow and arrow, were engraved with scenes of Eskimo life, such as ships trading with Bering Sea Eskimos, or important events in the artist's own life.

Engraved ivory cribbage boards: The first boards may have been carved early in this century by Happy Jack, an Eskimo from Little Diomede Island who had lost both feet in a hunting accident. Long, sinuous walrus tusks were used for this popular souvenir.

Ivory, bone, antler, wood, and baleen story knives: A knife was usually carved by a male relative for a young Eskimo girl, who used it to draw on the ground as she told a story, which always began with the sketching of a house floor plan. Girls apparently found it difficult to tell a story unless they were drawing at the same time.

Coiled baskets: Poorly made in the 19th century, the grass baskets of the Yup'ik women began to improve in the early years of this century. The technique involves coiling a bundle of compressed rye-grass stems, and stitching together succeeding levels of the coil. Traditional designs were simple geometric patterns.

Wooden masks: Eskimos made a variety of masks, representing human faces, or half-animal/half-human faces. Worn by dancers in ceremonies rather than in war, masks honored the spirits of animals or birds about to be hunted, or evoked angry or dangerous spirits. Some masks covered almost the whole body.

Aleut weaving: Aleut women made exceptionally delicate baskets, mats, boot liners, hats, and mittens using wild rye grass, the blades of which were dried and cured and split with a fingernail. Different weaves developed on Atka and Attu islands, where the women wove some of the finest baskets in the world. Even exceptionally skilled weavers took 15 hours to add an inch in height to a three-inch-diameter basket. Before contact with westerners, baskets were decorated with eagle down, feathers, baleen, and colored grass; afterward, threads of silk and wool were incorporated. To supply the 19th-century market, weavers made card cases, covered bottles, and lidded baskets. Production declined in the years after World War I when a number of basketmakers died, but it has since been revived.

Bentwood hats: Made of a single piece of wood, steamed and bent into a triangular shape, these hats were worn by wealthy Aleut leaders. The visorlike front was both blessing and hazard: it shaded the wearer's eyes when he was hunting at sea, but might have caught a gust of wind and overturned his boat. The hats were painted, and decorated with ivory amulets, feathers, beads, or bristles of a sea lion, of which each animal has only four. Hats aquiver with bristles indicated the owner's hunting skills.

Gut parkas: Made from sea lion, walrus, bear, and whale intestine carefully seamed in horizontal strips, these Aleut garments were lightweight and completely waterproof. They were called *kamleikas* by the Russians who, impressed by their efficacy, wore them. Some were decorated with strips of sea-lion esophagus and loops or patterns of tufted and embroidered hair.

THE INDIANS OF ALASKA

Historically, the two groups of Indians in Alaska—the Athabascans of the Interior and the Tlingit, Haida, and Tsimshian of Southeast—were as different as socialists and capitalists.

The Athabascans were the first peoples to cross the land bridge to North America, and are related to the Navajo and Apache far to the south. In Alaska, they settled mostly in the Interior along rivers, though some had villages around Cook Inlet or the Gulf of Alaska.

The seafaring Haida, whose homeland was the Queen Charlottes, settled on Prince of Wales and Dall islands before contact with Europeans. Their language is a linguistic loner, totally unrelated to any other. In Alaska, the Haida were known as the Kaigani. Today, about 1,000 Haida remain in Alaska, 300 of them in Hydaburg, a village founded in 1911.

The Tlingits (*klink*-its), whose language is in the Na-Dene family of Athabascan tongues, occupied the territory from Yakutat Bay to Portland Canal, including portions of Prince of Wales Island that were not controlled by the Haida. Fierce warriors, they fought the Russians and were never defeated. Undaunted by seeing their village at Angoon wiped out by the U.S. Navy in 1882, they sent two war canoes to Seattle a few years later to recover a totem pole stolen by a tourist. About 10,000 Tlingits remain in Southeast; another 1,000 live in Anchorage.

The Tsimshians arrived in Alaska in historic times. A group of 823 left Prince Rupert, British Columbia, and followed their leader, Anglican missionary William Duncan, to Annette Island, southwest of present-day Ketchikan. There, in 1887, they founded New

Metlakatla, a model community where they operated a sawmill and cannery. Annette Island is the only reservation in Alaska, and its 1,000 Tsimshians were the only Natives who exempted themselves from the Native Claims Settlement Act.

ARTISTS AND ACQUISITORS

Life for the inland Athabascans was hard. Famine was frequent and cannibalism was not unknown. Their territory was the coniferous forest that the Russians call *taiga*, or land of little sticks. They were forced to keep moving to hunt caribou, moose, and rabbit— sources of food that were always on the move. They also caught salmon, using a trap that funneled fish into an enclosure.

Though they created permanent villages, their mobility called for a variety of portable or temporary housing, including ice caves. The Kutchin, whose territory extended well into the Arctic Circle, built villages of log houses with gable roofs. To live on the land, they carried a *nivaze*—a domed tent of caribou or moose hides over a spruce framework, which two families would use—or a tepee of four poles and a single skin. Because the Athabascans had to survive in freezing temperatures, they wore carefully tailored clothing of caribou and moose hides, which they decorated with beads and quills. Expert in making snowshoes and dogsleds, they were nowhere near as artistically prolific as their southern neighbors.

Great artists that they were, the Tlingit and Haida in Alaska were above all else capitalists. Creating, accumulating, and displaying wealth ruled their existence. Living in the naturally abundant Panhandle, they had both the means to get rich and the leisure to make magnificent works of art that declared their wealth. Their societies were hierarchical: things were ranked (interior houseposts were more valuable than exterior ones) and so were people—from the lowest slave to the leader of a house, who constantly strove to maintain his position.

Tlingit and Haida tribes were divided into two groups that anthropologists call moieties. The Tlingit moieties were Raven and Wolf (or Eagle in the north); the Haida divisions were Raven and Eagle. Individuals inherited the moiety of their mother, and had to marry a member of the opposite—in other words, the father's—lineage. The leadership of a house (which was a grouping of several families living together) passed usually to a maternal nephew.

The moieties were obliged to perform certain tasks for one another. For example, when a man wanted a crest carved, his wife's brother did the work or paid an artist to do it. When a man died, members of his wife's lineage dressed his corpse and cremated it. If he had been an important individual, they would tear his house down and build a new one for his family. Obligations, once met, had to be reciprocated. Funerary services, for instance, were repaid with a potlatch.

Christian missionaries saw in the potlatch an excess of feasting and wasteful gift-giving. They did not understand its complex roles. Among the Tlingit, the ceremony maintained social order

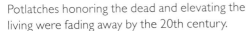

Potlatches honoring the dead and elevating the living were fading away by the 20th century.

and defined the relationships among people. Its impetus was to honor a dead relative and to pay the debts incurred by his funeral. At the same time, the right of the host to succeed the deceased was declared and witnessed by the guests.

Among the Haida, the ceremony fulfilled the role of our credit unions and life insurance policies. By potlatching them, a Haida repaid members of his own moiety who had helped him in some way. Giving his wealth away was an investment because in a few years, the guests would repay him with interest. If he died, they would care for his orphaned children. The totem pole raised at a Haida potlatch validated what had taken place.

Outlawed in Canada between 1884 and 1951, the ceremony simply faded away in Alaska by the turn of the century. The last great potlatch was a cross-racial revival held in Wrangell in 1940 to commemorate the restoration of Chief Shakes Tribal House on Shakes Island in the inner harbor. To pay for the event, at which he was named the seventh Chief Shakes, Tlingit Charlie Jones adopted the Wrangell Chamber of Commerce into his tribe and accepted its financial contribution.

Unlike their neighbors to the south, the Athabascan tribes were not much interested in art. They did excel in beadwork and tailoring, and made containers of birchbark and woven baskets. The Haida, Tlingit, and Tsimshian surrounded themselves with art, their best-known works being monumental wood carvings. Most visitors to Alaska will encounter at least one totem pole, if not one park where groups of poles are dramatically displayed. *(See* How To Read a Totem Pole, *page 128.)* Native Indian artifacts of note in museums include the following:

Chilkat blankets: The Chilkat, a northern Tlingit group, excelled at weaving these blankets from the wool of mountain goats. It took the wood from three goats to make one blanket. They twisted bark of yellow cedar trees with strands of spun wool to form the warp threads. The geometric totemic designs were woven by women following pattern boards painted by men.

Materials such as hemlock bark, iron, wolf moss, woolen trade cloth, and urine produced the yellow, black, and blue dyes. Chilkat blankets had a higher status than button blankets.

Coppers or tinnehs: These two- to three-foot-long plaques of beaten copper covered with black paint or graphite, with engraved or carved crests, were always made in the same shieldlike shape. They can be recognized by ridges that form a T. Among the Southeastern Indians and particularly among the Tlingit, they seem to have been used like money, their value increasing as they were traded or sold. Their symbolic value was also powerful; individual coppers had sentimental names, and their histories were remembered. At feasts, as a demonstration of his wealth, a chief might break off pieces which themselves became valuable and might be bought by a rival who would attempt to accumulate the whole copper. Sometimes, insults were avenged by giving a piece of a copper to the offender. Coppers are sometimes incorporated into a totem pole carving.

Labrets: Women of high rank inserted these oval wood or stone ornaments into a slit in their lower lips. They can be seen on several totem poles in Alaska.

Ceremonial spoons: Families treasured these carved and decorated wood or horn implements, which were used to ladle food at feasts and ceremonies.

Masks: Southeast Indians always carved masks to be worn in ceremonies. Their masks are less complicated than those of the south coast; there are fewer mechanical masks but more minimally painted portraits. Tlingit shamans were buried with their religious paraphernalia, which included masks they had worn while practising their healing and ceremonial arts.

Bentwood boxes: Made of a single plank, kerfed at the corners, and steamed and bent into shape, these boxes were watertight and could be used to store liquids or to cook foods (by heating liquid inside the box with hot stones). They were elaborately painted with family crests.

Beadwork: Athabascan women were expert at decorating skin clothing and footwear using porcupine quills, flattened with the teeth, and carved wood beads or seeds. Later, they incorporated tooth shells and glass beads in trading with Southeast Indians and westerners.

Baskets: Athabascans cooked food or carried water in birch-bark containers. They also made coiled and geometrically decorated baskets of willow roots, carefully dug and split. Tlingit spruce-root baskets, in twined weaving, were decorated with red and black patterns. Some baskets had lids that rattled because loose stones had been hidden in the weaving.

Eagle, Raven or Thunderbird crests can
often be distinguished atop totem poles.
(See How To Read a Totem Pole, *pages 128–29.*)

HOW TO READ A TOTEM POLE

The totem pole was the perfect expression of lofty status among the hierarchical Indian societies on the northwest coast. Standing tall in front of a house, a pole made a public declaration of ancestry, affiliations, and real or imagined events that had shaped a family's history.

The Tlingit, Haida, and Tsimshian raised several types of poles. An early form was inside their longhouses, where as many as four poles supported the roof. Outside, a frontal pole framed the doorway or sat to one side of it, flush against the house. Memorial poles, with one figure at the top, or with top and bottom figures, were erected to commemorate a leader. Mortuary poles had the same function, but also contained a box or niche for the body or the ashes of the deceased.

The totem pole reached a peak of artistic expression in the mid-19th century. Carved of red cedar by a commissioned artist, totem poles were raised by wealthy leaders and stood in front of, but not right up against, their houses. At a feast or potlatch after the raising of a pole, the owner would explain the significance of the figures.

Begin examining a pole at the top where you'll likely see the crest figure of the owner, the common ones being Raven, Eagle, or Thunderbird. The legend of Raven and how he gave the world light by stealing the sun from a stingy chief is depicted on several Alaskan poles. Raven sits on the box in which the chief kept the Sun. Another figure you will easily recognize at the top is the Watchman. In the body of the pole, look for the figures described below.

Raven: The large and straight beak is the key. The figure is usually upright, with wings close to its sides.

Eagle: Again, look to the beak. Eagle's is shorter than Raven's, curved and comes to a downturning point.

Thunderbird: Though the beak resembles Eagle's, curved horns on top of the head are unique to Thunderbird. The wings may be outspread. Kolus, Thunderbird's younger brother, has straight, horizontal tufts.

Watchmen: These crouching human figures sit atop Haida (and sometimes Tlingit and Tsimshian) poles surveying sea or land to warn of approaching danger. They wear high hats that look like segmented stove pipes. The segments, called skils, might indicate the number of feasts or potlatches given by the chief for whom the pole was carved. Skils sometimes appear as part of the body of the pole.

Bear: Flared nostrils or a short snout, a full set of squared-off teeth (and perhaps some sharp incisors), and a protruding tongue are the tip-offs. Bear's ears are small.

Wolf: Can be distinguished from Bear by its longer, slender snout and ears, and its many large teeth.

Beaver: With its two big incisors, a stick between its paws, and a cross-hatched tail, Beaver is easy to identify.

Frog: Crouched in sideview or diving, Frog shows a toothless mouth, a goofy grin, and big round eyes.

Whale: Look for blowholes carved as human faces. The grey whale has a short fin on its back and long side fins. A long back fin, short pectoral fins, and fiercer expression indicate a killer whale.

Mosquito: A long, downturning proboscis is the obvious clue.

Human beings: People usually don't wear clothes, though a chief may sport a hat with a number of skils. Europeans are dressed and may have heavy, wavy beards. Uncle Sam is readily identifiable atop the Centennial Hall pole in Juneau; Abraham Lincoln is the top figure on a Saxman Village pole.

Transformations: Check out a creature's limbs; they may be clearly human. You may be seeing an animal with human characteristics or a human with animal characteristics— and getting a glimpse into the spiritual world of Southeast Indians where magical transformations took place, and animals became human by shedding their skins.

PORTS OF CALL AND OTHER SPECIAL PLACES

Southeast Alaska . . . is not so much a collection of separate places as an intricate web of life bound together by weather and the movement of tides. An eagle rises with a fish clutched in its talons. Sitka black-tailed deer move silent as shadows through the lush undergrowth of the forest. A grizzly prowls a stream bank, looking for salmon. A pod of orcas, or killer whales, surfaces and moves in search of seals. This is a corner of the earth not yet overwhelmed by people.

— Art Davidson, *Alakshak: The Great Country*

The majority of cruise passengers explore Southeast Alaska, the Panhandle that forms ten per cent of the state. This strip of land paralleling the northwestern coast of mainland British Columbia embraces a thousand islands scattered off the thickly treed shoreline. It is separated from the Alaskan Frying Pan by a mammoth ice field; by the St. Elias Mountains, among the world's loftiest coastal ranges; and by the seasonal rain that keeps Southeast fresh and evergreen. Despite the lushness, this is as real an Alaska as the barren tundra Up North. The belligerent, snow-drenched winter weather, enveloping wilderness, and capricious seas combine to make life here raw, unpredictable, on the edge. True, there are 70,000 Southeasterners—including Tlingit, Tsimshian, and Haida Indians, but no Eskimos—which makes it sound more populated than seekers of the wild may wish. But to put that in context: the 17-million-acre Tongass National Forest, America's largest, with its black-tailed deer, brown bear, and bald eagles, encompasses about

A reflected field of cotton grass—one of Alaska's extraordinary landscapes.

three-quarters of the region. It is literally Southeast's backyard. And there are only about 50 miles of all-weather roads in the entire region. Even if you travel nowhere else but the Panhandle, you have encountered a true Alaska, unlike anything in the Lower 48.

Venture farther, by luxury train, motorcoach, or plane, and you'll witness other, equally fascinating treasures of the 49th state. In the Interior looms Mount McKinley—The Great One—within one of the biggest wildlife sanctuaries on the planet, Denali National Park. On the Arctic Ocean at Prudhoe Bay, amid the caribou-rich tundra of the North Slope, American petroleum companies wrest black gold from the continent's largest oil field. West across the Arctic Circle, on the Bering Sea, Nome retains its flavor as the most riotous of pioneer gold-rush towns, and Kotzebue is a vital Eskimo community whose inhabitants herd reindeer and still hunt walrus and other sea mammals for subsistence.

What follow are mini-portraits of the ports (including British Columbia's Vancouver and Victoria), inland communities, and other pleasures you can experience by ship or on shore excursions. Features of special interest to cruise-ship passengers—such as tours and visitor attractions—and specific places they're most likely to visit are indicated by SMALL CAPITAL LETTERS. Because cruises have varying itineraries, listings are alphabetic for easy reference.

ANCHORAGE: ALASKA ALL AROUND

The grizzly was on the prowl that October day in 1991. Not a surprising sight in most of Alaska, but this chocolate-brown, three-year-old, quarter-ton bear was making its way through the throngs on the streets of downtown Anchorage. Unfortunately, because so many people came to watch—a local radio station gave updates on the grizzly's progress—biologists had to kill the animal, rather than take a chance on tranquillizing it. The incident was another reminder that the state's largest and most sophisticated city, holding nearly half its population, is still a mere step away from the wilds of South Central Alaska.

There's a standing joke that Anchorage is only half an hour from Alaska. It is ringed on three sides by the Alaska and Aleutian ranges and the Talkeetna Mountains, and juts into the twin arms of Cook Inlet, all of which moderate the snowfall and temperatures. Sealed away perhaps, but more than 100 flights from two-score cities arrive each day at the international airport, the springboard for cruise passengers heading to Fairbanks, Prudhoe Bay, Nome, Kotzebue, and Seattle.

Despite its youth—slightly more than seven decades old—Anchorage acts like the older brother of Alaskan communities. The only big city in the state seems reliable and a little driven. Born of conventional commerce, a railroad town, it has a much less checkered past than its siblings. Anchorage maintains a cast of respectability despite its undesirable districts (Spenard Road near the airport, with its escort-service clientele, comes to mind). In cultural terms, this is a highly livable community with a dozen musical groups, among them a symphony orchestra and ballet and opera companies; the highly regarded Alaska Repertory Theater; a museum of history and art; and the artistic activities generated by the campuses of the University of Alaska, Anchorage, and Alaska Pacific University. The $70-million Performing Arts Center opened in 1988 to a first season featuring Rudolf Nureyev, Itzhak Perlman, and Leontyne Price. In fact, Anchorage has been declared second only to Honolulu in *The Livable Cities Almanac*. The author based much of his ratings on life expectancy, which in Anchorage's case he attributes to a diet high in fish.

Fishing, of course, is what locals and visitors do a lot of here, recreationally, along with the more focused food fishing of Native peoples, who make up five per cent of the quarter-million urban population. Anchoragites also rock-climb and kayak, ski and snowshoe. Every second home seems to have a boat or float plane, a camper or snow machine, to escape the city's 1,700 square miles for the wilderness on their doorstep. An extensive network of bi-

Anchorage's big-city office towers are
humbled by the encircling mountains.➤

cycle paths threads the city. Even in town, there are perceptible signs of what's Out There, such as moose wandering by a suburban backyard. A dozen miles south on the Seward Highway, more than 130 species of waterfowl, from arctic terns to sandhill cranes, can be viewed from a boardwalk along Potter Marsh, the ANCHORAGE COASTAL WILDLIFE REFUGE. And the lakes around Anchorage International, one of the nation's busiest airports, support high flyers of another kind: nesting Canada geese, ducks, and terns.

Anchorage, the state's transportation hub, started life as a tent city hewn out of the wild to serve the crews building the Alaska Railroad from Seward to Fairbanks in 1915. Before then, the peninsula between Turnagain and Knik Arms of Cook Inlet had been a sometime home to Eskimos, who were displaced by the

Main Street, Anchorage, 1964:
A major quake rearranges the city.

Tanainas, an Athabaskan tribe. These nomads were on hand to trade sea-otter furs with Capt. James Cook in 1778. Because the British explorer could find no passage out of the inlet's arm, it came to be known as Turnagain. The other arm, Knik (pronounced Kuh-nik), bears an Eskimo word for fire. Gold brought more white men here, but it wasn't until the railroad came through that anyone bothered to stay. As many as 7,000 laborers and entrepreneurs lived under canvas and later in log cabins before the settlement was officially incorporated in 1920. While the area had been known as Ship Creek and Knik Anchorage, the settlers wanted to name the port Alaska City—but the Post Office settled on Anchorage. Even then, observers were noting that it didn't resemble any typical Alaskan town.

A local newspaper publisher once remarked that Hitler, Tojo, Stalin, Mao Zedong, and Ho Chi Minh had been the greatest developers of Anchorage. And it's true that the strategically sited town profited from the building of army and air force bases during World War II and further military expenditures in the decades since. In 1957, when oil was found on the Kenai Peninsula south of Anchorage, and later at Prudhoe Bay, there were other booms as petroleum companies moved in and built the office towers that dominate the cityscape. Seven years later, the city—along with many other communities in a 500-mile swath of southern Alaska—was first shattered by North America's worst earthquake of the century (see The Bad Friday Quake, page 139) and then revitalized in the aftermath of reconstruction. EARTHQUAKE PARK (at the far western end of Northern Lights Blvd.), a residential neighborhood flattened in 1964, has an interpretative display of the Big One. In the 1970s, Anchorage became headquarters for many of the large Native regional corporations created under the Alaska Native Claims Settlement Act; one of them, Cook Inlet Region, Inc., constructed a glass-sheathed landmark building.

Today, as oil money ebbs, increasing tourism helps stabilize the city's roller-coaster economy. Many visitors use Anchorage as a base en route to the rest of the state—to the Kenai Peninsula in the south, for instance, or to Denali National Park in the Interior.

The journey north takes them through Alaska's breadbasket, the MATANUSKA VALLEY, unique in its lush growing conditions. The Mat-Su, as it is nicknamed, was carved during the last Ice Age, and its fertile soil and long summer days produce brobdingnagian vegetables—3-pound beets, 10-pound celery, 83-pound cabbages. As the center of the agriculture industry, the valley has experimental farms and, at Palmer (pop.: 3,000), the preserved remnants of the farming colony of transplanted Midwesterners formed during the Depression.

For others, Anchorage is a way station en route to the rugged east coast or the glacier country to the west. The easily accessible PORTAGE GLACIER, with its all-weather icebergs afloat in Portage Lake, is an hour away; and COLUMBIA GLACIER spreads across 440 square miles in Prince William Sound. *(See* Glaciers: The Power and the Glory, *page 57.)* Columbia lies off the ice-free port of WHITTIER. This engaging small town of only about 350 has a rich history: Russian-Native trading, gold-mining, and its survival of three tidal waves from the quake that killed 13 residents. Perhaps the most interesting piece of its past happened over two years during World War II. Because the saltwater port of Seward was considered too open to Japanese attack, the Army secretly dug a total of three-and-a-half miles through the Chugach Mountains to create two tunnels connecting military bases in Anchorage and Fairbanks to Whittier. (Two crews burrowing from opposite ends met in the middle only six inches off course.) During the Cold War, the armed forces returned, departing finally in 1960. Most of the townspeople now have condos in "the city under one roof," a 14-story tower formerly occupied by a thousand servicemen when it was the tallest building in Alaska.

That was then. Now the whole state has grown up, especially its major city. Whittier's high-rise has been supplanted by taller buildings in Anchorage, whose skyline looms like an urban reflection of the mountainscapes surrounding this large but livable city on the doorstep of the Alaska wilds.

THE BAD FRIDAY QUAKE

It was the real thing: the most powerful earthquake ever to be recorded in North America this century. At 5:36 P.M. local time on March 27, 1964—Good Friday—the planet's crust burst a seam 500 miles long and 150 broad along the Aleutian Islands and the southern Alaska mainland. The shock waves jarred the earth over half a million miles. A series of tidal waves surged down the west coast. In all, the quake and resulting tsunami killed 28 people in the Lower 48 and 103 in Alaska—where 4,500 people were left homeless and the damage totalled an estimated half a billion dollars.

In the Pacific Ocean around Alaska, the plates forming the upper crust of the earth thrust downward at an angle beneath the edges of the plates in the lower crust. When these plates shift suddenly, the seismic energy creates the tremors the state is famous for, and, infrequently, a quake. In 1964, the sea bottom here shot up 30 to 50 feet, the largest such vertical lift ever measured. The force of the quake moved local mountains by as much as 50 feet and elevated 50-mile-long Montague Island by at least 30 feet. The shock registered the equivalent of 9.2 on the recently revised Richter scale (80 times the energy of the San Francisco cataclysm of 1906).

The epicenter was 1,200 feet below Prince William Sound, about 80 miles east of Anchorage, a city with footings of unstable clay. Within five minutes, 30 downtown blocks and a posh new suburb of Alaska's largest and swiftest-growing urban area lay in shambles. On the north side of 4th Avenue— the main street—an entire block of shops dropped 20 feet into a fissure; those on the south side survived. Nearby, an unoccupied six-story apartment crumbled, and the new five-story J.C. Penney store rocked back and forth before its front collapsed, killing two people. A hundred homes in Turnagain-on-the-Sea tumbled down cliffs above Cook Inlet. Because school was out and most stores were closed, and possibly because the city sits 100 feet above sea level, only nine died.

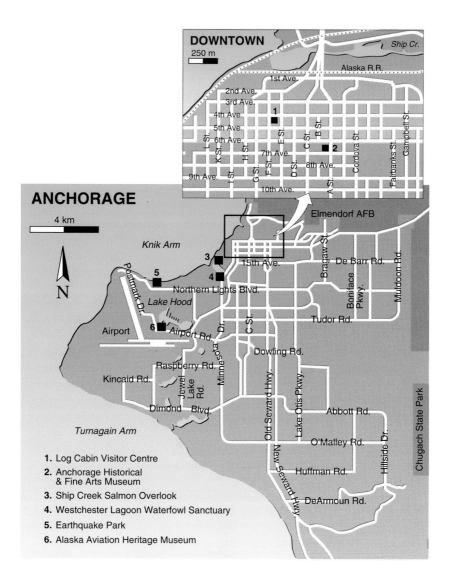

DOWNTOWN

250 m

Ship Cr.

Alaska R.R.

1st Ave.
2nd Ave.
3rd Ave.
4th Ave. **1**
5th Ave.
6th Ave.
7th Ave. **2**
8th Ave.
9th Ave.
10th Ave.

L St.
K St.
J St.
H St.
G St.
F St.
E St.
D St.
C St.
B St.
A St.
Cordova St.
Fairbanks St.
Gambell St.

Elmendorf AFB

ANCHORAGE

4 km

N

Knik Arm

3
15th Ave.

5
Northern Lights Blvd.
4

Lake Hood

Airport
6
Airport Rd.

Postmark Dr.

Bragaw St.
De Barr Rd.
Muldoon Rd.
Boniface Pkwy.

Tudor Rd.

Minnesota Dr.
C St.

Dowling Rd.

Raspberry Rd.

Kincaid Rd.

Jewel Lake Rd.

Dimond Blvd.

Turnagain Arm

Old Seward Hwy.
Lake Otis Pkwy.
New Seward Hwy.

Abbott Rd.

O'Malley Rd.

Hillside Dr.

Chugach State Park

Huffman Rd.

DeArmoun Rd.

1. Log Cabin Visitor Centre
2. Anchorage Historical & Fine Arts Museum
3. Ship Creek Salmon Overlook
4. Westchester Lagoon Waterfowl Sanctuary
5. Earthquake Park
6. Alaska Aviation Heritage Museum

WALKABOUT

LOG CABIN VISITOR CENTER, 4th Avenue and F Street, is a charmingly rustic trader's dwelling with a green sod rof and, in front, a 5,000-pound boulder of the state's gemstone, jade. Here's where you can find a handy map and other directions for a self-guided downtown walking tour that helps you relive Anchorage's past and directs you to craft shops.

ANCHORAGE HISTORICAL AND FINE ARTS MUSEUM, 121 W. 7th Ave., a five-story atrium, with dramatic dioramas of state history; six permanent art collections of Native peoples, white exploration, and development of Alaska; and more than 30 new shows every year.

THE HERITAGE LIBRARY MUSEUM, in the National Bank of Alaska at Northern Lights and C Street, shows Alaskana books, artifacts, paintings, and photos.

SHIP CREEK SALMON OVERLOOK AND WATERFOWL NESTING AREA, off Whitney Road just southwest of downtown, is on the site of the Tanaina Indian fish camps, where spawning salmon head upstream throughout the summer, and geese and ducks hang around all year.

LAKE HOOD and the neighboring Lake Spenard, southwest of downtown, may be too far by foot, but they're a popular tour-bus attraction. The air harbor here is the biggest floatplane base in the world, with 800 or more daily takeoffs and landings in High Summer as tourists and locals take sightseeing and fishing flights.

THE ALASKA AVIATION HERITAGE MUSEUM, 4721 Aicraft Dr., has vintage planes and flight uniforms, historical photos, and half-hour films on pioneer aviation.

DENALI NATIONAL PARK:
THE COMPLEAT WILDERNESS

You are on the open tundra of Sable Pass 3,900 feet high, and the astonishing land around you belongs to no one but the grizzly bear. Whole families of this most compelling emblem of the wilderness live here in Denali National Park and Preserve, fully protected from their only enemy: humans. You are not allowed to step outside the shuttle bus that brought you to the pass (nor would you want to, given the grizzly's mercurial reputation), but from its windows you can watch patient sows with their cavorting cubs, often twins or triplets who have little fear of the people staring at them, round-eyed with wonder. Perhaps only 300 grizzly bears exist in the Lower 48. Alaska has as many as 43,000—and the five miles along Sable Pass are the finest place in the world to observe them.

Elsewhere in Denali, where people are allowed to roam and the grizzlies are almost as likely to appear, the park staff have tried to ensure that direct contact between bear and human is slight. After placing radio collars on some grizzlies who pillaged backpackers' food supplies, the biologists would later check up on them by concocting a meal that might attract a hungry bear. If a problem grizzly showed up in their camp, they'd shoot it with painful but harmless plastic shotgun slugs—a process repeated until the bruin lost all taste for domestic dining. But since 1955, the bears have not had to deal with any humans hiking around the off-limits Sable Pass area, which is why it remains such a superb setting to see the animals in all their wild dignity.

Yet there is so much more to the natural drama of Denali than the grizzly. This sub-Arctic park is reputed to be the largest protected ecosystem in the world, 9,375 square miles of mountain and forest, river and valley—bigger than the state of Massachusetts. Straddling a 160-mile stretch of the Alaska Range, it encircles Mount McKinley, at 20,306 feet North America's highest peak,

Denali can be austerely beautiful or,
in the brief summer, lush and welcoming.

which also soars above its base farther than any other mountain in the world (7,000 feet more than Mount Everest does from its foot). Until 1989, when a University of Alaska team remeasured it with satellite equipment, McKinley was thought to be 14 feet taller. No matter: it deserves its Athabaskan designation as the High One, Denali—which gave the park its newest name. Every year about 1,000 mountaineers test their skills on McKinley, half of them achieving the summit, but at least 70 have died on its steep slopes in storms or from falls or cerebral and pulmonary edema.

Denali is second only to Portage Glacier as the most-visited tourist attraction in Alaska. Not surprisingly: among Denali's 37 species of mammals, 155 of birds, and 450-plus of plants there are more big animals to be seen more easily than in any other U.S. parkland. Caribou mingle with Dall sheep on the mountains while moose stroll through the parking area at the Eielson Visitor Center. Trumpeter swans, ptarmigan, and golden eagles abound; golden plover visit from Hawaii, arctic terns from South America. The tundra and taiga are swathed in electric-colored blankets of short-lived summer vegetation, such as the lavender of mountain saxifrage and the golden waves of tufted cottongrass. No wonder Denali has been selected as a United Nations International Biosphere Reserve.

Although the park has fine natural hiking routes, there are only a few signs, marked trails, and designated campgrounds. There's a quota system for hiking the back country. Private vehicles are limited to local landowners and registered campers travelling only to their camps. Otherwise, the U.S. Park Service strictly controls the single 87-mile road, mostly gravel, on which the shuttle buses run regularly. (Your first glimpse of Mount McKinley on a clear day is Mile 9, looking to the southwest.) To minimize disruption of wildlife and to avoid traffic hazards along the twisty roads, park officials regulate the number of bus trips each summer. Cruise-ship passengers on land excursions may take either a NATURAL-HISTORY or TUNDRA WILDLIFE TOUR by bus. (Some also opt for RIVER RAFTING, HORSEBACK RIDING, or a HELICOPTER FLIGHTSEEING TRIP over park, mountain, and glacier.) The many pairs of passengers' eyes on a bus can spot animals more reliably than a couple of people in a private vehicle will. You might catch sight of foxes, coyotes, lynxes, martins, and beavers. Or wolves wandering the banks of the Toklat River, golden eagles and gyrfalcons launching from Polychrome Pass, and early in the season, within the first hour of the tour, perhaps a grizzly stalking calving moose.

Since its birth in 1917, Denali has been a natural laboratory. It was here in 1939 that pioneering wildlife biologist Adolf Murie began to record the reality of wolves, chronicling their kills of the weak, young, and old among their prey, and changing the common attitude that they threatened herds of domestic and wild stock by hunting down animals in their prime. Today, park rangers and visiting biologists continue the field work—for example, discovering the biggest breeding ground of golden eagles in Alaska. And they continue to respect Denali's wolves. One ranger travelling by dog sled in winter had to endure a night of wolf howls outside his cabin. They meant no harm, he told his companion. They'd simply picked up the scent of the female huskies and wanted to be with them. Still using dogs to get around (and giving dog-sled demonstrations behind the Park Service headquarters in summer), the park staff have a lab so large that even some veteran rangers have never visited some of the more remote areas.

And the park keeps getting larger. Created only a year after the National Park System, and designated from the start as wilderness, it was then named Mount McKinley. In 1922, the year the first official tourist visited, it was enlarged to the Nenana River on the east, and ten years later embraced Wonder Lake on the west—which is the reflecting pool for the mountain in so many photographs that you might feel you've seen it before. (Other good photo viewpoints: Eielson Visitor Center and Stony Hill.) It wasn't until 1972 that a new all-weather paved road between Anchorage and Fairbanks skirted the park's eastern border, generating twice the number of visitors. And eight years later, when it was renamed Denali, 2.5 million acres were added to the park—for a total of 6 million acres—to provide areas for Native people's subsistence hunting and trapping as well as snowmobiling. An additional 1.3

million adjacent acres were declared a national preserve, where hunting for sport and the landing of aircraft are permitted. Next door lies Denali State Park, whose 324,000 acres yield similar wildlife experiences and striking vistas of the Alaska Range.

Those lofty mountains have always intrigued explorers and climbers. McKinley and its mates are so high that they latch on to the moisture from the Gulf of Alaska and cool it, creating snow at about the 14,000-foot level that sustains plentiful glaciers, including a half-dozen around McKinley. Southwest of it stands Mount Foraker, at 17,400 feet. Captain Vancouver, writing in 1794 from Knik Arm, said he could view on the far northwest horizon "distant stupendous mountains covered with snow, and apparently detached from one another." Natives in the Interior had already named the grandest one Denali, while other tribes knew it as Dolyeka and Traleyka. The Russians called it Bulshaia Gora (Great Mountain) and on their maps labelled it Tenada. Its first English name was the prosaic Densmore's Mountain, for Frank Densmore, an American gold prospector who saw it in 1889. Another prospector named William Dickey passed through the area seven years later, reporting: "We named our great peak Mount McKinley after William McKinley of Ohio, who had been nominated for the presidency, and that fact was the first news we received on our way out of that wonderful wilderness. We have no doubt that this peak is the highest in North America and estimate that it is over 20,000 feet high." (An alternative story says that, to spite prospectors who were trumpeting the cause of silver, he named it for the president who championed the gold standard.)

In 1902, federal geologists came here on foot and horseback, mapping the region so thoroughly that their work held up for half a century. And in 1903, much-loved U.S. District Judge James Wickersham and four others attempted the first climb of McKinley. *(See* The High One: A History, *page 148.)* The most controversial ascent was the Sourdough Expedition seven years later, when two gold miners with basic gear and no specialized climbing experience surmounted the more difficult North Peak (19,470 feet)— scaling more than 8,000 vertical feet and returning to base camp in an extraordinary 18 hours. They were among a quartet of miners who took a Fairbanks bartender's $500-per-person challenge that they couldn't make the top of McKinley. Shod in insulated rubber boots and moccasins and wearing bib overalls and long underwear under their parkas, they carried snowshoes, home-built crampons, and primitive ice axes. After reaching their final camp at about 11,000 feet on March 17, three of them toting hot chocolate and doughnuts started for the summit on April 1. In -30° weather, Billy Taylor and Peter Anderson crested the peak and, in a pyramid of rocks below it, planted a pole with the American flag. But when one of their party later claimed that all seven had climbed both the North and South peaks, most people doubted the whole story of the successful ascent—especially when a later climbing party two years later reported no sign of the sourdoughs' flagpole. In 1913, however, Taylor and Anderson were vindicated when an expedition under Episcopalian missionary Hudson Stuck

Tour buses taking visitors through Denali
(then McKinley) park in the 1930s.

THE HIGH ONE: A HISTORY

1902: Alfred H. Brooks, leading a U.S. Geological Survey party, is the first white man to set foot on the slopes of Mount McKinley—and believes he may be the very first of any race because the Alaskan Native "has a superstitious horror of even approaching glacial ice."

1903: Judge James Wickersham and four others from Fairbanks make the first ascent, reaching the 8,100-foot level.

1910: Two members of the Sourdough Expedition, climbing on a bet, reach the summit of the North Peak.

1913: Rev. Hudson Stuck and four others, including Indian boys aged 14 and 15, are the first to surmount McKinley's South Peak—and confirm the sourdoughs' success.

1947: Barbara Washburn is the first woman to reach the top.

1954: While making the first ascent by Ruth Glacier and the South Buttress, leader Elton Thayer is killed in the descent down Karstens Ridge.

1967: Ray Genet, Dave Johnson, and Art Davidson make the first winter ascent; Genet, who launched the mountain's first guiding service, is later lost on Everest.

1984: Japanese explorer Naomi Uemura makes the first winter solo ascent but dies in a storm during the descent.

1988: Vern Tejas makes the first full solo winter climb; on his next trip as a guide, a young woman collapses and dies while descending from the summit. Three Frenchmen with artificial legs reach the summit.

1991: In a 16-day expedition, 12-year-old Taras Genet—Ray Genet's son—becomes the youngest mountaineer to conquer McKinley.

became the first to ascend the South Peak and sighted the pole still standing on the North Peak.

It was the Reverend Stuck who, after his climb, summed up the magnificence of Mount McKinley so eloquently: "There was no pride of conquest, no trace of that exultation of victory some enjoy upon the first ascent of a lofty peak, no gloating over good fortune that had hoisted us a few hundred feet higher than others who had struggled and been discomfited. Rather . . . that a privileged communion with the high places of the earth had been granted . . . secret and solitary since the world began. All the way down, unconscious of weariness in the descent, my thoughts were occupied with the glorious scene my eyes gazed upon, and should gaze upon never again."

What he saw, and what visitors to Denali National Park and Preserve can still enjoy more than eight decades later, is a compleat wilderness in harmony with itself, one of the few such parks left in the world where the rawness of nature can be experienced without much interference from humankind.

FAIRBANKS, THE GOLDEN HEART

The second-largest city in Alaska—Fairbanks, near the geographical heart of the state—is a place of hope, of golden dreams realized and dashed only to be dreamt of again. A place of optimists. The 31,000 inhabitants *must* be, given the location of their community only 90 miles south of the Arctic Circle, which spawns their long, laborious winters. In December the sun may appear for less than four hours, seasonal temperatures regularly plummet below -40°F, and the strongest air inversions in the world (three times worse than Los Angeles') can create ice fog and winter pollution for weeks at a time. That combination of factors means that the smog you breathe is frozen. Yet during the summer—and the warm, dry summer always comes—Fairbanks lives in perpetual, moonless light, and welcomes the visitors who now fuel its feast-or-famine economy. Outsiders do appreciate its frontier charms, its waning and waxing legacy of gold and oil, and its hopeful, if cantankerous people. A city of extremes, locals say with pride. Where for three years in a row, voters rejected an official bond issue to finance a much-needed new hospital, only to spontaneously launch a citizens' campaign to raise more than enough funds privately. As a former Alaskan governor, Jay Hammond, once described it, this is a place "where ideas flourish, where debate, sometimes strident, searches for truth, regardless of how many sacred cows are milked dry or barbecued in the process."

The Interior encompasses one-third of Alaska, between the southern Alaska Range and the northern Brooks Range. Fairbanks, lying amid the spacious Tanana River valley, is the Interior's service and supply center, its hub, spreading north into the summer-green hills from the downtown floodplain of the Chena River, where stern-wheelers take you on riverboat tours. The past and present commingle here. Big-city concrete office towers hulk over small-town wooden buildings and western bars. Not far from the core, you can visit the ghosts of gold dredges that were still producing half a century ago, and the very-much-alive Trans-Alaska Pipeline that continues to create wealth for the state. And nearby is the University of Alaska's research range, Poker Flat, where scientists take advantage of the isolation—the immense, natural geophysical laboratory—and launch rockets to plumb the secrets of earth's atmosphere. Fairbanksans are still looking up at the stars, and dreaming optimistically.

Felix Pedro was one of the first dreamers here. In 1900, after mining coal in the U.S. Midwest and hunting gold in British Columbia and the Klondike, the hard-luck Italian-American arrived in Tanana River country. It had been prospected for years with little success. Pedro plugged on in the valley, encouraged by traces of yellow, joined by sourdoughs who worked at a nearby trading post on the Chena River above its junction with the Tanana. Finally, in July 1902, Pedro hit pay dirt and discreetly shared his find with a few friends—and the unscrupulous trading-post proprietor, Elbridge Barnette, who let the whole world know.

In a rush that would repeat itself throughout Fairbanks history, thousands flocked to what was Alaska's biggest gold field—a field of broken dreams for many who wanted the quick payback and weren't prepared to work for the mining companies that had to dredge the gold from deep below the permafrost. One of them was Otto Nilsson, who half a century later talked about how he, Felix Pedro, and others met to organize a mining district: "After the meeting I went out to stake my claim. I passed up creeks worth $130,000 a season. I staked on Little Eldorado and worked the creek thirty-four years, but I never found a pay streak." According to Nilsson, they named the townsite that boomed around the trading post for one of the prospectors' friends, Senator Charles Fairbanks of Indiana, who later became Vice-President under Theodore Roosevelt. Another story claims that legendary Alaskan Judge James Wickersham asked the first mayor to name the place for Charles Fairbanks. The mayor was Elbridge Truman Barnette, who grew wealthy enough to open a bank before running off with a million dollars' worth of deposits in 1911.

By then, despite devastating flood and fire, Fairbanks was a boom town with electric lights, steam heat, and sewers. Because of long-term jobs with the large mining companies, it had a settled populace that was remarkably law-abiding for Alaska—a characteristic unchanged over the next six decades. After the gold was gone, the massive military spending of World War II and then the Cold War kept the city stable. Eielson Air Force Base still numbers more than 5,000 people, who build on the city's aviation heritage—it was here that Alaska's first bush-pilot mail service began. In 1967, Fairbanks was flattened when the usually mild Chena River flooded, wreaking $200 million in damage. But just a few years later, construction began on the pipeline from Prudhoe Bay, and the population of Fairbanks went to 65,000 from 40,000. Governor Hammond had to send in an emergency force of legal specialists to control the surging crime wave. It ended in 1967 as quickly as it began, the prostitutes and muggers one step behind the departing construction workers.

Now the university, the most northern in North America, and tourism are among the city's mainstays. A must-see is the UNIVERSITY OF ALASKA FAIRBANKS MUSEUM, which features a superb art collection and sophisticated natural-history and gold-mining exhibits, including an enormous bear and more nuggets than you've ever seen. The university's renowned Geophysical Institute studies earthquakes, the atmosphere, and the aurora borealis— the "dawn of the north." The colorful, magical northern lights are created when the sun's rarified gasses erupt and send their electrically charged particles into space, to be picked up by solar winds. Approaching earth's upper atmosphere, they're caught by the magnetic field lines in the polar regions; electrons emit green light when striking an oxygen molecule in the ionosphere, red light when colliding with a nitrogen molecule. A university geophysicist describes the lights as a "gigantic neon sign with a high-volume electrical discharge." Eskimos thought they sounded like whispering spirits; scientists now acknowledge that they can make a noise like an electrical transformer's. Fairbanks witnesses

The aurora borealis colors the sky around
Fairbanks an average of 240 nights a year.

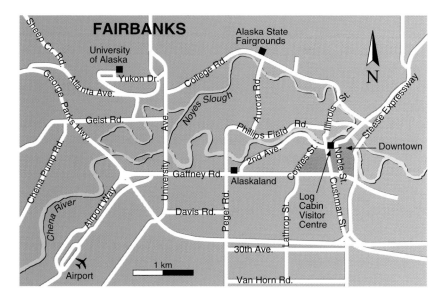

WALKABOUT

LOG CABIN VISITOR CENTER, 550 1st Ave., close to a monument marking where the city was born, offers self-guided walking tours of historic downtown Fairbanks. Stroll 2nd—Two Avenue, in local parlance—for a hint of the grittiness that the city suffered during the pipeline invasion. And on the block between 3rd and 4th avenues and Noble and Laces streets looms the Alaska National Bank Building, the Interior's original steel-girder skyscraper, which inspired Edna Ferber's Alaskan novel, *The Ice Palace*.

ALASKALAND, Airport Way and Peger Road, with shuttle bus service from downtown, is an interesting pioneer theme park with old structures from Fairbanks, entertainment, and a popular salmon bake. Noteworthy are the Gold Rush and Mining towns, the Alaska Native Village, and the sternwheeler *Nenana*.

them an average of 240 nights a year, most brilliantly in the spring and fall. Some Japanese couples honeymoon here because of folklore suggesting that a marriage consummated under the aurora's lights will be a happy one.

RIVERBOAT CRUISES take you back in time as the *Discovery*, steered by a third-generation stern-wheel captain, navigates the Chena and less-ladylike Tanana rivers where the two-story paddle-wheel boats once carried freight and passengers to the gold fields. Some tours offer a stopover to see a prominent musher and sled dogs and to visit a replica of a camp of the local Athabaskan Natives.

Outside town, GOLD RUSH TOURS can include a visit to a five-story-high old dredge that dug up gold-filled gravel, and to a working gold mine with a narrow-gauge railway, tent city, permafrost drift tunnel, and mining relics. At both destinations, you can pan for the yellow flakes. Running near the city is the TRANS-ALASKA PIPELINE, and motorcoach excursions provide good views of the unique construction of this ongoing reminder of Fairbanks' boom-and-bust, dream-and-endure history.

JUNEAU, A CAPITAL CITY

Bridget A. Smith, a lecturer in psychology on the local campus of the University of Alaska, has written an entertaining mystery novel called *Death of an Alaskan Princess*, which offers an insider's perceptions about modern-day Juneau and its past. Among them: "... the history of the town can be discerned by the careful observer—narrow streets intended for horses, the absence of right angles as the town grew organically up and around the mountains, the predominance of wood as a construction material giving way to a few buildings built in the thirties of stone when it looked as if it would be a permanent community." Now all this, she writes, is "piously preserved."

Delivering float-plane passengers to the People's Dock, the chatty woman driving the tour bus comments on the two almighty facts about Juneau—its status as the state capital and its relative isolation as a seaport with no road links to the rest of Alaska: "One out of every two folks in the workforce is employed by the government. We have 29,000 people and 25,000 cars—going nowhere."

These complementary insights combine to present an attractive portrait of Alaska's third-largest city. Yes, Juneau may appear a little devout in paying attention to its past, but a lot of its history is still firsthand—with many original buildings standing downtown, recorded in the National Register of Historic Places. Yes, this is a relentlessly government town and it *is* cut off by land, but the security of regular paychecks combined with the sense of separation may explain why there are so many vehicles for only 160 miles of local roads (and why there are 2,750 recreational boats). And the comparative wealth and relatively high educational levels of those in government service have obviously given them the discretionary income and the appreciation for things cultural, including an extravagant amount of art on public display in the streets.

Greater Juneau—at 3,100 square miles the largest U.S. city in size—stretches along a skinny bench of land that extends to the Mendenhall Valley, the suburb ten miles northwest where much of the population lives. The city and borough are squeezed between the Gastineau Channel of the Inside Passage and the 3,500-foot peaks of Mount Juneau and Mount Roberts, which from time to time release avalanches on the community. The Coast Mountains rise to the north and east, the Chilkat Range to the northwest, and the summits of Admiralty Island to the south. Behind the city stretches the 1,500-square-mile JUNEAU ICEFIELD, which feeds 38 glaciers, among them the mighty—and accessible—MENDENHALL. You can visit the ice cap and glacier by plane, jet-turbine helicopter and bus, and even take a raft trip down the Mendenhall River. *(See Glaciers: The Power and the Glory, page 69.)* Along the line of Coast Mountains runs a series of domes of igneous rock deep below the earth. These batholiths are rimmed by caches of minerals dissolved by heat and water and then deposited in solid form into veins and lodes. The mineral of most interest, gold, is found locked in bands of quartz.

It was gold that brought a couple of bad ole boys to Alaska from the mines of the Pacific Northwest in 1879. Richard Harris had been described "an inveterate drunkard" by one boss, and the word on Joseph Juneau, in those politically incorrect times, was that "between hooch and squaws he never had a cent to get away on." Both in their forties, they landed in Sitka and went to work prospecting for a German mining engineer. After spending all their grubstake and losing their boat, they convinced a Tlingit Indian to take them back to Sitka. Kowee, related to the local Auk tribe, took them first to a small stream he knew off the Gastineau Channel, where he led them to a vein of quartz bursting with gold. On their second trip there in 1880—the engineer had no one else to send but the hopeless pair—they made Alaska's first major gold strike, which Harris later described: "We knew it was gold, but so much and not in particles, streaks running through the rock and little lumps as large as peas or beans." They staked their claim and a townsite of 160 acres. This was the first Alaskan town to be founded after the U.S. bought the territory from Russia. Originally the mining camp was called Harrisburg, but when a horde of competing prospectors soured on its namesake for making multiple claims, they rechristened it Juneau. Dick Harris died broke in an Oregon sanitorium, and Joe Juneau splurged his $18,000 gold earnings within two years.

Hard-rock mining and milling companies superseded the placer miners. Of those working claims on Douglas Island, just across the channel from Juneau, the Treadwell Mine was most successful. For 35 years, miners dug out its glory hole—a huge open pit 450 feet deep that led to tunnels half a mile down—until, in 1917, the ground caved in below the flourishing company town of Treadwell, and three million tons of sea swallowed up the mine. In little more than six decades, three local mines produced $158 million worth of low-quality gold using high-tech methods. The last one to close, based on the original Harris–Juneau claims, was the Alaska–Juneau. The A–J's hundred-plus miles of tunnels yielded about $4 million worth of gold a year for a decade until a wartime labor shortage shuttered it in 1944. The rusting hulk of its crushing and recovery mill can still be seen on the slope of Mount Roberts above the site of the GOLD CREEK SALMON BAKE. (You can enjoy another salmon bake at a mountain lodge in the shadow of a glacier.) While ample gold supplies remain in the area—GOLD PANNING is a common visitors' pastime—and there are ongoing plans to revive the mines, the mineral hasn't figured prominently in Juneau's economy since.

Fishing has, however—commercial halibut and salmon fishing is resurging as stocks recover from a decline in the 1980s. A familiar tour destination is the $7-million GASTINEAU SALMON HATCHERY, three miles north of town, where you can watch through underwater windows as pinks and chum fight their way up the largest fish ladder in the state and get checked for maturity. Ripe females are dispatched and relieved of their eggs, which are fertilized with milt squeezed from the males' bellies. Juneau's SALTWATER SPORTFISHING is the most popular in Alaska, offering a quarter of all the sport

The New England colonial-style
Governor's mansion in Juneau.

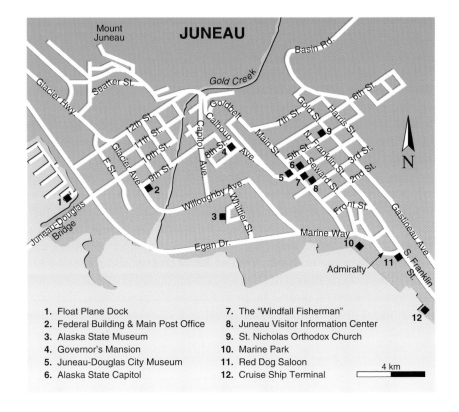

JUNEAU

Mount Juneau

Basin Rd.

Glacier Hwy.
Seatter St.
Gold Creek
Goldbelt
6th St.
12th St.
11th St.
10th St.
9th St.
Glacier Ave.
F St.
E St.
Calhoun Ave.
Capitol Ave.
8th St.
7th St.
Main St.
Gold St.
N. Franklin St.
5th St.
Seward St.
3rd St.
2nd St.
Harris St.
6th St.
Willoughby Ave.
Whittier St.
Front St.
Marine Way
Egan Dr.
Admiralty
Gastineau Ave.
S. Franklin St.
Juneau-Douglas Bridge

N

1. Float Plane Dock
2. Federal Building & Main Post Office
3. Alaska State Museum
4. Governor's Mansion
5. Juneau-Douglas City Museum
6. Alaska State Capitol
7. The "Windfall Fisherman"
8. Juneau Visitor Information Center
9. St. Nicholas Orthodox Church
10. Marine Park
11. Red Dog Saloon
12. Cruise Ship Terminal

4 km

WALKABOUT

JUNEAU VISITOR INFORMATION CENTER, 134 3rd St., a log cabin modelled on the city's first church, has a Walking Tour guide that features historic Juneau.

PUBLIC ART: A sampling of many possibilities includes *Harnessing of the Atom Totem Pole* (Calhoun & Main) symbolizing the U.S., Russia, the harnessing of energy, and the Raven Creator; *Windfall Fisherman* (outside Courthouse, Main Street), a full-sized bronze of an Alaska Brown Bear; *Raven Discovering Mankind in a Clam Shell* (City Municipal Building, Marine Way), a wall mural depicting the Tlingit legend.

JUNEAU-DOUGLAS CITY MUSEUM, Veterans Memorial Building, 4th & Main: A motherlode of gold-mining lore, hands-on exhibits and video shows.

ST. NICHOLAS ORTHODOX CHURCH, 326 5th St.: Although there were no Russians in Juneau, local Tlingit chiefs asked the Eastern Orthodox bishop in Sitka to baptize them, and this octagonal church was built with Russian funds in 1894. Tlingit families have been worshiping here continuously since.

king salmon taken in the sea and the saltchuck. The kings range local waters throughout the summer, with the largest—18 to 50 pounds—peaking in late April through June. Some companies offer another adventure on the water: a LYNN CANAL CRUISE/FLY TOUR to Skagway by sightseeing boat and back by plane. The glacier-dug channel, broad and deep, is 67 miles of Native and Gold Rush history; seals, sea lions, humpback and killer whales; and valley and hanging glaciers amid the snow-streaked mountains.

Since 1912, Juneau has been the official capital and, with statehood in 1959, government emerged as the biggest local business. But for more than two decades, the locals had to live with threats to move the capital to somewhere more central—the most active suggestion being the somnolent southcentral community of Willow (pop: 200). The move would have shrunk Juneau's population by two-thirds and shut nearly half its businesses. In 1982, state voters finally decided not to spend $2.8 billion to relocate the capital, and Juneau bloomed anew. By summer, when the cruise ships arrive, the state legislature has finished its session, but you can visit the old marble-columned STATE CAPITOL (4th Street) and admire the white, New England colonial GOVERNOR'S MANSION (atop the Calhoun Avenue hill), which has housed Alaska's governors and their families since 1912. Out front, a totem pole tells the Tlingit legend of the creation of the ubiquitous mosquito.

If you have time, one way of savoring the history of Juneau— and the rest of the state—is a visit to the ALASKA STATE MUSEUM (395 Whitter St.). Among its treasures: original sketches from the Cook and Bering voyages, a Tlingit clan house and a 40-foot Eskimo whale-hunting boat, and the engrossing eagle-nesting tree. Cruise visitors can also partake of the Perseverance Theatre's conveniently scheduled LADY LOU REVUE, a rollicking musical paean to the characters that Robert Service, the Poet of the Yukon, enshrined in *The Shooting of Dan McGrew* ("and watching his luck was his light-o'-love, the lady that's known as Lou"). And for something completely different, stop in at the RED DOG SALOON (Marine Way and South Franklin Street), a Gold-Rush replica with swinging doors, sawdust on the wood floor, and a polished bar with brass beer spigots. It's abrim with wilderness trophy heads, antique guns, nineteenth-century lifebuoys, flags from foreign vessels, and thousands of personal calling cards, some a century old. Joe Juneau's isn't among them.

THE KENAI PENINSULA: THE GOOD LAND

Mini-Alaska. The whole state on a small scale. Anchorage's Backyard. Alaska's Playground. They've all been used to describe, with only a little hyperbole, the 16,000 square miles of the Kenai Peninsula, a place of mountain peaks and mammoth fields of ice, numberless fjords and fish-choked rivers, a national forest, and state and national parks and wildlife refuges. It begins just south of Anchorage, along the Seward Highway, and residents of the state's largest city often use it as a weekend retreat. Every summer this stampede helps more than double the peninsula's population of 40,000 centered in four main towns. Along with its popularity, there's another reality some visitors might find worrisome upon first hearing. It was in the Kenai where one of the first post-war Alaskan oil finds began producing, and still plays a prominent economic role. And it was here, along Prince William Sound, where the world's largest oil spill washed up, some of it staining the shores of Kenai Fjords National Park.

Yet the happy truth is that neither oil nor tourism has left much of a mark on the peninsula. You realize, for a start, that this is an area in which Rhode Island, Delaware, and Connecticut could fit quite comfortably. That almost 85 per cent of it is under federal protection as the national park, the Chugach National Forest, and the Kenai National Wildlife Refuge. That most of the year-round population is scattered thinly in the towns of Kenai, Homer, Soldotna, and Seward. That the oil fields are offshore in Cook Inlet, on the far-western verge of the Kenai, where cruise passengers on land tours don't usually visit. And that in 1989, winds prevented the spill from the oil tanker *Exxon Valdez* from sullying much of the park's shoreline at the time, so that virtually no visible blemishes are left now. (Nevertheless, the park staff has mounted informative oil-spill displays at their base in Seward.) Given all these factors, the Kenai Peninsula more than deserves its Athabaskan name, *Yaghanen*, or The Good Land.

Athabaskans and some Eskimos lived here first, and continue to make up about ten per cent of the population. In 1791, a Russian trading ship following the sea-otter routes reached the mouth of a river the Natives knew as *Kaknu* and the Russians named *Kenay*. There, a village of the Athabaskan Dena'ina tribe stood on a cliff above Cook Inlet. Today the town of Kenai is the peninsula's largest (pop: 6,500), the service base for the inlet's oil fields, and a port for the regional fishing fleet. The Russians, after settling in Kenai, spread across the peninsula, founding Seldovia and then Ninilchik, which became a retirement colony for their hunters who had taken Native wives and refused to return to Mother Russia. The first Americans were pursuing rumors of a richness in coal; the second wave sought gold. Neither promise panned out, although more than 3,000 prospectors flooded into the optimistically named communities of Hope and Sunrise in 1896. You can still pan for gold—mostly for fun—in the Chugach National Forest.

Those who settled here farmed the land, raised foxes for furs, and fished for herring. It wasn't until 1957, when Atlantic Richfield found oil and then gas in Cook Inlet, that the economy heated up. And in 1980, the creation of the Kenai Fjords National Park attracted the attention of visitors from beyond the state, generating the tourist dollars that keep the locals afloat. They are an intriguing bunch: one writer who lives in Homer recently described his town as "a jumbled-up community of fishermen and computer nerds, hippies and fundamentalists, artists and Cat skinners (bulldozer operators)." Among the peninsula population are a gaggle of Libertarians who don't want the government to intrude in their lives, and a prospector whose ad in an Anchorage newspaper for a mail-order bride attracted 8,000 replies from around the world.

The *real* wildlife in the Kenai is self-evident once you cross the slender isthmus at Portage and either turn east along the spine of the Kenai Mountains to the national park or continue south and west to Cooper Landing (pop.: 400). Getting to the first of the centers serving the Sterling Highway, only two hours from Anchorage, you pass lookout points for Dall sheep and mountain goats. The Landing, named for a 19th-century miner and still rife with log cabins, acts as base camp for half-day RAFTING EXPEDITIONS down the rapids-rich Kenai River. Cruise passengers visiting here also have a choice of HORSEBACK RIDING, FLIGHTSEEING, HIKING through an alpine back country alive with moose, mink, beaver, and bald eagles, or FISHING for red salmon in prime spawning grounds nearby. World-renowned for its runs of king salmon, the river occasionally lures so many anglers that Alaskans refer to the scene as "combat fishing." There's also salt-water fishing for salmon, Dolly Varden, and such bottom fish as halibut from the revitalized port of SEWARD (pop.: 2,400).

On Bad Friday 1964, it was three strikes—and Seward was all but out. First, the tremors of that terrible earthquake. Then the fires erupting in an oil storage-tank farm near the new port. And finally a series of tidal waves, the second one the worst, roaring up Resurrection Bay: a wall of water 30 feet high, alight with burning oil, surging into town more than 100 miles an hour, flinging aside boxcars and their engines like so many model trains. Houses lay shattered, cars squashed, boats snapped in two. A 4,500-foot swath of waterfront sank into the bay. No one was killed, but the combination of quake, fire, and tsunami left the port and the rail line—the region's economic underpinnings—in ruins. Ironically, Seward had been slated to receive an official All America Cities Award for industry and civic improvement the following week.

It took the city a couple of decades to recover and rebuild, with a $10-million, supposedly earthquake-proof, dock; and the railroad returned to its pre-quake strength. Today, one of the few reminders of the disaster is the slide show Seward Is Burning, at the public library (5th Avenue and Adams). In its low-slung, frontier-town attractiveness and the vitality of its renewed economy, Seward could well be at least a contender for a national award again. Not that all of it is model Small-Town America: the main street may have more drinking establishments per capita than anywhere else in the state. But step outside to absorb the views of the bay in front and Mount Marathon behind and you might agree that the city still earns the encomium of one of its founders, John Ballaine. He recalled "that shining afternoon as we glided easily in those majestic scenes up to the timber-covered site I had chosen for the future terminal city—the future gateway in and out of Alaska's great interior."

It is that: a year-round ice-free harbor for ships to and from Outside; the southern terminus of the Alaska Railroad leading to Fairbanks and beyond; as well as the gateway to the increasingly popular Kenai Fjords National Park. In 1903, Ballaine was the first agent of the Alaska Central Railroad, which decided to use Resurrection Bay as the sea terminal. He suggested naming the new townsite for Secretary of State Seward. The rail line made a couple of false starts before evolving into the Alaska Railroad in 1923. Seward was also the original start of the Iditarod Trail to the bountiful gold fields of Nome, a dog-sled course blazed through the land during 1910–11. (In 1915, 46 dogs pulled a record ton and a half of gold south to the port.) Today, the annual Iditarod Trail Sled Dog Race runs from Anchorage to Nome *(see* Nome—No Place Like It, *page 179)*, but you can see Mile 0 of the first trail marked on a plaque at the southeast corner of 4th and Railway.

Three blocks southwest of Mile 0 is the Seward Railroad Car (3rd and Jefferson), the Pullman dining car in which President Warren C. Harding rode to drive the last golden spike of the Alaska Railroad. Now it's the Chamber of Commerce Information Cache, which offers a walking-tour map of such areas as the Resurrection Bay Historical Museum; the University of Alaska's Seward Institute of Marine Science, with its live specimens and tours; and Millionaires Row, the half-dozen elegant houses the founders built from materials shipped in from the Lower 48. Mount Marathon rears up 3,022 feet over the city; every July 4 since 1915, suicidal runners have raced up the peak and down, some in less than 45 minutes.

The restored Small Boat Harbor, at the north end of 4th Avenue, is action central of Seward's fishing industry, which operates the largest halibut-receiving station on the U.S. West Coast. (Fish can grow so big here that they're often shot upon landing to prevent them from damaging the boat.) Throughout the summer, there are derbies for halibut, king salmon, and silver salmon (first prize $10,000), with the entries weighed in at the harbor. And sometimes out on the water, beyond the fish boats and sailing vessels, you might spot sea otters.

Near the Harbormaster is the Kenai Fjords Visitor Center, with its fine displays of the Harding Icefield and the less-visible attractions of nearby KENAI FJORDS NATIONAL PARK. Few federal parks in America seem as protected as Kenai, surrounded as it is by the Caines Head State Recreation Area to the east, Kenai National Wildlife Refuge to the west, Chugach National Forest to the north and east, and Kachemak Bay State Park and State Wilderness to the southwest. Near the park entrance, a typical first stop is EXIT GLACIER. One of eight large glaciers formed in the Harding Icefield, Exit flows into the Resurrection River Valley, which reveals all the typical levels of plant life found on glacier-carved land. Beware of ice falling from the face: in 1987 a half-ton chunk killed a California woman who came too near.

While the park itself may be one of the state's smaller ones, its steep-sided fjords and the range of sea and bird life make it one of the most sublime. But because so much of the land is uncongenial for the casual visitor, it's best seen by boat. Your sea voyage girdles Kenai, taking you along Resurrection Bay near the forest shoreline where Aleksandr Baranov, who named the basin, launched Alaska's first shipyard. Here he built small but sturdy boats in the 1790s to compete against the sea-otter hunters of other nations. Guides will likely point out artifacts of the more recent past—concrete bunkers that supported gun emplacements and searchlight stations during World War II. They might even mention that it was here on this bay—and not a fjord near Murmansk, Russia—that Sean Connery's nuclear submarine cruised at the start of *The Hunt for Red October*.

But the man-made pales beside the natural world. This can be one of the finest places in Alaska for viewing marine life. A couple of thousand sea otters cruise the region, and you'll often see some, along with Dall's porpoises, harbor seals, sea lions, orcas, and a variety of whales, including fins, seis, and minkes. And many of the 200,000 or so sea birds that make this their summer home— auklets, tufted and horned puffins, cormorants, and even the black-legged kittiwakes (with their black wing tips and yellow bills). Black bears and grizzlies prowl the shores and mountain goats pose on the slopes, where waterfalls plummet beautifully into the bay.

A gem of a park. Or in the words of a frequent visitor, a former state fishery biologist, it's nothing less than the crown jewel of the Kenai Peninsula.

KETCHIKAN: FIRST CITY

Her name was Dolly Arthur, and she was Ketchikan's most famous madam, a feisty Idaho waitress who came to Alaska in 1914 and for half a century operated a house of ill repute. "I realized I could make a lot more money from the attentions of men than I could waiting tables," she once recalled. Today, Alaska's First City—the southernmost major port and the traditional first stop for cruise ships—is a tamer place, notable for salmon and halibut fishing, the state's largest collection of totem poles, and its handiness to the feral majesty of Misty Fjords National Monument. But to re-live the essence of old Ketchikan, which a California newspaper once called "Uncle Sam's wickedest city," you have only to stroll the boardwalk of south-side CREEK STREET. The Creek, where it's said both the salmon and the fishermen came up to spawn, still had a score of brothels when local authorities shut them down in 1954. Dolly's House, No. 24, is now a privately run folk museum teeming with her memorabilia, including secret panels to hide money and Prohibition liquor, a discreet nude photograph of the solidly built proprietor, and her equally overupholstered, fringe-and-satin bedroom.

The plank boardwalk of craft and souvenir shops, below Boston Smith Hill, stands on pilings high above the creek that may have given Ketchikan its name. It *may* have come from a Tlingit Indian phrase for "salmon creek that runs through town"; or perhaps "spread wings of a prostrate eagle" for the shape of a sandspit at the creek mouth; or (if you prefer) for the 19th-century Tlingit named Kitschk, who had a summer fishing camp here that came to be known as Kitschk-hin—Kitschk's stream. And there are at least three other tales of origin. For certain, it was born as a white settlement in 1887 with the opening of a salmon cannery, the first of 13 canneries and cold-storage facilities that helped make Ketchikan the self-proclaimed Salmon Capital of the World, the center of a fishing industry propelling the Southeast economy until the mid-1950s. And—it can't be avoided—this is also one of the Rain Capitals of Alaska, with more than 13 feet of rain a year, though May through August are the least-wet months.

Ketchikan spreads for several miles along the the southwestern verge of Revillagigedo Island (which Captain Vancouver christened for a Mexico viceroy and which locals abbreviate to Ruh-*vil*-la). Revilla, bigger than Rhode Island, is ringed by the 150-mile Behm Canal, one of the most picturesque and fish-rich waterways in the Panhandle. The borough of 14,300 people borders 50-mile-long Tongass Narrows, where cruise ships pull up to docks that rise and fall with the 20-foot tides. (Downtown basements often fall victim to these tides.) Never more than ten blocks wide as it backs up against 3,000-foot Deer Mountain, it's a city of wooden staircases ascending rocky hillsides to ragged rows of houses on stilts, with steep, dormered roofs and shake and clapboard sheathing. The harbor below swarms with float planes and pleasure and fish boats.

Ketchikan was once the hub of the North Pacific halibut fleet. Today's commercial fishery focuses on salmon. Although pinks are more abundant, kings and cohos are the prizes here in SPORTFISHING EXPEDITIONS on up-to-date charter boats with enclosed

Creek Street boardwalk, once the domain
of Ketchikan's famous madams.

cabins and knowledgeable skippers. You can take other WATER-BORNE EXCURSIONS: in sea kayaks around the port and across the narrows to a rain-forest island; in massive Indian-like canoes on a quiet mountain lake; or in a yacht that motors alongside the city's most historical sites and introduces you to the local fishing industry.

This is an ideal setting in which to absorb Native culture. Either of two land cruises just outside town will bring you face to face with the vivid story-telling medium of totem poles, among 113 in the Ketchikan area. Century-old Tlingit and Haida Indian poles, authentically recreated replicas, and a representative clan house line the shore at the TOTEM BIGHT STATE HISTORIC PARK, the site of a traditional Tlingit summer camp on Tongass Narrows. The communal house has carved corner posts, an impressively painted façade, and a cedar entrance pole recounting tales of Raven creating daylight in the dark world. On the quiet beach walk beside the poles, there's a chance of spotting seals and other sea mammals, bald eagles—and ravens.

SAXMAN TOTEM PARK, just south of Ketchikan, has more standing totem poles than any other place—over two dozen—and even more in the way of entertainment. Originally the Tlingit village of Fort Tongass, it was renamed for a Presbyterian minister who taught there late last century, and drowned while seeking a new site for the community. In the lean late-1930s, the Civilian Conservation Corps brought poles from old villages to Saxman and restored them. The collection has such curiosities as President Lincoln, in a stovepipe hat, as a symbol of the first white man seen by the clan, and U.S. Secretary of State William Seward, wearing a potlatch hat, on a pole that was meant to shame him because he didn't exchange gifts during his local visit in 1869. There's a carving shed where masters of the art create new 40-foot works; a Beaver tribal house, the first clan house to rise in half a century; a handicraft store and interpretative center; and culturally faithful performances by the Cape Fox Dancers.

A flightseeing tour is a fine way to comprehend the 2.3 million acres of MISTY FJORDS NATIONAL MONUMENT, which even some jaded

Alaskans insist is one of the more spectacular sights on earth. There are no roads in; planes and boats are the only options to view the sheer mountains quilted with snow, hanging valleys, white sand beaches, three major rivers, and countless streams that are among the state's best for rearing fish. It embraces eastern Revillagigedo Island and some of the mainland between the fjords of the Portland and Behm canals. Protected from logging, its forests are western hemlock, yellow and red cedar, Sitka spruce, a bit of silver fir, and even the northernmost stands of Pacific yew, prized for its use in cancer treatment.

From a float-equipped bush plane, you can watch twin waterfalls tumble from the bowl of Big Goat Lake, where mountain goats and brown bears ramble. You might fly close to the fortresslike granite flanks of a valley carved by a glacier and land at the head of long fjords to sit silently on the black saltwater of Rudyerd Bay. At its entrance, on the Behm Canal, a volcanic plug 20 stories tall

By the 1930s, about 1,200 fish boats fed Ketchikan's canneries and cold storage.

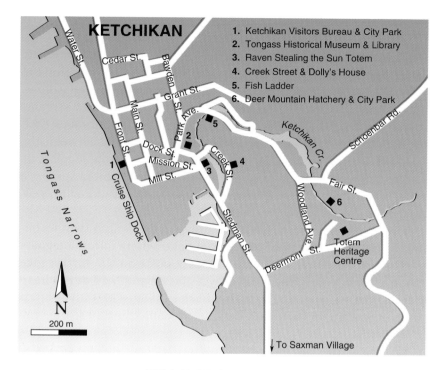

KETCHIKAN

1. Ketchikan Visitors Bureau & City Park
2. Tongass Historical Museum & Library
3. Raven Stealing the Sun Totem
4. Creek Street & Dolly's House
5. Fish Ladder
6. Deer Mountain Hatchery & City Park

WALKABOUT

TOTEM HERITAGE CENTER, a quarter-mile up Deermount Street, houses an intriguing collection of house posts from old Native villages and 33 original totem poles from the 19th century.

DEER MOUNTAIN HATCHERY on Ketchikan Creek, across the footbridge from the Totem Heritage Center, welcomes visitors with a description of the breeding and raising of coho and king salmon. The kings and pinks spawn in the creek in late summer, using the fish ladder to surmount the falls.

TONGASS HISTORICAL MUSEUM, in the library complex at 629 Dock St., focuses on Native art and craft and the fishing industry, as well as local history; generally open during cruise visits.

A TRAMWAY rises up the cliff from Creek Street to a Tlingit-styled hotel built by the Cape Fox Indian Corporation on Boston Smith Hill, which offers commanding views over Tongass Narrows and the city.

vaults from the water, a basking spot for seals. The ubiquitous Captain Vancouver named it New Eddystone Rock for a similar formation on a lighthouse rock off Cornwall, England. It's part of the wonder of a national monument which, given its mist-shrouded enchantment, might just as well have been called *Mystery* Fjords.

KOTZEBUE: THE LIVING ARCTIC

Shore Avenue, Kotzebue. Twenty-six miles above the Arctic Circle. Inupiat Eskimos repairing kayaks and umiaks sprinkled along the shore of Kotzebue Sound on the Chukchi Sea. The water illuminated with a strange summer light, not unlike the alpenglow of mountains. Beyond the flattened sea, silver-domed peaks on Cape Krusenstern National Monument melting into clouds. A sky as wide and high as the world. There are salmon and walrus meat drying on racks under a sun that, from early June, won't set for 36 days. Telephone poles take the place of trees; the scrub brush promises more than it ever delivers. Along the gravel road of Shore Avenue, which some locals call Front Street, are the Arctic Dragon restaurant and the Native-owned Nullagvik Hotel, whose dining room serves reindeer stew.

Kotzebue perches on the tundra 550 miles north of Anchorage and 200 south of Siberia, linked to Outside by daily flights and, for three summer months, by sea-going deep-draft vessels bringing in fuel and food supplies for the year. (River sediment in the Sound forces these ships to anchor many miles offshore.) The commercial and transportation center for northwestern Alaska, it's the state's largest community of Eskimos and one of its oldest. They represent three-quarters of the 3,800 population. For six centuries their ancestors made this a trading center, calling it Kikiktagruk— "almost a peninsula"—and *their* ancestors may have been living here, on the Baldwin Peninsula near the mouths of three rivers, since 8000 B.C. The current name comes from—well, it's nicely explained in a mysterious movie called *Salmonberries*, starring singer k.d. lang, which was filmed here in 1990 and went on to win the major award at the 1991 World Film Festival in Montreal. The singer plays a young woman called Kotzebue; the local librarian tells her the city was named for Otto von Kotzebue, the third of 17 children of the successful German playwright August von Kotzebue. She doesn't mention that his son Otto was sailing for the Russians, searching for the Northwest Passage, when he came upon the village in 1816.

Today's English-speaking Inupiat live in relatively easy coexistence between two worlds, herding reindeer and watching TV by satellite, hunting walrus and whale and working even farther up north in the Red Dog zinc-and-lead mine co-owned by their Native corporation, the Northwest Alaska Native Association (NANA). But urban pressures intrude in the unlikeliest ways. With the immensity of the Arctic all around, the city is hemmed in on this narrow spit of land three miles long—and it's running out of room for housing. There's as much of a spartan quality to the unadorned wooden structures as there is to the landscape, in which minuscule willows may be one inch tall. Done in Polar Pre-fab, the commercial buildings and the dwellings—some of them 41-plexes—can be dun-colored or occasionally, to relieve the starkness, pastel. Besides the comfortable NANA-built hotel, Kotzebue has a 50-bed hospital, a bank, recreation center, library, video stores, biweekly tabloid newspaper *(The Arctic Sounder)*, radio station KOTZ, a University of Alaska campus, and schools for 700 students with a full-sized gym (basketball's the big sport).

Although the prime employer is the borough school district, the local success story is NANA, organized under the Native-claims legislation of 1971. Its investment portfolio includes local seafood processing, reindeer harvesting, jade mining, and tourism, and statewide oilfield services and mineral drilling. In 1989, the corporation launched a joint venture with Cominco, Inc., which quickly became the western world's largest zinc producer. At its peak, the Red Dog Mine to the north is expected to employ

Visitors to Kotzebue can join the
Inupiat in the high-flying blanket toss.

about 360, injecting millions of dollars into the local economy. With the cost of food here more than twice that in Anchorage, residents need the money. They spend some of their discretionary cash on a popular pastime, bingo. Yup'ik storyteller John Active describes watching as a player in the bingo hall "raised his head up over the smoke, looked around quickly, then ducked down again. He looked like a seal. No, a ptarmigan."

On the Fourth of July, the people of Kotzebue celebrate with Native games, a whale-blubber-eating contest, and the presenting of awards for the biggest beluga caught during the season. A week later, artisans from around the borough gather at the Arctic Trades Fair to show their handicrafts and perform traditional dances. Visitors throughout the summer can see dancers, meet with artists, and take part in blanket tosses at one of three not-to-be-missed attractions: the NANA LIVING MUSEUM OF THE ARCTIC. It has an ambitious multimedia program featuring ultra-realistic dioramas, which explain the local culture and wildlife, and offers a tour of a jade factory. At the CULTURAL CAMP, youngsters demonstrate traditional hunting and fishing, cooking and sewing. More offbeat, the OOTUKAHKUKTUVIK CITY MUSEUM—you may have to pronounce it before they let you in—is chockablock with such indigenous artifacts as a coat of many bird feathers and a rain parka made from walrus intestine.

Above all, Kotzebue is a place for strolling through the dwarf fireweed and the cottongrass, for soaking up the accessible Arctic setting and its way of life. Summer is good walking weather, cool, seldom rising above 60°F. As you wander, consider the winter climate, when the temperature can plummet to 52° *below.*

NOME—NO PLACE LIKE IT

"It is the liveliest, speediest, swiftest mining camp ever seen in Alaska. All sorts of sharks are making fortunes," wrote a pioneering prospector in 1899, when Nome was briefly the gold-rush capital of the world. Nearly a century later, the city continues to be a modest gold-mining center and—though short of sharks—one of the zaniest, zestiest of Alaskan communities. It's the kind of place where locals golf with an orange ball and an iced tee on the frozen Bering Sea in March; swim between ice floes in its numbing 35-degree waters just after breakup on Memorial Day; play baseball in the midnight sunlight in June; and in summer build homemade rafts of any materials to run the Nome River and win a fur-lined honey bucket.

At the turn of the century, one hopeful American prospector came to town on a bike he'd ridden down the frozen Yukon River and across the tundra, while a Norwegian attempted the trip on ice skates. Ever since, Nome has had a history of attracting characters. These days, most everyone flies in on the 90-minute hop from Anchorage, and 60 per cent of its 4,500 people are Eskimos, a fiercely independent group who finally abandoned the spartan life on nearby King Island in 1959. Yet the western Arctic city lures adventuresome visitors and has a decidedly mixed bag of residents. Because Nome sits only 190 miles from Siberia, the tourist traffic along the sea on Front Street might include Russians, although cab drivers and shopkeepers no longer accept their devalued rubles as they once did. Meanwhile, trade across the Bering Strait (and the International Dateline) is slowly growing since the border reopened in 1988: one Nome entrepreneur has installed meat processors on Siberian farms to make sausages from reindeer—in return for the animals' horns which he exports to South Korea for use as aphrodisiacs.

Landlocked Nome, 150 miles south of the Arctic Circle, lies exposed to the elements on the southern verge of the Seward Peninsula overlooking Norton Sound, an extension of the Bering Sea. It may take its name from an Eskimo phrase, *Kn-no-me*, meaning "I don't know" (supposedly the answer to "What's the name of this place?"). But more likely it comes from nearby Cape Nome, itself a misinterpretation of the markings on a 19th-century British map of the area when *? Name* was misread as C (for Cape) Nome.

In the westernmost time zone in the U.S., on about the same latitude as Fairbanks, Nome is milder than its coastal neighbor

Kotzebue—which in summer means average lows of 40°F and highs in the 50s, with an occasional heat wave of 75. The surrounding permafrost terrain is classically treeless. (In December, convoys head down to the tree line east of the city to cut scrubby-looking spruce for the whole community's Christmas.) Summer briefly brings a riot of wildflowers, sedges, and grasses reaching ankle height in the encircling hills. Off the three dirt roads leading out of town, the Arctic tundra supports moose, musk-ox, and reindeer. (Local reindeer herds played the part of caribou stampeding during the 1983 Disney film, *Never Cry Wolf.*) Nearby lakes and streams run thick with salmon, arctic char, and grayling. The Seward Peninsula attracts 180 kinds of birds, many of them Asiatic species seldom seen in North America. And in the sea there are seals, whales, and the plentiful walrus.

Only Alaska Natives are allowed to legally possess ivory from the tusks and teeth of walrus, which they carve into works of art and offer for sale locally. Some of the ivory is mineralized and fossilized, the remnants of prehistoric mammoths and mastodons. Such artifacts of Eskimo culture are shown to effect in the CARRIE McCLAIN MEMORIAL MUSEUM (in the library building on Front Street), along with an intriguing exhibit of gifts from Russia, and the inevitable Gold Rush displays.

In 1898, the site where Nome now stands was an empty beach of black sand. That autumn, two Swedish-born prospectors and a Laplander—the legendary three Lucky Swedes—panned $1,800 worth of gold in a few days at Anvil Creek, three miles inland. By the following summer the beach was a tent city of hopefuls from the Klondike, the Lower 48, and the rest of Alaska. One day an elderly gold-panner decided to try the sand at his feet and found grains of gold right there along the shore. By summer's end, while prospectors extracted $1 million from the creeks, 2,000 elbow-to-elbow miners along the beachfront had taken twice that much more easily, using pans and the ingenious rockers that worked like swinging sluice boxes. There was a third wave of discovery when geologists realized that the water had once reached higher levels on the land and that more gold was to be found below those ancient beaches. Within a dozen years, the Seward Peninsula had given up more than $60 million in gold.

By 1900, the fledgling town counted among its many businesses 20 saloons, 12 general stores, and a bookshop, and its population included 11 doctors, 16 lawyers, and a masseur. It needed each of those specialists to deal with the physical and legal conflicts that erupted with the greed for gold. The new-money miners set the partying standard for present-day Nome, importing troupes of entertainers from Seattle and throwing lavish dinners catered by their own Chinese chefs. Even Wyatt Earp ran a bar and promoted local boxing matches, two decades after the gunfight at the O.K. Corral. (However, John Wayne playing a Nome gold-rush miner in *The Spoilers* never made it here; nary a foot of that classic 1942 film was shot in Alaska). At the turn of the century, the recorded population was 12,488, one-third of all whites living in Alaska. Nine thousand of them had dug the sands on a single day in 1900. But fire, storms, and outright thievery—some of it through the courts—reduced those numbers, as did the decline in production six years later. And by 1915 only 1,000 people remained in Nome.

The allure of gold continues to keep the city lively. The Alaska Gold Company is the major operator in the area. Some gold dredges still run during the summer, and you can photograph the wooden hulks of several old ones within walking distance of town. GOLD PANNING on the beach remains a popular tourist pastime; all you need is a pan bought locally. Is there any precious metal left in that played-out sand? The local Convention and Visitors Bureau warns that "while panning for gold is most assuredly fascinating, and fun, don't count on it to pay for even a small part of your trip—let alone your subsistence." Of course, they don't mention that in 1964 a visitor found a 1.29-ounce nugget at the end of Nome's seawall.

The 3,350-foot seawall was built of tons of granite to stop the ocean from devouring the foreshore and Front Street along with it. Over the years, the city has survived many blows, including a storm that nearly knocked it flat in 1913 and a fire that caused $2

million worth of damage in 1934. It was during a diphtheria epidemic in 1925 that 20 mushers drove relays of dog teams to bring serum 674 miles from Nenana, near Fairbanks, over part of a mail route that had been carved 15 years earlier. Today the IDITAROD TRAIL SLED DOG RACE—the so-called Last Great Race on Earth—starts at Anchorage and follows some of the same treacherous path, crossing two mountain ranges, snaking along the Yukon River, and arriving in Nome over the pack ice of Norton Sound. The actual distance now is nearly 1,100 miles, and the run can take two weeks, although consistent winner Susan Butcher and others have done it in little more than 11 days. High tech has overtaken the event: starting in 1993, vets implanted computer microchips in the dogs' necks to register them as entrants, rather than painting their fur, and officials at checkpoints used scanners to record their numbers as they ran by. Because the race takes place in March, summer visitors have to be content with viewing the arch of the finish line next to City Hall and perhaps get an unseasonal ride in a dog sled. There are usually sled dogs tethered along the east end of 6th Avenue to take pictures of but not to pet—they can be temperamental.

If you happen to be here in mid-June, the MIDNIGHT SUN FESTIVAL will more than make up for missing the Iditarod celebrations. To commemorate the summer solstice, there's a parade, a bank holdup and trial, Eskimo dancing and blanket tossing, the overnight softball tournament, and the mad Nome River Raft Race. And as you might expect of a raunchy old mining camp, it's a day-and-night, week-long wingding.

In Nome of the early 1900s, legendary Wyatt Earp
owned "the only second class saloon in Alaska."

THE PRIBILOF ISLANDS, A PLACE OF SURVIVORS

They are survivors, the handful of humans and the hundreds of thousands of mammals who inhabit the two specks of basalt and lava sand amid the Bering Sea 300 miles off the southwest Alaska mainland. The Pribilof Islands, even more remote than the isolated Aleutians to the south, are wind-blasted, treeless chunks of volcanic rock. The Pribilofs have become the unlikely home of the world's largest community of Aleut Natives and the more logical breeding ground of the greatest concentration of NORTHERN FUR SEALS. That means about 800 resident Aleuts but perhaps 1.1 million braying, brawling, basking fur seals—which, combined with harbor seals, Steller's sea lions, sea otters, and walruses make these islands the premier gathering place of mammals on the planet. They are also nesting grounds for nearly 200 avian species who form what may be the most extraordinary colony of SEA BIRDS anywhere.

ST. PAUL, the main population center, is the largest of the four islands, a mere 44 square miles. Off its coast sit deserted islets named Walrus and Otter and, 40 miles southeast, St. George Island. While lying at about the same latitude as Moscow, the Pribilofs have a reasonably moderate climate, thanks to currents from the south. True, summer temperatures seldom rise to 60°F and the land is usually fog-bound and light-starved, but when the sun does appear, it shines on endless blankets of blue lupines, yellow Aleutian poppies, and wild celery. And, come late spring, it also shines on the innumerable fur seals that are the only reason anyone ever came here to live.

Making their home in the open sea in winter, the female seals and their young migrate as far as Japan or southern California while the males remain in the Gulf of Alaska. Mature bulls begin returning to the Pribilofs in May, establishing their turf as beachmasters, awaiting the arrival of the pregnant females in June—occasionally lifting them in their jaws and flinging them into the territory they guard from other battle-scarred males. Within a few days, the females give birth to single black pups and, soon after, are ready for mating again. By September, all the seals have left the area.

The Aleuts and the fur seals have a symbiotic relationship—as hunter and hunted—yet they also share a history of cruelty inflicted upon them: near-extinction, and ultimate survival. *(See* The Native Way, *page 116.)* Today, visitors will find a welcoming Native community where elementary-school kids are learning the Aleut language, young adults are doing traditional dances, and their elders are using seal pelts to create handicrafts.

Their story starts in 1786 when Russian fur merchant Gerasim Pribilof was anchored in the Bering Sea during a thick fog. Either that, or as a well-known drunk he might have been off course. In any case, Pribilof heard the caterwauling of tens of thousands of northern fur seals. Three-quarters of the world's stock, breeding on what would become known as the Pribilofs, they represented the most valuable prize in the North Pacific; their skins were the gold standard among furs. To harvest them, the Russians enslaved people from the Aleutians, forcing them onto the hilly, uninhabited islands far out in the sea. In that ruthless process, here and elsewhere in Alaska, they helped reduce the Aleuts to an endangered species. *(See* A Little Alaskan History, *page 22.)* After 1876, the United States continued the seal harvest and within two decades, royalty income from the coveted seal pelts returned the national treasury nearly as much as America had paid for all of Alaska.

In the middle of the 19th century, Russian Baron Ferdinand Wrangell had instituted a program of cautious conservation of the fur seals, estimated to number four million at the time of the sale. And in an enlightened move in 1870, the U.S. Congress made the Pribilofs a protected federal reserve, curtailing the annual harvest to 100,000 male animals a year old or older and prohibiting any killing by firearms. Sealing rights were leased to the Alaska Commercial Company, which agreed to open schools and provide free dried salmon and firewood for the 400 Aleuts on the islands who would carry out the harvest. But for the next decade and a half, the federal government ignored the Pribilofs, along with most of Alaska, while American and Canadian sealers shot pregnant females as well as males on the open seas. With the population reduced by 90 per cent, the northern fur seal was approaching extinction. It wasn't until 1886 that the U.S. began to seize sealing ships in the Bering Sea; and finally in 1911, it signed an international treaty with Russia, Japan, and Great Britain, on behalf of Canada, limiting seal harvesting to the land, under rigorous controls.

By then the Aleuts had become efficient butchers, killing the animals so humanely with clubs and knives that even the Audubon Society would eventually defend their methods. ("The process is at least as humane as the millions of killings we sanction daily in slaughterhouses across the country," *Audubon* magazine has remarked.) In 1957 the four nations set limits on the quantity of non-breeding males to be harvested—anywhere from 20,000–30,000 a year—in an agreement that wildlife experts around the world praised as a model of migratory wildlife conservation. Yet continuing pressure from environmentalists led to the end of commercial harvesting in 1984. Since then, the Aleuts have been allowed only an annual subsistence harvest of about 1,600 bachelor seals.

That left many of the Pribilovians, direct descendants of their shanghied ancestors, unemployed—literally at sea. Despite a $20-million government settlement, it took nearly a decade for them to replace the seal economy with one based on fishing and tourism. Under a new fishery-management agreement, the U.S. fishing industry allocates seven per cent of Alaska's ground-fishing resource to local communities. Residents of the Pribilofs contract with a fishing company, which employs them in catching and processing Pacific cod, pollock, rockfish, and flounder. "It's been a big shot in the arm for them," says Dave Cormany, Pribilof Islands program manager for the National Marine Fisheries Service. "People are starting to look toward the future, becoming very active in reviving the tradition and culture of the Pribilofs."

St. Paul has an airstrip, a hotel, a restaurant, the frame Russian Orthodox church of Saints Peter and Paul, and tidy rows of houses along red volcanic-cinder roads for the island's trucks and all-terrain vehicles. The modern school, which goes up to Grade ten, has an auto-repair shop, an electronics laboratory, and computers. TV sets are everywhere, and microwaves are not uncommon. But step just outside the community, and you're at an immense seal rookery, observing the indefatigable bulls with their harems. Or watching birds by the millions, in one of the best birding sites in the world. The sea cliffs are among the world's few nesting areas for the red-legged kittiwake, the red-faced cormorant, and eight species of auks, including the tufted puffin. The islands are home to winged visitors from Siberia and Hawaii, and such local species as a rare sandpiper and several colorful Asiatic finches. There are wild reindeer in the bush, and arctic blue fox scavenging the beaches where sea lions breed with other mammals. All of them, like the seals and the Aleuts, are survivors in this place which resembles nowhere else on earth.

PRUDHOE BAY: WHERE OIL MEETS MAMMAL

At 21 places along its route, the Trans-Alaska Pipeline dips underground for about 60 feet and then resurfaces to continue its zigzag course across the tundra. There are no "walk" or "don't walk" signals at these spots, but they are pedestrian crossings of a sort.

Freedom of movement for Alaska's mammals was one of the many environmental issues raised by the building of the pipeline. As a result more than 500 animal crossings were provided. But the caribou herds created a difficult problem. The herds had to be free to migrate to their calving grounds. Biologists had experimented with various mammals' reactions to a pipeline. They found that moose would scramble on their knees under low pipes, but caribou wouldn't enter the enclosed space under a raised pipe nor use a ramp to get over it. Even a mother, separated from a bawling calf, would stay on her side of the line. Buried pipeline under level crossings was the only answer for the herds, and engineering them created one of the wonderful peculiarities in the 800-mile pipeline from North America's largest oil field, at Prudhoe Bay on the North Slope, to the port of Valdez on Prince William Sound.

The caribou are still plentiful along the DALTON HIGHWAY to Prudhoe Bay *(see* Driving the Dalton, *page 188),* and a trip to the source of the oil shows how man and mammal are cohabiting around a community that exists for a single purpose: to extract from the Salerochit Formation about a quarter of the petroleum produced in America. Fronting the ARCTIC OCEAN on Alaska's northeastern coast, nine-mile-wide Prudhoe Bay (usually pronounced *Prude*-oh) was named by Sir John Franklin for a fellow British explorer-scientist, the Baron of Prudhoe, during an expedition that took Franklin down Canada's Mackenzie River to the sea. The population center is the private company town of DEADHORSE, the Dalton's northern limit. A few miles from the ocean (whose bone-numbing waters you can dip fingers or toes into), it is operated by several multinational oil corporations who bring workers here for a few weeks at a time to labor intensively for stratospheric rates of pay and then fly Outside as fast as they can for rest and recreation. Aside from mountains of food and the latest videos, there are few of the amenities you'd expect in a town equipped for up to 8,000 people, and workers seldom have time to consider the starkly magnificent tundra and the plenitude of wildlife—whales, polar bears, and caribou—surrounding them.

Thanks largely to Prudhoe Bay, Alaska vies with Texas year by year as America's leader in oil production. The vast fields here have estimated recoverable reserves of at least 16 billion barrels of oil and 26 trillion cubic feet of natural gas. It was in 1968 that Atlantic Richfield announced a wildcat well, Prudhoe Bay State No. 1, creating a stampede of the world's oilmen, many of whom came to Anchorage with cash in hand to bid for leases the following year—quadrupling the state's revenues overnight. Within two decades, half the estimated oil reserve had been pumped south. To

The Trans-Alaska pipeline, here elevated, wends its way from Prudhoe Bay to Valdez.

make the most of the remainder, a $2-billion waterflood project has been forcing extra oil out of the rock. Meanwhile, a Central Gas Facility—the world's biggest gas plant—produces tens of thousands of barrels of natural gas each day. And though the known petroleum reserves are in decline, in recent years there has been a revival of exploratory drilling on the North Slope.

While security prevents visitors from wandering the docks or local roads, guided tours show you the most relevant areas of the oil-drilling activity and the environmental measures the petroleum companies take as they pump the black gold to Valdez. The oil that comes out of the ground at Prudhoe Bay is hot—about 180°F. Inside the 48-inch pipeline, it cools to about 145°. Slightly more than half the line is above ground, supported between 78,000 pairs of upright piping (for which four million feet of hole had to be drilled). Above ground, the pipeline wears an insulated jacket to protect it and keep the oil warm enough to flow after an interruption. When it goes under the tundra, the pipe is buried in stable ground to protect the permafrost. To keep the ground frozen at the caribou crossings, the excavated ditch around the pipe has been surrounded with sheets of Styrofoam and filled with gravel. But in some cases, the engineers had to go one step further. They have laid underground pipes through which brine is pumped to keep the frozen ground of Alaska frozen.

Alaska presented unique challenges for the pipeline engineers: temperatures that range from -80°F to 95°; three mountain ranges; earthquake and avalanche zones; and 800 river and stream crossings. Their solutions were inventive and sometimes novel. The line's zigzag pattern is intended to give flexibility in controlling movement from earthquakes or thermal expansion and contraction. Zinc anodes placed beside buried sections of pipe attract electrical currents in the earth's surface (the same currents that generate the northern lights), returning the currents to the earth and reducing the risk of damage to the pipeline. In earthquake zones, where the pipe is raised, it is free to slide from side to side on its vertical supports. At Atigun Pass through the Brooks Range, the highest point on the line, the pipe is buried to protect it from avalanches and swathed in 21 inches of insulation inside an 8-foot-wide concrete sarcophagus to protect it from corrosion.

In the late 1960s, before construction had begun, estimates were that the line would cost $900 million. By the time the final design was finished in 1974, Alyeska Pipeline Service Company—the consortium of seven oil companies that built and still operates it—had revised its estimate to $8 billion, which was what the line cost when it was finished in June 1977.

On average, 1.7 million barrels are pumped through in a day, and, moving at six miles an hour, it takes a little over five days for the oil to reach Valdez, where it is stored before being pumped into ocean-going tankers. By 1992, nine billion barrels had been taken from the North Slope fields.

Safety features have been incorporated with Alaska's delicate environment in mind. Pump stations along the route monitor the flow, and computers at Valdez can indicate a drop in pressure, signalling an operator to close valves at the pump stations. Inside the line itself, valves will close if the oil flow stops or reverses. These measures are supposed to limit the size of a spill. In February 1978, when the line was sabotaged, 16,000 barrels escaped east of Fairbanks.

Each year, the interior of the pipe is examined with a "pig," a cylindrical device carrying sophisticated measuring instruments. Some pigs clean the inside of the pipe; some check changes in shape or look for corrosion. The newest ultrasonic pig takes 27 million readings in a mile, detecting and recording changes in the thickness of the pipe wall. When, in 1989, it revealed small spots of corrosion at points along the line, Alyeska handled the problem by increasing the amount of drag-reducing agent it normally injects to reduce turbulence in the oil and make it easier to pump. This temporary increase lowered the pressure in the pipe and allowed repairs to be made. In 1991, 8.5 miles of pipe were replaced in the Atigun Pass floodplain. This was the largest construction project on the pipeline since startup in 1977.

While the oil continues to flow, so do the caribou. The Nelchina herd, which had decreased to 10,000 before the pipeline

DRIVING THE DALTON

It's a two-day trip on the damndest highway you've ever driven along. Gravel for all but 39 of its 414 miles, the Dalton Highway takes you through the taiga forest and treeless tundra of the Alaska wilds north of Fairbanks, over the Brooks Range and the Yukon River, across the Arctic Circle and the Continental Divide, through the GATES OF THE ARCTIC NATIONAL PARK AND PRESERVE and the ARCTIC NATIONAL WILDLIFE REFUGE, across Alaska's highest mountain pass, into the summering habitat of hundreds of thousands of caribou in the Porcupine and Central Arctic herds—and on the whole trip you won't pass through a single population center unless you count WISEMAN (pop: 25) and America's northernmost truck stop, COLDFOOT.

The Dalton began life in 1974 as the North Slope Haul Road to truck supplies for the Prudhoe Bay oil fields and the northern section of the Trans-Alaska Pipeline, whose route it generally parallels. Named for James Dalton, a pioneering Arctic engineer involved in exploring the North Slope for oil after World War II, the 28-foot-wide highway took only five months to build—at a cost of three million man-hours and $125 million, with $30 million of that for the 2,290-foot-long, wood-decked Yukon River Bridge (at Mile 55.6 on the way up, 358.4 on the way down). The Yukon is Alaska's longest river, meandering 1,400 miles between the Bering Sea and the state's border with Canada's Yukon.

Ownership of the highway—still called the Haul Road—has reverted to the state, which has only recently allowed limited public access with permits as far as Deadhorse. Heading north in the air-cushioned comfort of a luxury tour bus, you'll see the sign marking the Arctic Circle—latitude 66°33'—at Mile 115. Sixty miles on is Coldfoot, the halfway point, an overnight stop for tourists and truckers. The name comes from those prospectors who followed gold plays on the Koyukuk River in 1893 and got cold feet when winter arrived. In 1989 the temperature here sank to -82°F and stayed below -62° for 17 days; the following summer it rose to 97°—a difference of 179 degrees that set a continental record. The buildings are leftovers from pipeline construction camps: a motel, a café with personalized coffee mugs and a message board for truckers, and a service station whose pumps often fuel bush planes as well as tour buses and the big tractor-trailers.

Ten miles north, on the middle fork of the Koyukuk River, the historic mining town of Wiseman—now not much more than a museum and general store—was settled in 1911 when people began to leave Coldfoot as they sought gold on Nolan and Wiseman creeks. After passing Sukakpak Mountain, the old border between Eskimo and Indian lands, you're into the 8.4 million acres of the Gates of the Arctic National Park and Preserve, named for Mount Boreal and Frigid Crags that form the landmark gateways.

You're amid the BROOKS RANGE, the world's most northern mountain network, which sweeps across the top of Alaska from the Mackenzie River in Canada's Northwest to Kotzebue on the Bering Sea. At Mile 244, you reach the summit of 4,800-foot ATIGUN PASS, the highest on the continent, where avalanches are common in winter. Driving down from the Continental Divide, you can often spot Dall sheep and caribou, grizzlies and wolves, as you approach the North Slope and the pipes and rigs of Prudhoe Bay.

was built, grew to 45,000 animals in 1992. Scientists, watching the animals' behavior over a period of three years, observed that 99 per cent of the caribou successfully cross the pipeline.

SITKA: BEAUTY *AND* CULTURE

Sitka is more than just a pretty place. As stunningly situated as this Southeastern community is—facing the open Pacific, set amid snow-crested mountains and endless fjords—Sitka has also been a cultural center for centuries. The numerous Tlingits who lived here had developed the most sophisticated civilization of any Natives in the Great Land. Their well-constructed houses, gift-giving potlatches, and elaborate dances performed before long voyages demonstrated the richness of their world. The local tribe lived in the village they called Shee Atiku –"people on the outside of

Sitka perches on the open Pacific, against the backdrop of Fuji-like Mount Edgecumbe.

Shee," which is the island now known as Baranov, the present site of Sitka. Here, in 1799, Aleksandr Baranov of the Russian–American Company established Mikhailovsk, Fort St. Michael (named for the Archangel Michael). In 1802, the Tlingits slaughtered most of the men and enslaved the women in this fortress colony of Russian fur traders. Two years later, Baranov forced the Tlingits to flee—in Tlingit history, only because they misinterpreted the Russians' white flag of surrender for a sign that they'd be erased as clean as snow. A mile west of the old fort, Baranov created New Archangel—more commonly called Sitka, a contraction of the Tlingit name. A hyperbolic writer of the era dubbed it "the Paris of the Pacific," replete as it was with fine art and Flemish linen, good wines and Virginia tobacco, a theater and multilingual lending library. One Yankee trader described its aristocratic administrators as "highly educated, refined in manners, intelligent and courteous. Most of the gentlemen spoke French and English in addition to their own language."

Contemporary Sitka maintains the cultural tradition: not only has it freeze-framed the past in such artistic ventures as the New Archangel Russian Dancers and the Tlingit Gajaa Heen Dancers but since 1972 it has also staged a summer music festival that attracts superb musicians from around the world. And an annual symposium of international writers has been held at Sheldon Jackson College, the campus where James Michener based himself for three summers while researching his popular documentary novel *Alaska*.

Sitka, Russia's capital in the New World, was the Russian–American Company's first permanent settlement. The precedents continued: one governor was the first to export Alaskan lake ice, shipped in sawdust, to chill the drinks of Californians; another set up the first wholesale conservation program in North America, restricting the hunting of fur seals and the now-endangered sea otters that had brought the Russians here in the first place. And when Russia sold Alaska to America in 1867, Sitka became the first capital of the new territory of Alaska. (Juneau assumed the mantle in 1900.)

All this compelling history is heralded throughout modern-day Sitka (pop: 8,600). SITKA NATIONAL HISTORICAL PARK, at the eastern end of Lincoln Street (named for you-know-who), became the first federally designated park in 1910, marking the Battle of Sitka in which Baranov and his Aleut allies had taken the Tlingit fortress a century before. It's an entrancing place today with Tlingit and Haida totem poles theatrically set amid looming hemlock and Sitka spruce in a mile-long seashore loop—the local Lover's Lane. Other cedar poles, rising up to 80 feet in front of the Southeast Alaska Indian Cultural Center, are replicas of those collected for the 1904 Louisiana Purchase Exposition, one of them incorporating the ominous figure of a white man with a rifle. The center offers demonstrations of silver and bead work and wood-carving, and an illuminating ten-minute show of watercolor slides about local history.

Neighboring the park is the SHELDON JACKSON MUSEUM, on the campus of the private college set up in 1878 to train Alaska's Native peoples. The state's oldest educational institution now grants arts degrees and teaching certificates. The museum is an octagonal structure, dating back to 1895, the first concrete building in the territory. It is named for Alaska's original General Agent for Education, a Presbyterian missionary who crisscrossed the state in the late 19th century performing good works, such as introducing reindeer from Siberia to help hungry Eskimos. Along the way, he collected thousands of Native artifacts, from kayaks and reindeer sleds to masks and bentwood boxes—the finest collection of its kind in Alaska and among the most significant in the world.

Across from the Jackson campus (at 1101 Sawmill Rd., north of the Indian River bridge) is a unique treatment facility for birds revered by Native people: the ALASKA RAPTOR REHABILITATION CENTER. Every year, volunteers care for up to three dozen injured eagles, hawks, falcons, and owls, sending the most serious to avian experts in the Lower 48, releasing the rehabilitated to the wild, and using non-releasable raptors for captive breeding programs. The majority of cases are bald eagles, 80 per cent of them hurt intentionally or accidentally by humans and by such unnatural objects as fish hooks and powerlines. One of them was Buddy, a hatchling raised by humans and later abandoned in a Southeast village in 1988. After the center's staff taught him to fly and fed him on "ratsicles" (frozen rats), he became an educational tool for the center, travelling across the U.S. and even—by state ferry—to the annual gathering of balds at Chilkat River near Haines, Alaska.

The RUSSIAN BISHOP'S HOUSE (on Lincoln across from Crescent Harbor)—the oldest intact building in Alaska—is the only one remaining from the Russian colonial era and one of only four original Russian structures still standing in North America. As a missionary in 1824, Father Ivan Veniaminov began fashioning an alphabet for the Aleuts, taught them brickmaking and other trades, and took farflung kayak trips for months at a time to convert an estimated 10,000 Natives to his faith. American observers referred to him as Paul Bunyan in a cassock. A decade later, he moved to Sitka, where he eventually became Russian Orthodox Bishop of Alaska before returning home as all-powerful Metropolitan of Moscow and, after his death, being canonized as St. Innocent. The manse he lived in here has been restored, with the help of archeologists and historians, at a cost of about $5 million. The 1842 structure of squared spruce logs and planks features a first-floor museum of Russian-American artifacts; the second story has been authentically returned to its early grandeur, even to the original gold-embossed, crushed-velvet upholstery.

The most imposing reminder of Russian times is the onion-domed, spruce-and-clapboard ST. MICHAEL'S CATHEDRAL in downtown Sitka. America's first Russian Orthodox cathedral stood for 188 years before a fire destroyed it in 1966—but not before local residents rescued its superb iconography and art, including the Sitka Madonna, to which miraculous powers have been attributed, and a couple of important two-century-old oils on canvas covered in impressive silver *rizas*. Fund-raising in Alaska and Washington raised more than $500,000 to painstakingly rebuild a near-replica of the cathedral—recasting the spire's bronze bells from those melted in the fire—but this time incombustible cinder blocks lie beneath its wooden sheathing. The mother church for the 20,000 Alaskans who still follow the Russian Orthodox faith serves a local

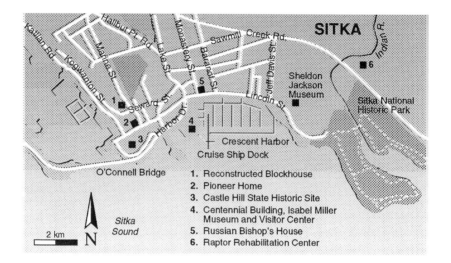

Sheldon
Jackson
Museum

Sitka National
Historic Park

Crescent Harbor
Cruise Ship Dock

O'Connell Bridge

Sitka
Sound

2 km   N

1. Reconstructed Blockhouse
2. Pioneer Home
3. Castle Hill State Historic Site
4. Centennial Building, Isabel Miller
   Museum and Visitor Center
5. Russian Bishop's House
6. Raptor Rehabilitation Center

WALKABOUT

The SITKA VISITOR BUREAU, in the Centennial Building off Harbor Drive, beside Crescent Boat Harbor, has a city map with highlights to see; in the same building, the ISABEL MILLER MUSEUM shows a detailed model of Sitka in 1867 as well as such historical items as logging and mining equipment and a whalebone chair.

The wooden BLOCKHOUSE, on a downtown hill at Kogwanton and Marine, is a replica of the original stockade that once separated Natives from the European community. Next to it is the RUSSIAN ORTHODOX CEMETERY with 400 graves a century and a half old, among them that of Princess Maria Maksutova, the effervescent wife of Alaska's final Russian governor (who fainted when the Stars and Stripes replaced the Russian double-eagle flag).

The state's first retirement home, SITKA PIONEERS HOME, on Lincoln Street next to the Post Office, welcomes visitors who want to chat with aging sourdoughs and buy their handicrafts in a gift shop.

congregation of about 300, most descended from Russian-Tlingit ancestors.

Many shore excursions include a spirited performance of the NEW ARCHANGEL DANCERS, a highly polished group of local women whose repertoire includes heritage dances of Russia, Ukraine, and Armenia. Taught by professional folk-dance specialists, and costumed in such authentic garb as Georgian gowns and Cossack boots, they even pull off the traditionally masculine stunts of sky-high leaps and knee-popping squats.

The small state park of CASTLE HILL (up the staircase beside the Post Office on Lincoln) handily sums up the three phases of Sitka history. Kiks Adi Natives had their ancestral home here before the Russians arrived, and Baranov built his castlelike headquarters on the outlook. And it was on this site that Russia formally transferred the territory to the United States, which had paid just under two cents an acre for a land twice as big as Texas.

The hill overlooks the quiet waters of Sitka Sound and Mount Edgecumbe, a dormant volcano whose elegant peak reminds many visitors of Mount Fuji. The mountain ascends on Kruzof Island, one of hundreds of small islands whose human-scale fjords lend such beauty to SIGHTSEEING NATURE CRUISES and MARINE EXPEDITIONS. A typical destination is Silver Bay; the 18-mile voyage—during which Steller's sea lions and humpback whales may be glimpsed—passes by the remains of the Liberty Prospect Mine, dating back to Alaska's first gold strike in 1872, and one of two modern pulp mills within the Tongass National Forest, a prime plank in Sitka's economic base. Another cruise might lead to Salisbury Sound, 25 miles north, for the chance of observing and photographing tufted puffins and auklets, porpoises, killer whales, and sea otters basking like Sirens, as well as such land animals as Sitka black-tailed deer and brown bears. A more adventurous exploration of the sea starts on a catamaran speeding through the islands and shifts gears as you board versatile Zodiac-type rafts that offer close-ups of ocean life—especially when a scuba diver surfaces with an octopus or sea cucumber for your inspection. Anglers with enough time will find that the inlets surrounding Sitka are ideal for

SPORTFISHING for halibut—and this is a hot spot for the prized king salmon.

As you cruise through these beautiful waters, consider the small but determined sub-culture of local surfers: wearing wet and dry suits, transporting their boards by skiff, they head out to the coast, which shelters Sitka Sound, and tackle the fearsome and frigid waves of the open Pacific.

SKAGWAY, THE LOST FRONTIER

You want characters? Authentic Alaskan characters in a town that looks as if it were lifted from a tale by Robert Service? A place that was seriously considered as the off-center home of *Northern Exposure*, the hit TV series about this state of relentless individuals? Welcome to Skagway.

There's the ivory trader who advertises himself as *Corrington—The Legend—The Man*. The woman who came to visit and wound up buying the Red Onion Saloon, a pint-sized donkey, and a pot-bellied pig. The balmiest of the 700 permanent residents who hired a couple of planes to fly in Big Macs from Juneau's first McDonald's, and others who successfully wielded a petition and a phony newspaper front page imploring Alaska's rural TV network to bring back the eccentric series *The Simpsons*—their soulmates, obviously. And not to forget the kazoo-crazy, award-winning Big Hammer Marching Band, which disrupts every Fourth of July celebration, sending people scurrying from the smoke of their mock nuclear meltdown or neglecting to let the police know about a make-believe bank holdup erupting in simulated gunshots and dynamite blasts.

All of which is one reason why Skagway—at the northern end of the Inside Passage—may be Southeast's most popular cruise port. Amid the imposing St. Elias Mountains, it sits at the head of Taiya Inlet on the 75-mile Lynn Canal from Juneau. Aside from an average annual rainfall of a mere 26 inches (one-sixth of Ketchikan's), the town's most obvious lure is its gold rush past.

During the late 1890s, it was the staging area for the Klondike Stampeders who tried to surmount the wicked White Pass Trail to the Yukon, one of the two Trails of '98 across the Coast Range. As the century turned, Skagway became the starting point of the narrow-gauge WHITE PASS & YUKON RAILWAY line to Whitehorse—which after several years' interruption in the 1980s has resumed its enthralling run over the picturesque pass as a tourist attraction between here and Fraser, British Columbia. *(See* Alaska's Lively Railways, *page 202.)* Cruise-ship passengers can take a briefer trip behind old No. 73, a steam engine, which eventually gives way to diesels powerful enough to climb to the summit, at the international border with Canada, and wend back down the mountain.

Now, as part of the widely scattered Klondike Gold Rush National Historical Park (with branches in Seattle and Canada's Dawson City), Skagway has enshrined its history. The park service is spending millions on restoration. Although much of the town may be a tarted-up replica of the real thing, every building along two blocks of the main street was put up between 1897 and 1900. These days the whole place is paved, but Broadway's street surface is a special mix similar to the dusty gravel that tourists used to trip over only a few years back. There's the Sweet Tooth Saloon Café, The Rushin' Tailor, and THE RED ONION, which opened in 1898. Then it was a saloon and brothel (red lights and mannequins dressed as trollops still stare from the second-story windows); now it's a watering hole that often hosts cruise-ship musicians playing jazz on a busman's holiday. THE MASCOT SALOON MUSEUM (Broadway and 3rd) will tell you almost as much as you wanted to know about gold-rush bars. One of them, at 2nd, JEFF SMITH'S PARLOR, belonged to the town's legendary bad man, Jefferson Randall (Soapy) Smith.

If Skagway has characters today, they descend in spirit from the bearded, beak-nosed Soapy, a con man from the U.S. South. He picked up the moniker in the Lower 48 from his penny-ante racket of selling soap to suckers who hoped to win the $20 and $50 bills

The White Pass & Yukon Railroad twists through terrain that's "too steep for a billy goat." ➤

supposedly wrapped inside the bars. In 1897, Smith came to a site that had been settled a decade earlier by William (Capt. Billy) Moore, a shrewd riverboat skipper and prospector who had claimed 160 waterfront acres and built a wharf. (MOORE'S CABIN, the oldest local building, is still on 5th Street east of Broadway). With the Klondike gold strike, about 100 stampeders led by surveyor Frank Reid decided to commandeer Moore's land—although he did sell the wharf for $175,000—and lay out a town. It came to be known as Skagway, a Tlingit name variously believed to mean, among other things, "home of the north wind" and "the end of salt water." The day after Smith arrived in the windy, tidewater settlement, he and five fellow crooks rescued a bartender from hanging—Soapy announced there'd be no lynch mobs in *his* Skagway. This pretence at principles made him popular enough that he soon ran the lawless town, operating a crooked gambling parlor and overseeing a string of strongarm men, pickpockets, and rip-off artists. Soapy himself was not above a good swindle, such as collecting $35,000 in contributions for a new preacher in town and then having him robbed overnight.

Meanwhile, Canada's North West Mounted Police were running the Yukon *(see page 230)*, and when Superintendent Sam Steele visited Skagway in 1898, he was appalled at the difference. The town of 15,000, he said, was "little better than a hell on earth": "At night, the crash of bands, shouts of 'Murder!,' cries for help mingled with the cracked voices of singers in the variety halls. . . ." It wasn't until July 8, 1898, when a new arrival who had been robbed of his gold dust protested loudly, that Soapy's reign ended. At an evening meeting called by more honest citizens to discuss the victim's complaint, a drunken Smith arrived to harangue them—only to be met by Frank Reid, who had helped relieve Capt. Billy Moore of his land. After a shootout, Smith was dead and Reid lay dying.

Skagway incorporated in 1900 and, with Soapy and most of the stampeders gone, it settled down to the business of being a reputable port and a railroad town. For the next eight decades, the White Pass & Yukon carried the natural resources from Canada's

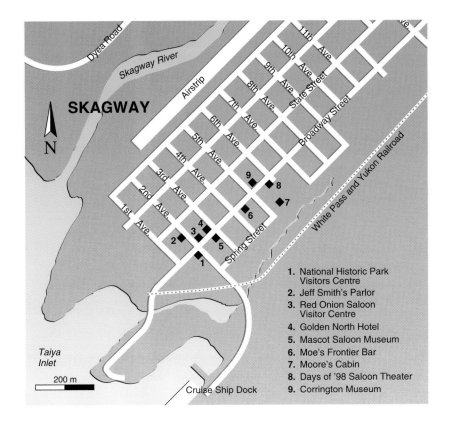

SKAGWAY

N

Dyea Road
Skagway River
Airstrip
11th Ave.
10th Ave.
9th Ave.
8th Ave.
State Street
7th Ave.
6th Ave.
Broadway Street
5th Ave.
4th Ave.
3rd Ave.
2nd Ave.
1st Ave.
White Pass and Yukon Railroad
Spring Street
Taiya Inlet
200 m
Cruise Ship Dock

1. National Historic Park
   Visitors Centre
2. Jeff Smith's Parlor
3. Red Onion Saloon
   Visitor Centre
4. Golden North Hotel
5. Mascot Saloon Museum
6. Moe's Frontier Bar
7. Moore's Cabin
8. Days of '98 Saloon Theater
9. Corrington Museum

WALKABOUT

VISITOR CENTERS are located at the Arctic Brotherhood Hall (home of a sourdough fraternal order established in 1899), on Broadway between 2nd and 3rd—the one with 20,000 sticks of driftwood on its façade— and the National Historical Park Visitor Center across the road. Both centers have ambitious walking-tour maps of downtown.

Strolling Broadway, look for the three-story, yellow onion-domed GOLDEN NORTH HOTEL, which with an 1898 birthdate might well be Alaska's oldest. It's fitted out with Gold Rush furnishings and, yes, there's the fabled ghost of Mary, a gold miner's wife, on the premises. THE DAYS OF '98 SALOON THEATRE, Broadway and 6th, has the longest-running entertainment in the state: the melodrama featuring Soapy Smith has been involving audiences for nearly seven decades. MOE'S FRONTIER BAR, on Broadway between 4th and 5th, is where the locals go to down a few, or more.

ALASKA'S LIVELY RAILROADS

They called it "the toughest 110 miles of track in the world," a right-of-way hacked out of a mountainside and laid through gorges on topography that was "too steep for a billy goat and too cold for a polar bear." But by July 1899, the first steam train of THE WHITE PASS & YUKON RAILROAD—the northernmost line in the western hemisphere, with one of the steepest grades on the continent—chugged into Skagway carrying a payload of half a million dollars in Klondike gold. Railway workers, braving deep snows and up to -60°F weather, had dangled by rope from sheer cliffs as they positioned blasting powder to dynamite their path through the Coast Mountains between Skagway and Whitehorse in the gold-rich Yukon Territory. And even after it was all done—the tracks from the two towns met at Carcross, Y.T., on July 29, 1900—the operators still had to contend with the inevitable avalanches and, eight decades later, a decline in mining that would stop the railway even colder.

The tale of the WP&Y is typical of Alaska's lively rail history, which cruise-ship passengers and others can revisit in trips through flabbergasting scenery and fascinating heritage sites. The state-owned ALASKA RAILROAD grew out of the financial failure of the Alaska Central Railway, a 70-mile line that a Seattle consortium built to the port of Seward in 1903. It was taken over by the Alaskan Northern Railway Company, which the Alaska Railroad bought in 1915 as it began construction of nearly 500 miles of track from Seward on the Kenai Peninsula, through the new rail town of Anchorage, to Fairbanks. The Loop District through the Kenai Mountains demanded a series of tunnels and cloverleafs over weblike wooden trestles—some of the most complicated engineering in railway history.

Today, the Anchorage-Fairbanks line passes through Denali National Park and affords superb views of Mount McKinley and a variety of wildlife. On this route during the summer, major cruise lines offer luxe accommodation on special double-decker domed rail cars pulled by the railway's regular diesel engines. The Alaska Railroad also runs a summer shuttle service between Portage and Whittier on Prince William Sound. Year-round, it offers freight and passenger service both to Whittier and on the half-day trip from Anchorage to Fairbanks, where moose meandering down the tracks can slow its progress. Some of the half-million passengers use its flag service: homesteaders, who much of the year travel by snow machine or dog sled, can stop a train in the middle of the wilderness.

Two visionaries created the White Pass & Yukon. Sir Thomas Tancrede, spokesman for a group of British financiers, had decided that a railroad to the Klondike couldn't be strung across the St. Elias Mountains. He hadn't yet met Michael J. Heney, an Irish-Canadian railway contractor, later known as the Irish Prince. When they did run into one another in a Skagway bar, Heney convinced Tancrede during one long night that the project was viable. Construction started in May 1898; two months later, a train travelled the first four miles—an excursion run, like today's trips. The track topped the summit by the following February, and the Yukon River's headwaters at Lake Bennett by July 6.

The WP&Y's history has since been as up and down as its route. It toted stampeders and their freight until the Gold Rush ebbed, rallied again during World War II to supply the Alaska Highway project, and afterward grew into an integrated system with container ships, pipelines, and trucks to haul ore from Yukon mines. Until 1982, when metal prices sank worldwide, the mines closed—and the railway with them. Until 1988, when tourism to Skagway had soared high enough to justify reopening it as the White Pass & Yukon Route exclusively for excursions.

Cruise passengers can take the Scenic Railway of the World to the top of the pass and back, on mountain flanks through a box canyon and a tunnel, past the nearly two dozen glacier-fed cataracts of Bridal Veil Falls, and along the Deadhorse Trail of '98. And those taking land cruises from Whitehorse, Y.T., can get aboard the railway at Fraser, British Columbia, and journey to Skagway on *The International*.

North to the coast. But when the Yukon's lead and zinc mines closed in 1982, the railway went down with them. By then the National Park Service had begun restoring the town's boardwalks and false-front buildings. Summer tourist traffic quickly became the major industry. Cruise-ship companies now offer a cornucopia of excursions here. Among them:

A HISTORICAL TOWN TOUR by motorcoach or antique automobile will take you through the compact town center (watch for 1st and State, where Smith and Reid killed one another), and perhaps stop at the granite-faced TRAIL OF '98 MUSEUM on the second floor of the former Skagway courthouse. Built originally as a Methodist college in 1899, it is chock-full of Native artifacts (some made of duck and salmon skin); mementos of the Victorian life-style the town enjoyed; tools of the gambling trade; and the story of Soapy and his nemesis—who lie buried in the GOLD RUSH CEMETERY just outside town, not far from pretty Reid Falls. Many tours provide an opportunity for photographs at the SKAGWAY OVERLOOK, just on the edge of town, with its inspiring view of the community, the valley, and the Lynn Canal.

THE WHITE PASS TOUR by motorcoach leads to the 3,292-foot summit through the well-named Tormented Valley, a route that runs near the White Pass & Yukon rail line, past glaciers, and on to the U.S.–Canada border. This tour can include a visit to the LIARSVILLE TRAIL CAMP, a replica of a turn-of-the-century tent town including sled-dog demonstrations, campfire tales, and a chance to pan for gold. A longer YUKON TERRITORY TOUR heads up over the pass and across the border to Carcross and Lake Bennett for a visit to the Frontierland Theme Park and Museum of Yukon Natural History. *(See* Yukon, *page 225.)*

A HELICOPTER EXCURSION offers an exciting view of the alternative Chilkoot Trail to the gold fields, where you may spot contemporary climbers, and lands you on a glacier. Various FLIGHTSEEING TRIPS, ideal for photographers, explore nearby Glacier Bay, the Chilkat Mountains, and the Chilkat Bald Eagle Preserve near Haines—where a bus takes you along the coast on an eagle-watching expedition, and large rafts cruise gently down the Chilkat River through the 49,000 acres dedicated to the magnificent birds. *(See Wild Alaska, page 96.)*

As in most Southeast ports, SPORTFISHING for salmon and halibut in Skagway is fine, especially from the deck of a roomy cruiser. Another seagoing option is a LUXURY BOAT CRUISE to the head of Lynn Canal along steep-mountained fjords and a visit to the log cabin and private salmon hatchery at Burro Creek, where modern homesteaders run their own hydroelectric plant. And only a walk away are the remains of a homestead dating to gold rush days. The two contrasting sites, a century apart, nicely sum up the Skagway area, a place that has always been peopled with adventuresome, independent characters.

TOK, THE SLED DOG CAPITAL

Alaska's Eskimos may have been using dogs to pull sleds as long ago as the late Middle Ages, archeologists suggest. Certainly, when Bering came through in 1741, sled dogs were crucial to Natives' winter survival, the huskies hauling freight and hunters through the wilderness of snow and ice. They continued their key role until the 1970s when snow machines, the so-called iron dogs, threatened them with extinction. What saved the animals was the resurgence of competitive mushing as a sport. At the turn of the century, gold miners in Nome raced teams of dogs for large sums of cash; soon after World War II, Anchorage's Fur Rendezvous and Fairbanks' North American Championships provided decent purses for sprintlike competitions. But it wasn't until Joe Redington, Sr., of Knik mortgaged his homestead and put up a $20,000 purse for the first long-haul Iditarod Trail race in 1967 that the state's official sport became legitimate. Full-time professionals now win prizes totalling $500,000 a year and even attract annual coverage on TV. And today, when the dogs are more numerous than they were in 1900, the Alaska Highway community of Tok is the acknowledged Sled Dog Capital. About a third of its

900 residents are somehow involved with breeding and training the animals.

Tok (rhyming with *spoke*) is also known as the gateway to Alaska from Canada: 125 miles northwest of the border, it's a key junction between the Alcan route to Fairbanks and the Tok Cutoff of the Glenn Highway to Anchorage. The unincorporated town began as an Alcan construction base in 1942, and the official story is that it was called Tokyo Camp for its proximity to the Tokyo River, until wartime feelings abbreviated the name. Another tale is that it comes from the Athabaskan for "peace crossing" because the area was, and remains, a trading center for tribes in the Upper Tanana valley.

Women from nearby villages still create NATIVE CRAFTS: beaded necklaces, moccasins of tanned moose hide cured in the smoke of rotted spruce, and baskets of birch bark stitched together with spruce root and dyed with everything from food coloring to berry juice. They sell these and other Athabaskan crafts in Tok's gift shops, which also offer soapstone carvings and fur hats and earmuffs.

THE ALASKA PUBLIC LANDS INFORMATION CENTER, near the junction, is an entertaining stop, with its interpretative exhibit of a fire that swept the Tok River in 1990; an impressive floor map and a room devoted entirely to a historical time line; and a wildlife museum featuring walrus, wolves, and an eight-foot grizzly.

Predictably, the town's many mushers offer visitors SLED DOG DEMONSTRATIONS, including training sessions and rides. The animals might be blue-eyed, snowshoe-footed Siberian huskies, the most common of competitors, or the bigger Alaskan malamutes bred to pull large loads—or a cross of such breeds as wolf, Labrador, and even Irish setter. Tok's trail (20.5 miles) is the site of the Race of Champions, a contest that originated in 1954 as a bet between two roadhouse owners and now ranks as the third leg of the sport's Triple Crown after the Anchorage and Fairbanks races. With the largest field of any sprint race in the state, it features more than 100 teams in two heats in two days during late March. Championship racers might have anywhere from 7 to 16 dogs in their teams and, because they can't replace them during a heat, often end up with fewer than they began with—losing animals to aching muscles and sore feet. Most nights in summer, a local inn shows *Spirit of the Wind*, an Alaska-produced film documenting the state's best-known dog racers.

Dog mushing has become big business in Alaska. Competitors attract corporate support, professionals rent their dogs to amateur racers (for $10,000 and more a team), and breeders sell pups for $500 and veteran animals for twice that. Although they may spend as much as $30,000 maintaining their teams, the few top racers—such as Susan Butcher and Rick Swenson—can make a good living. Butcher, born in Cambridge, Massachussetts, not only wins the Iditarod consistently, she and Joe Redington, Sr., were the first to ascend Mount McKinley by dog team.

VALDEZ: LITTLE SWITZERLAND

The city you visit now is not the Valdez destroyed in the great earthquake of 1967. Old Valdez lay four miles east, and today there's little there left to see. Gold had launched it in 1897, copper kept it alive for a while, and now another natural resource, oil from Prudhoe Bay, is pumping life through the arteries of the new city that rose to replace the pioneer South Central town.

About 120 miles due east of Anchorage, Valdez earns its name of Little Switzerland as one of Alaska's more beautiful urban settings—with a port off Prince William Sound at its feet and the Chugach Mountains rearing up around it like the Alps—as well as one of the more affluent cities in the state. For a place of only 4,000 people, it's well served with such recently developed amenities as a Civic Center, a teen center, and a growing community college. Normal temperatures in High Summer here are in the low 60s. In winter, the snow falls by the ice bucket: an average of 25 feet a year compared to Anchorage's 6; in January 1990, a record 47.5 inches landed in a single day.

Port Valdez, on which the city's busy SMALL-BOAT HARBOR fronts, was named in 1790 by Spanish explorer Don Salvador Fidalgo for Spain's marine minister, Antonio Valdes y Basan. (Alaskans unaccountably pronounce the civic name Val-*deez*) The most northerly ice-free port in the western hemisphere, it's the southern end of the Trans-Alaska Pipeline, which descends Thompson Pass behind Valdez to deliver oil to the $50-million container terminal. Supertankers berth at the 800-foot-deep anchorage and, on their way to the Lower 48, ply tricky Valdez Arm, the estuary leading to Prince William Sound. There's also a land link to the Alaska Highway system and Fairbanks via the old gold-rush trail and wagon road, which became the Richardson Highway.

During the Klondike gold stampede of 1897–98, about 3,500 people, their horses and dogs, landed at the port to carve an All-American Route to the Yukon Territory. They had to cross the virtually impassable, mile-high Valdez glacier to the Kluteena, Copper, and Yukon rivers. Their foes were fog and wind-whipped snow and rain, crevasses and avalanches, and sunburn and snow blindness from light bouncing off the ice. Once over the glacier, only about 200 stampeders managed to survive the Kluteena's fearsome rapids. Most who didn't die turned back, heading south for the safety of home below the 49th parallel. By the winter of '99, those still left in the tent town at Port Valdez were dying horribly of scurvy. After spending a total of $3.7 million, the gold seekers had failed to establish an alternative U.S. passage to the Klondike.

But the relative few who did surmount the glacier found copper in the Wrangell Mountains during the early 1900s. The notorious Alaska Syndicate of American financier J.P. Morgan and the Guggenheim mining family purchased rights to the copper lode and planned to use Valdez as the terminus of a railroad from the mines. When it switched to another site, promoter Henry Reynolds created the Alaska Home Railroad of Valdez to compete with the Syndicate's line through KEYSTONE CANYON. The Syndicate disliked rivals; its guards met Reynold's men in the canyon and shot five of them, killing one. (Today, you can take a WHITE-WATER RAFT TRIP on the glacial Lowe River through the steep-walled canyon, or a SCENIC MOTORCOACH TOUR through this gorge where Bridal Veil Falls tumbles nine stories.) Lacking funds, Reynold's railroad soon failed. Another, launched by British-backed Michael Heney—who had pushed the White Pass & Yukon line between Skagway and Whitehorse—was bought out by the Syndicate, which retained Heney to complete the track from the copper mountains to the port of Cordova, southeast of Valdez.

In the 1920s, the Richardson Highway was paved, and for the next four decades Valdez survived only as the major cargo route to the Interior. Then, on Good Friday 1964, the hard-pressed town of 1,100 was shattered by earthquake and battered by a giant wave that rolled 30 miles up the inlet, crashed on to the land, knocked down power lines that ignited fuel tanks and sent flames spilling across the port. Thirty-one people died, 225 homes were levelled or damaged. In its wake, residents decided to re-create Valdez on a new site four miles west along the port.

Valdez has the most northerly ice-free harbor in the western hemisphere.

Little more than a decade later, it finally came into its own as the OIL PIPELINE TERMINUS. A tour of the 1,000-acre Alyeska Marine Terminal across the bay reveals the sophisticated complex demanded to store up to 9.18 million barrels of crude oil from Prudhoe Bay and load it from four berths on the mega-tankers that take it around the globe. The statistics of the place are astonishing. It took $1.4 billion and a workforce of 4,300 to build the terminal (but only about 265 people to operate it). There are three fixed berths each of which can load a ship with 100,000 barrels an hour, and a single floating berth, loading four-fifths that fast, which weighs 6.5 million pounds. The capacity of each of the 18 holding tanks is 510,000 pounds, enough fuel to fly a 727 jet around the world 376 times.

By 1989, the property taxes on the tank farms and loading docks were accounting for 94 per cent of the city's revenues, and oil salaries were a major contribution to the local economy, with income from fishing a far second. That was the year the dark side of this dependence on petroleum surfaced. On the twenty-fifth Good Friday since the great quake, the supertanker *Exxon Valdez* went aground 25 miles from the port, on Bligh Reef, known until then for the state's finest silver-salmon fishing. Three hours before, a city council committee had been warned that it was just a question of when—not if—a major oil spill would pollute Prince William Sound. In the worst such spill in American history, the ruptured ship spewed 10.1 million gallons into the fish- and mammal-rich waters along 1,100 miles of coastline. Although the port itself was spared, 9,000 workers valiantly cleaned up the beaches of the sound; Valdez' summer population leapt to 12,000. Today, though enviromentalists remain watchful, government biologists agree with Exxon that the remaining oil seems not to pose any lingering threat, and a chief government scientist reports that the ecosystem of the sound and the adjacent Gulf of Alaska have emerged from the spill largely intact.

The VALDEZ VISITOR CENTER (200 Chenega Ave.) offers, along with city maps, a cross-section of the pipeline and the first barrel of oil that flowed from it. VALDEZ MUSEUM (217 Egan Dr.) is a good place to comprehend not only the construction of the line and the marine terminal (revealed in an illuminated model) but also the aftermath of the city's two disasters: the earthquake and the oil spill. Diverse displays feature a "pig," an instrument-toting cylinder that travels through the pipeline; the bar from a 19th-century saloon; and "please-touch" sea otter pelts and Columbia Glacier ice. Tour options from Valdez offer the opportunity to see glaciers up close on a THOMPSON PASS AND WORTHINGTON GLACIER DRIVE and COLUMBIA GLACIER FLIGHTSEEING by helicopter, which also lands on Shoup Glacier.

And if you take a tour of the ice fields, remember to salute those argonauts who tried to scale Valdez Glacier during the gold rush, sunburned, snow-blind, blanketed by fog, and sometimes buried by avalanche.

VANCOUVER THE BEAUTIFUL

The bread-and-butter letter was more like a mash note. Addressed to the editor of *The Vancouver Sun* following the 1993 summit meeting between U.S. President Bill Clinton and Russian President Boris Yeltsin, it read: "Please allow me to use your newspaper to thank the people of Vancouver for their extraordinary warmth and hospitality during the Russian-American summit of April 3 and 4. While your city's remarkable beauty is well-known—and was on incredible display throughout the weekend—it was your spirit and your excitement that set the stage for our meetings. Vancouver's open affection and enthusiasm helped President Yeltsin and me take important steps forward toward building a world of peace and friendship. I will never forget Vancouver and its people. Thank you." It was signed Bill Clinton.

Vancouver, British Columbia, has that kind of effect on many people. British Columbians have been called the Californians of

Vancouver's downtown Canada Place complex is
the major terminal for Alaska-bound cruise ships.➤

Canada: eccentric, effervescent, self-confident Far-West frontiers-men. B.C. itself has been described as the sandbox in the Cana-dian schoolyard, Lotusland, the Promised Province. And its principal city (pop.: 1.7 million and rising quickly)—Canada's third-largest—has long been lumped alongside Rio and Hong Kong as having the world's most luxuriant sea-and-mountain setting. The combination of this backdrop, a mild, mostly snow-free cli-mate, and in recent years the nation's most vibrant economy, has made Vancouver the fourth-swiftest-growing metropolis in North America, next to Orlando, Florida, and Sacramento and San Diego, California.

Perched on the Pacific below the Coast Mountains, Vancouver is Canada's largest seaport, where ships from 90 nations berth every year to load 66 million tons of bulk cargo: grain and forest products, petroleum and minerals, coal and chemicals. (That yel-low mountain you can see across the harbor on Burrard Inlet is sulphur.) Some of those vessels, of course, are the world's most magnificent cruise ships, which make this their summer home port for the voyage up the Inside Passage to Alaska. In fact, the major cruise terminal is part of the CANADA PLACE complex in the inner harbor, smack in the middle of downtown, that was the centerpiece of the Russian-American summit. It also houses a ho-tel, office tower, the immense screen of an IMAX Theatre, and the Vancouver Trade and Convention Centre.

Because of its pivotal location, Vancouver has become a center of international trade and investment, with Japan second only to the United States as a trading partner. High-tech manufac-turing may soon rival the traditional forestry and mining indus-tries as the city's economic propellant. Tourism already does, attracting more than $1.5 billion a year. And the temperate weather, the surrounding natural splendors, and experienced local movie crews help Vancouver vie regularly with Toronto as the continent's third-busiest film capital after Los Angeles and New York.

A lot of those movies use old GASTOWN as a location. Just a brief walk from Canada Place, the neighborhood is the birthplace as well as the original nickname of Vancouver. In the early 1860s, a sea captain started a sawmill here amid the forests along Burrard Inlet. Logging camps drew Gassy Jack Deighton—christened for his loquaciousness—to set up a saloon on the new townsite of Granville (now the name of the city's main north-south street). In 1886, when the settlement became the western terminus of the nation-spanning Canadian Pacific Railway, it was reborn as Vancouver, after the British naval captain who first saw it in 1792. Two months after incorporation, the 1,000 residents watched it burn down; by year's end, as the railway and the port jump-started the economy, it was rebuilt into a home for 8,000. Vancouver began to truly boom in 1898 when Americans used the city as a way station on the long trail to the Klondike gold rush.

Today, Gastown's old Romanesque and Italianate warehouses and low-rise office buildings are becoming inner-city condos for professionals and artists. But the area remains a visitors' mecca of inviting restaurants and curio shops along cobblestone streets—and it's hard to miss the world's first steam-powered clock at Water and Cambie streets and, at the other end of Water, the statue of Gassy Jack in Gastown's first civic center, Maple Tree Square.

The new city's first resolution, back in 1886, was to petition the Canadian government to acquire 1,000 acres of a military reserve on a forested peninsula along Burrard Inlet. They became STANLEY PARK, one of the greatest urban oases in North America and the single tourist attraction in Vancouver that simply must be seen. With thick forests of spruce and hemlock, western red cedar and massive Douglas fir, riotous rose gardens, and 200 species of rhododendron, it's at once an unspoiled and yet carefully cultivated natural park. And it sprawls on the fringe of downtown, a few minutes' drive from Canada Place. Here, locals play cricket, soccer, and rugby on grassy fields, swim and fish off its beaches, golf and play tennis, feed the resident Canada geese, and in the odd cold winters skate on frozen Lost Lagoon (named in a poem by Pauline Johnson, the daughter of an Indian chief, because the water once disappeared during low tide). The park has restaurants, totem poles, two small zoos, the VANCOUVER AQUARIUM—

VANCOUVER

1. Canada Place
2. Gastown
3. Chinatown
4. Dr. Sun Yat-Sen Classical Chinese Garden
5. Granville Island Market
6. Queen Elizabeth Park
7. VanDusen Botanical Garden

among the continent's finest—and best of all, a 5.5-mile paved seawall path. Here you can walk or cycle in sight of a bevy of the world's ships offshore, awaiting berths, entertained by an abundance of migrant waterfowl and occasional sightings of such marine life as seals and killer whales.

There's a lushness about this rainforest land (which receives less summer rainfall than any other major Canadian city except Victoria). QUEEN ELIZABETH PARK on Little Mountain (33rd Avenue and Cambie) has waterfalls in sunken quarry gardens, a Henry Moore sculpture, a wide-screen vista of city and mountains, and the BLOEDEL FLORAL CONSERVATORY under a geodesic dome, with free-flying tropical birds and exotic plants, including an exceptional array of Japanese bonsai. VANDUSEN BOTANICAL GARDEN (37th Avenue and Oak Street) provides 55 eminently walkable acres of lawns, ponds, sculpture, children's garden, plant maze, gift shop, and restaurant, and Canada's biggest collections of rhododendrons and hardy ornamental plants. THE UNIVERSITY OF BRITISH COLUMBIA BOTANICAL GARDEN (6804 S.W. Marine Dr.) features alpine, native, food, and Asian plantings as well as the medicinal plants of the 16th-century-style Physick Garden. The seaside setting of the major provincial university makes for the most glorious campus in the nation. The monumental MUSEUM OF ANTHROPOLOGY stands here (6393 N.W. Marine), inspired by the cedar houses of Northwest Coast Natives, and showcasing one of the world's most extensive displays of their sophisticated traditional and contemporary art. It's all imaginatively arranged inside the award-winning building and on the totem-strewn grounds, which are planted with grasses and other vegetation the First People once used.

Perhaps the most serene of all Vancouver's urban sanctuaries is the DR. SUN YAT-SEN CLASSICAL CHINESE GARDEN (578 Carrall St.), the first authentic Ming Dynasty garden outside China. This is a place of gnarled trees and seasonal flowers, of pavilions and ponds of koi fish, of bridges and sculpted rock, built by 52 Chinese artisans from such traditional materials as limestone rocks and colored river pebbles. It's now an integral part of historic CHINATOWN (centered on Pender and Keefer streets, between Main and Gore), North America's second-largest after San Francisco's. Observers say Greater Vancouver is well on its way to becoming the continent's first Asian city. Already a third of the population in suburban Richmond, home to the Vancouver International Airport, is Chinese in origin, and about 70 per cent of all land in Richmond's downtown core is Asian-owned. In downtown Vancouver, on the former site of the successful world's fair, Expo 86, Hong Kong billionaire Li Ka-shing intends to build a 12-million-square-foot residential and commercial development. Meanwhile, the traditional Chinatown quarter in central Vancouver teems with turn-of-the-century Chinese architecture, restaurants reflecting all the regions of China, and shops selling porcelain and silk, exotic teas and life-enhancing herbs, and glistening barbecued ducks.

Another center of exciting street life is GRANVILLE ISLAND MAR-KET, a former industrial isthmus (on downtown False Creek below the Granville Street Bridge) which has been transformed into a village with its own hotel, community center, art school, brewery, floating-home village, and information center. All that, and art galleries and crafts studios, restaurants and theaters, playgrounds and children's shops—and one of the grandest public markets in North America. The indoor market is a good place to pick up a snack or picnic lunch (the seafood is superb), watch the buskers, or buy handmade gifts and west-coast food and wine specialties.

To top off a Vancouver visit, there's nothing more elevating than a skytram trip up GROUSE MOUNTAIN, the 4,000-foot peak in North Vancouver across the elegant Lions Gate Bridge. Along the way, your tour may stop in at the SALMON HATCHERY amid the forests of Capilano River Regional Park, where displays describe how two million salmon eggs are hatched here each year. Another nearby attraction is the CAPILANO SUSPENSION BRIDGE, a 450-foot length of scary-looking wood and cable—the world's longest suspended footbridge—that sways 230 feet above the tumultuous waters of the Capilano River Canyon. The ride in enclosed trams up Grouse Mountain may be even more dizzying, but once at the summit you can hike alpine meadows, which double as winter ski trails; catch a multimedia show and a loggers' demonstration; watch or try out tandem paragliding; snack, dine, or shop for souvenirs—and soak up the unforgettable view of Vancouver the Beautiful.

VICTORIA: EDEN ON THE PACIFIC

"The place itself appears a perfect 'Eden', in the midst of the dreary wilderness of the Northwest coast, and so different is its general aspect, from the wooded, rugged regions around, that one may be pardoned for supposing it had dropped from the clouds into its present position." In 1842 that was the considered opinion of James Douglas, chief factor of the fur-trading Hudson's Bay Company, after surveying the site for what would become Victoria. That attitude among newcomers toward the British Columbia capital seems as strong today as it was a century and a half ago. A few years back, the magazine *Condé Nast Traveler* ("Truth in Travel") announced that a readers' poll had declared the city's environment the most pleasant of any in the world—and ranked Greater Victoria, a city of 270,000, eighth-best overall, after places like Florence, Paris, and San Francisco.

Indeed, this Pacific port at the southern end of Vancouver Island (the largest island off the west coast of North America) appears as if it had dropped from a kinder, gentler time. Its low-rise downtown along the humming INNER HARBOR has a human scale; heritage buildings abound, and its impossibly clean streets brim with hanging baskets of flowers. You can escape the town center in a mere five minutes to be amid lakes and cricket fields, in the company of peacocks and royal swans, and the chickens and lambs of a children's petting farm, on BEACON HILL PARK (between Douglas and Cook streets along Marine Drive). Such gracious residential areas as OAK BAY and ROCKLAND look like Hollywood's image of middle-class neighborhoods in the 1950s. Then there's the weather: Victoria is the only urban center in Canada to have a frost-free winter, with daffodils trumpeting in late February; and summers here see less rain than any other sizable Canadian city. (James Douglas's assistant complained, mildly: "The climate is perhaps too fine . . . from June to Novr. we had scarcely anything else, than bright sunny days! Yet we were by no means oppressed by the heat, for the close vicinity of the sea & the cooling breezes blowing thence, made it very bearable.")

This is first and forever a government town, but its other preoccupation is tourism. Victoria has long ridden on its supposed resemblance to Olde England and a reputation as the nation's retirement capital—its gentility and good weather convincing visitors to return to live here. It's true that the inner city ringing the harbor area is overripe with British references. Bruce Hutchison, a distinguished man of Canadian letters, once said his hometown had made the 20 acres of the downtown an altar of the Victorian spirit. The tourist shops along GOVERNMENT STREET, the main drag, do feature Doulton china and Waterford crystal, Scottish woollens and English made-to-measure tweed suits. The ferries and floatplanes that land in the harbor (cruise ships and other large ocean vessels berth around the corner at Ogden Point) do have an inescapable view of the city's two turn-of-the-century stone monuments: the LEGISLATIVE BUILDINGS, seat of the provincial government, and the impressively restored EMPRESS HOTEL, still serving daily High Tea. Both were designed by an English architect in grand British Empire style (though the lights that outline the exterior of the legislature, strung for the Duke of Connaught's visit in 1910, give it a Disneyland touch).

Look beyond the city's façade, however, and you'll find a multicultural mélange typical of other Canadian centers, which surfaces in ethnic restaurants and the many nations reflected in residents' faces. If the city still lures warmth-starved Prairie farmers to retire here, its population has grown increasingly younger, while Halifax on Canada's East Coast has supplanted it, in percentage terms, as a haven for retirees. Victoria also attracts more than 2.5 million visitors a year from around the world, most of them American; its inhabitants can see the Olympic Mountains of Washington state, a quick ferry trip south across the Strait of Juan de Fuca.

It was Americans whom James Douglas was retreating from in 1842 when he arrived at the southern verge of Vancouver Island to seek a new site for a fort. The U.S. and Britain had agreed in 1818 to open up the region between California and Alaska to trading by people of both nations. Now American settlers and their political backers were calling for annexation of the Pacific Coast as far north as the Alaska boundary. Douglas of the Hudson's Bay Company—deciding to relocate Fort Vancouver from the mouth of the Columbia River in what is now Washington—found the idyllic site he called Fort Victoria in honor of the contemporary Queen. Three years later, he moved the trading company's Pacific headquarters there and became governor of Britain's new crown colony on Vancouver Island. In 1858, discovery of gold on the Fraser River on the British Columbia mainland brought 20,000 hopefuls, mostly veterans of the California gold rush, who stopped in Victoria before crossing the Strait of Georgia to the Canadian Eldorado. Victoria, soon a busy port handling the island's lumber and mineral riches, became a city in 1862; within three years, the muscle-flexing British opened a naval base here (now Canadian Forces Base Esquimault). After 1886, when the transcontinental railroad made Vancouver boom, Victoria no longer dominated the colony, though it remained the capital when British Columbia became a province five years later.

Thousands of the gold-seekers and railroad-builders were Chinese from the U.S. and Hong Kong. By 1884 they numbered nearly 17,000, half of Victoria's population, most of them indentured laborers living in CHINATOWN. The first such Chinese community in Canada, it inspired legends about opium dens, secret tunnels, and what is still the continent's narrowest street, Fan Tan Alley. Over the decades, the flourishing district around downtown Fisgard Street ebbed in vitality; fewer than 100 Chinese remained there by the late 1970s, when young artists were moving in while the city and the Chinese community began to revive the historic quarter. Heralding this renewed Chinatown of shops and restaurants is the Gate of Harmonious Interest, an archway of decorative Taiwanese tiles that spans Fisgard at Government Street.

The place to experience the history and environment of Victoria and the province is the ROYAL BRITISH COLUMBIA MUSEUM (675 Belleville St. near the Legislative Buildings), considered one of the seven best museums in North America. The First People displays are particularly poignant as you hear their celebratory potlatch songs, see flickering old movies of Natives in war canoes, and visit a Kwakiutl longhouse. There are stunningly lifelike dioramas of animal habitats, a simulated submarine tour of the ocean depths, and walk-through re-creations of Captain Cook's shipboard cabin, as well as an Old Town so realistic you might have slipped through a crack in time.

For more peeks into the local past, stroll through the city center, past the heritage brick buildings of OLD TOWN along Johnston Street, stopping at the award-winning Market Square complex of shops and restaurants. Or visit ANTIQUE ROW along Fort Street (from Douglas to Vancouver streets and beyond), where collectibles and old treasures compete with Canadian handicrafts, china, and crystal. In the Rockland area, you can tour CRAIGDARROCH CASTLE (1050 Joan Crescent), the multi-turreted mansion built of local sandstone for Robert Dunsmuir, British Columbia's coal king, to lure his Scottish wife to Vancouver Island. He died before the 20,000-square-foot mini-palace was finished in 1889, and in fact, work is still being done to restore its stained-glass windows and inlaid floors to their original beauty.

A lot less local, but still intriguing, are thatch-roofed ANN HATHAWAY'S COTTAGE (429 Lampson St. in Esquimault), a surprisingly authentic replica of the 16th-century home of Shakespeare's wife; and BUTTERFLY WORLD (1461 Benvenuto Ave. in Brentwood Bay), where some of the world's most exotic live butterflies court, lay eggs, and flutter by to be photographed in tropical settings.

It's just a couple of minutes' flight from the butterflies to what might well be the most astonishing private botanical showcase on the continent: BUTCHART GARDENS. The story goes that flower-crazy Jenny Butchart couldn't tell one bloom from another in 1904 when she and scads of Chinese workers began turning her husband's ugly limestone quarry into a formal, 50-acre garden. To transform it, she even rappelled down rock walls in a swinging ship's chair to plant ivy. Fountains and waterfalls, shrubs and evergreens accent the Japanese, Italian, English rose, and sunken gardens. Spring's daffodils, dogwood, and tulips yield to the roses, fuschias, and begonias of summer, while dahlias, zinnias, and chrysanthemums flourish in fall. Take tea in the Butchart home, browse the garden shop—and pleasure in a microcosm of the Eden that Victoria still is.

VICTORIA

1. Chinatown
2. Empress Hotel
3. Royal B.C. Museum
4. Legislative Buildings
5. Ann Hathaway's Cottage
6. Antique Row
7. Craigdarroch Castle

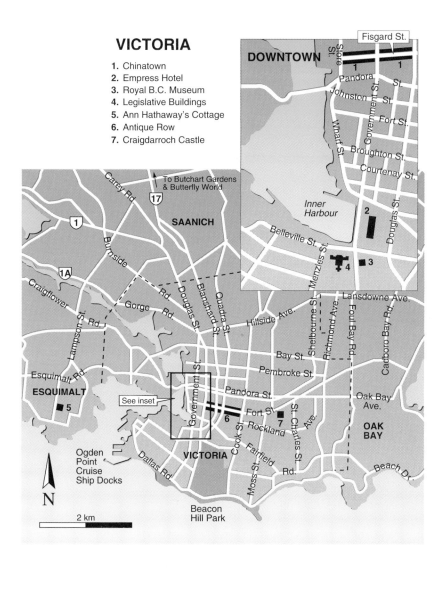

YUKON, CANADA

George Carmack was not interested in gold. He was a California-born white man who lived as an Indian, fishing and logging with his common-law wife, Kate, the daughter of a Tagish chief. Like most Indians, he considered prospecting a white man's game. Yet on Rabbit Creek in the Yukon one summer day in 1896, he was indeed searching for the stuff, prodded by his Indian friends Skookum Jim and Tagish Charlie. Jim had detected traces of gold in the gravel of the creek; now he and Carmack were panning for more. They found a nugget as big as a thimble, then enough surface gold to pack a shotgun shell—enough to make them think this could be the richest stake in the whole territory. Carmack convinced Jim that no Indian would be acknowledged as the discoverer, so on August 17 he declared himself the first man on the site. That entitled him to a double claim—1,000 feet of the creek.

George Carmack had caught the gold fever. He would carry it, spread it, until it became an epidemic infecting thousands around the world. It would be the wildest, gaudiest gold rush in history, three years of astounding good fortune and much bad luck, of greed and hardship and starvation and lavish spending.

Another man shares the credit for the discovery. Robert Henderson, a Nova Scotian who had hunted gold around the world for a quarter-century, had directed Carmack into the promising area around Rabbit Creek. Henderson had been panning a nearby creek he called Gold Bottom. Like Rabbit, it ran into a river the Indians called Throndiuck (Hammer-Water), for the stakes they hammered in at its mouth to hold salmon nets. The guttural Indian word became "Klondike" on the tongues of whites.

Henderson invariably obeyed the prospector's code: if a man found gold, he informed others. The philosophy was less generous than practical. Having others around lessened the loneliness

Whitehorse, the Yukon capitol, lies amid the
mountains and the historic Yukon River Valley.

of working in the wild; competition was no consideration because even the discoverer of a site could stake no more than two 500-foot claims. So Henderson, happening upon Carmack and his Indian friends earlier that month while going for supplies, had urged Carmack to make a claim on the Gold Bottom. But he offended Carmack by adding: "I don't want any damn Siwashes [Indians] staking on that creek." His slight would cost him a fortune.

BONANZA

When Carmack did stake his double claim as discoverer, the Indians each claimed 500 feet on the Rabbit—soon to be renamed BONANZA CREEK. Carmack and Tagish Charlie left Skookum Jim on guard and set off down the Yukon River to the community of Forty Mile to register their claims. At first nobody believed them, but within days prospectors descended on the creeks around the Klondike River. Robert Henderson wasn't among them: the slighted Carmack purposely neglected to tell him about hitting paydirt. And a few weeks later, when Henderson did learn of the spectacular find, the best of Bonanza had been staked.

Stampeders soon thronged into the territory, 186,000 square miles of wilderness, of mountains, forests, and tundra, of immense lakes and rapids-rich rivers. Bear and moose and caribou far outnumbered the inhabitants, most of whom were Indian tribes sharing dialects of the Athabaskan language. As prospectors converged on the area where the Yukon and Klondike rivers meet, trader Joe Ladue shrewdly guessed that land would become almost as valuable as gold. He staked out a townsite on swampy level ground on the Yukon's east bank and named it DAWSON, after a government geologist. The next summer of 1897, as the population passed 1,500, his house lots sold for thousands of dollars apiece.

That first winter, when Dawson was still a chaos of tents, there was virtual famine. "Food got scarcer and scarcer," A.T. Walden recalled in his autobiography, *A Dog-Puncher on the Yukon*. "The sharing of food was remarkable. Food was priceless, but there was no price on it. This was the Starvation Camp that the people on the outside never heard of." By May 1897, the camp had no food but flour. More prospectors came in by boat when the Yukon River broke up that month, but not until early June did the stern-wheeler *Alice* arrive with food—and with liquor that was served free the day the saloons reopened.

Scarcely a month later, the steamship *Excelsior* landed in San Francisco. Her cargo was Klondike prospectors and their embarrassment of gold. Their arrival jolted the continent—indeed, the world—and confirmed rumors that had been trickling out of the Yukon for months. The miners dragged ashore sacks and suitcases swollen with nuggets and dust. In Seattle another shipload of

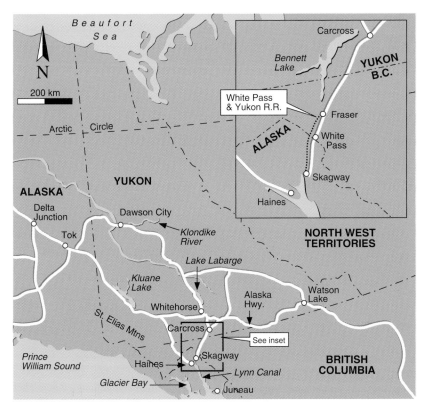

sourdoughs landed with more than two tons of gold. Together the two ships delivered $1.5 million worth.

The Klondike strike came at the end of an economic depression in North America, and men eagerly deserted homes and loved ones to follow the Trail of '98. The records brim with stories of gold-mad barbers deserting their shops, streetcar drivers abandoning their passengers, doctors forsaking their practices. The romantic name for such men was stampeders. In fact, most were tenderfeet—cheechakos in the Yukon jargon—and their inexperience would cause them incredible hardship.

A few could afford to go by ship to the Bering Sea port of St. Michael, in western Alaska, then by boat about 1,300 miles up the Yukon River to Dawson. But most trudged into the Yukon over the Coast Mountains, through the WHITE PASS or the CHILKOOT PASS. The White Pass trail began at the seaport of SKAGWAY, controlled by several hundred thugs and gamblers led by Soapy Smith. *(See*

A gold-rush laundromat and fortune-telling parlor.

Skagway, The Lost Frontier, *page 197.)* That fall of 1897, about 5,000 gold-seekers, including some women, attempted the 45-mile trek through the pass. The slippery trail was so narrow in places that competing pack teams could not squeeze by; traffic jams lasted for hours. The treacherous path became littered with discarded packs and the remains of most of the 3,000 horses that were forced up into the hills. Novelist Jack London, who took this Dead Horse Trail, reported that the animals died like mosquitoes in the first frost and were left to rot in heaps. It took only a few hours for a carcass to be mashed underfoot. In the White Pass, wrote Klondike chronicler Robert Service, "there is no mercy, no humanity, no fellowship. All is blasphemy, fury and ruthless determination." The climbers would pass a murdered man without pause.

"THIS SIDE OF HELL"

Most cheechakos reached the Klondike in 1898 over the awesome Chilkoot Trail—which one of them, Martha Black, later a Canadian Member of Parliament, called "the worst trail this side of hell." Raw rock in summer, slick ice and snow in winter, the Chilkoot was 600 feet higher than the White Pass and all but impassable by animals—in some places the trail climbed at a 35-degree angle. Its base was Dyea (*Die*-ay), an Alaskan town four miles north of Skagway. At the foot of the pass lay Sheep Camp, also in Alaska, its floating population of 1,500 living in tents, cabins, and the odd exotic dwelling such as a hut woven of branches by New Zealand Maoris. A lake of water behind a glacier burst into the Chilkoot Pass that fall, sweeping away scores of tents and drowning three men. In the spring an avalanche suffocated 60 persons under 30 feet of snow.

Through the winter and into the summer of '98, about 22,000 men and women clambered up the pass in what seemed an endless string of humanity. It was four miles from Sheep Camp to the Chilkoot summit—and Canadian territory. Canada's North West

Mounted Police (the forerunner of the Royal Canadian Mounted Police, the fabled Mounties) insisted that each person entering the Yukon have a year's food and equipment—a ton in weight. That meant making the climb 30 to 40 times, sometimes in blizzards and at temperatures of up to -58°F. Much of each load was food, but luxuries went over the Chilkoot on men's backs and up rope and cable tramways: pianos, a grindstone, newspapers, 10,000 bottles of mosquito lotion.

The buffalo-coated NWMP arrived on the Canadian side of the passes in February 1898, bringing law and order to the stampede. Their commander was Superintendent Sam (later Sir Samuel) Steele, a Mountie original with an impressive record of facing down rioters and outlaws. Steele's headquarters was at BENNETT LAKE, the bottom of both trails. There prospectors built or bought boats or rafts and at spring breakup set off for the Yukon River and Dawson. Near WHITEHORSE, at the boiling rapids of Miles Canyon, 150 vessels were wrecked and ten men drowned before Steele stepped in and enforced safety rules. In mid-1898—when he was responsible for law enforcement in all of the Yukon and British Columbia—Steele could boast that there had been only three murders in his territory.

Dawson, meanwhile, had endured a second starvation winter, with flour going from $6 a sack to $100. But after the supply boats arrived in the summer of 1898, the town boomed anew. The population reached more than 20,000 and the City of Gold was the biggest place west of Winnipeg, with telephones, electricity, and running water. Yet it looked primitive: tents, shacks, and log buildings were set on permafrost, which became a bog in spring. And it *was* primitive: a man won a bet that he could cross Front Street by jumping from one dead horse or dog to another.

Nonetheless, Dawson was unlike such unruly settlements as Skagway. On Sundays the town slept, saloons and theaters were shut, and working men were required to rest from their labors. (Two were fined for merely examining their fish nets.) The worst offenders were given a "blue slip" ordering them out of Dawson on the next boat. The town's 51 Mounties enforced laws that banned the carrying of firearms and the selling of liquor to minors.

But if it wasn't lawless, it wasn't very nice either. In the dance halls and saloons and gambling casinos, the motto was "never refuse a drink or kick a dog." The proprietors of these places prospered, as did many a female dancer-actress—some with such colorful names as Glass-Eyed Annie and Overflowing Flora. Behind the dance halls, the prostitutes of Paradise Alley worked from 70 shacks called cribs, and most of their money went to pimps who had paid their way to the Yukon. The Dawson currency was gold dust, carried in sacks, and signs in the gambling dens warned: "Don't overplay your sack." Diamond Tooth Gertie, a dance-hall girl, said it best: "The poor ginks have just got to spend it; they're that scared they'll die before they have it all out of the ground."

THE LUCKIEST CHEECHAKOS

Two fires levelled the core of Dawson in the winter of 1898–99. After the second, which destroyed 117 buildings, the town took on a different tone. Houses were built with finished lumber, sidewalks and roads were laid in macadam, schools were opened. The bubble of development would soon burst, but not before some latecomers, among the luckiest cheechakos, struck it rich—by disregarding the conventional wisdom that all gold was close to the creeks. Beginning in '98, new arrivals with no creeks to stake went into the hills and discovered broad veins with nuggets weighing half an ounce and more.

In the summer of '99, news of a gold strike at Nome lured Dawson people to Alaska—8,000 left in one week. The population continued to dwindle as mining by hand got harder. Most Yukon gold lay on bedrock, deep under muck and frozen gravel. The miners couldn't scoop it up in pans; they reached it in winter by burning wood—or later by driving steam through steel pipes—to thaw the ground. Then they tunnelled laterally, setting aside the precious gravel until spring. During runoff, creek water was used to wash the gravel through sluice boxes where the heavier gold settled to the bottom. Eventually, big companies began to buy up small claims and work them with mechanized dredges. At the turn of the century, a year's hand-mining produced $22 million in gold; in 1907 the yield was about $3 million. That year the last of the dance halls closed in Dawson.

The pioneers of the gold rush had long since left the Klondike. Joe Ladue, Dawson's founder, had come to earn enough to impress the parents of his girlfriend in Plattsburgh, New York; he went home with $5 million, married her, and within a couple of years died of tuberculosis. George Carmack, Skookum Jim, and Tagish Charlie all died wealthy. Carmack brought his Indian wife, Kate, back to the U.S. but left her for a prostitute. Kate sued him for abandonment, in one of the original palimony cases, but failed to have their common-law relationship recognized. And Robert Henderson, the unlucky man who learned about the Bonanza too late, left the Klondike to look for gold elsewhere in the Yukon and in B.C. When he died in 1933, he was still looking.

THE DRAMA OF DAWSON CITY

For more than three decades, the Canadian Government has been maintaining and imaginatively restoring Dawson City as a national historic site. Parks Canada has done its work well: though a lot of rickety old wooden structures line Dawson's wide streets beside new buildings, this community of 1,800 no longer feels like the ghost town it verged on being for much of its life. Fishing, trapping, agriculture, and even some latter-day mining help stoke the economy. But it's tourism that has preserved and re-created a photogenic, self-assured little city brimming with boardwalks, clapboard storefronts, and houses with gingerbread detailing and floral gardens. The theme, of course, is the Klondike Trail of '98. Yet Dawson is neither theme park nor historic leftover.

Dawson City is Yukon's second-largest center, after Whitehorse, which has about two-thirds of the Territory's 30,000 people living in and around it (in a land 15 per cent larger than

California). The city is set against a mountain backdrop—the 2,900-foot MIDNIGHT DOME, five miles distant, so-called because the sun shines on its peak at midnight every June 21. The city sits low on a permafrost plain near the junction of the Yukon and Klondike rivers, only 150 miles south of the Arctic Circle. The location prompts the local line: "This may not be the end of the world, but you can see it from here." Residents reveal their sense of humor about being in the boondocks by running the annual Klondike International Outhouse Race on Labor Day weekend in early September, placing outlandish-looking outdoor toilets on wheels and pulling them through the streets. The truth is that, like the rest of the Territory, this far-northern city is a pleasant place to be in summer. It's generally dry and warm, with the temperature rising as high as 85°F in July and the sun shining nearly 24 hours a day in June and 20 in July.

Not even avalanches could discourage the cheechakos who trudged up these trails.

Everywhere you wander in Dawson, there is drama, and melo-drama. This is, after all, a city that claims both Robert Service and Jack London as chroniclers of the Klondike. But in the decade after they and most of the stampeders left town at the turn of the century, mining technology improved and reduced the Territory's dependence on its capital city as a supply and service center. Gold production ebbed throughout the Klondike during World War I and for a couple of decades afterward; just as mining began to recover, along came World War II. And with construction of the Alaska Highway, Whitehorse flourished and robbed Dawson of its status as capital. Another highway, the Klondike, which runs the 333 miles between the two cities, pensioned off Dawson's port. Finally, in the 1960s, the last gold dredge stopped operating in the Klondike River Valley.

No wonder Dawson decided to resurrect its past. While fishermen, farmers, and trappers do contribute, it's nostalgic visitors from the south who keep the city healthy. They come to see the gold diggings, where the occasional miner still works a claim. Seven miles north along Bonanza Road, you can do your own gold panning over a water trough at CLAIM #33 BELOW DISCOVERY (meaning 33 claims below the historic find on Bonanza Creek in 1896 that set off the great stampede)—with a virtual guarantee of some flecks in every pan. Look for some of the original wooden claim stakes still standing here. Three miles farther north, you can see how the serious folk dug for gold on Bonanza. Here, DREDGE NO. 4—76 feet tall, 140 feet long, supposedly the largest wooden-hull dredge on the continent—now sits forlornly, no longer producing up to 800 ounces of gold a day from the river valley.

One of the last of the 250 steamboats to ply the Yukon River, the flat-bottomed, high-stacked S.S. *KENO* sits in drydock beside the river on Front Street, where you can tour the long white paddle wheeler, restored as a national historic site. A scaled-down stern-wheeler, the *YUKON LOU*, offers trips on the Yukon, along with a salmon barbecue and a visit to the cemetery of steamboats on Pleasure Island. The M.V. *YUKON QUEEN* features a riverboat dinner cruise just across the Alaskan border to Eagle, a richly historic old trading post with what may be more museum capacity per capita than anywhere else in the state.

Through displays and old documentary movies, the DAWSON CITY MUSEUM, on 5th Avenue at Church Street, recounts tales of the gold rush and the effects it had on the city. (Look for the bones of camels that crossed the gold-rush passes.) History comes rollickingly alive at two local dance halls. The original Palace Grand Theatre dates back to 1899 when Arizona Charlie Meadows

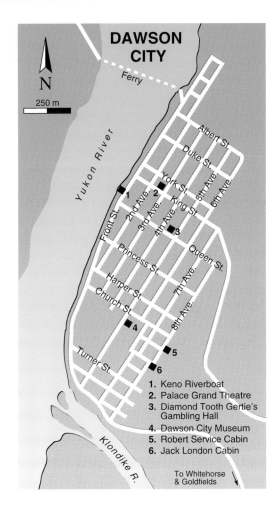

DAWSON CITY

Ferry

N

250 m

Yukon River

Albert St.
Duke St.
York St.
King St.
2nd Ave.
3rd Ave.
4th Ave.
5th Ave.
6th Ave.
Front St.
Princess St.
Queen St.
Harper St.
Church St.
7th Ave.
8th Ave.
Turner St.
Klondike R.

1. Keno Riverboat
2. Palace Grand Theatre
3. Diamond Tooth Gertie's Gambling Hall
4. Dawson City Museum
5. Robert Service Cabin
6. Jack London Cabin

To Whitehorse & Goldfields

From riverboats to gambling halls, gold-rush bards to lively museums, the national historic site of Dawson City presents the past in an agreeable, photogenic form.

built it from salvaged stern-wheelers to seat 2,200; the new one on King Street is a precise replica. Upstairs is a dressing room dedicated to singing, dancing Klondike Kate Rockwell, who wore a belt of $20 gold pieces and a tiara of illuminated candles (and who successfully sued theatre tycoon Alexander Pantages, originally a Dawson waiter, for breach of promise). Now the Palace Grand is the setting for an "Olde Tyme" music-hall show called the GASLIGHT FOLLIES. At DIAMOND TOOTH GERTIE'S GAMBLING HALL, 4th and Queen— named for dance-hall queen Gertie Lovejoy, who wore a sparkler between her two front teeth—there are can-can girls, honky-tonk piano music, and what for a long time was Canada's only legal casino, whose profits helped restore the city's heritage buildings.

Perhaps the most evocative places to visit in Dawson are the cabins that pay homage to the Klondike's bards. JACK LONDON'S CABIN AND INTERPRETATION CENTRE is the very basic lodging where the idealistic young writer and hapless gold-seeker from Oakland, California, actually lived for a few weeks. By his bunk, he wrote his name and a punning self-description—"miner author"—that would belie his success as creator of *The Call of the Wild* and many other works. Close by, the two-room ROBERT SERVICE CABIN reconstructs the life and work of the young bank teller who came to live in Whitehorse long after the gold rush had died, yet immortalized the Klondike with such books as *Songs of a Sourdough*, in which Dan McGrew got shot, and *The Trail of '98*, which he wrote in this log cabin. In both places, you can hear actors reading from the authors' verse and story. And, as you wander along Dawson's broad thoroughfares, you might recall Service's description of "the midnight melancholy of the haunted streets."

THE HISTORY OF WHITEHORSE

Yukon's metropolis, Whitehorse suffers the sometime smog and traffic jams of many small but bustling cities down south. But, tucked between the mountains and lilting hills of the Yukon River Valley at Mile 918 of the Alaska Highway, the capital city has a superb environment and advantageous suburban hiking and ski trails. This is a staging area for trips to such natural splendors as Kluane National Park, only two hours west, where 19,850-foot Mount Logan stands second only to Alaska's Mount McKinley as the continent's highest. And Whitehorse, as a government town with a relatively stable population, has built an infrastructure of amenities that visitors appreciate, such as ethnically diverse restaurants and a vital art and entertainment scene unexpected in a community nearly 100 miles north of Skagway, Alaska.

Boom and bust have been constants here, as in most northern centers, but Whitehorse seems to have risen above the cycles to endure with dignity. During the stampede of '98, it began as a tem-

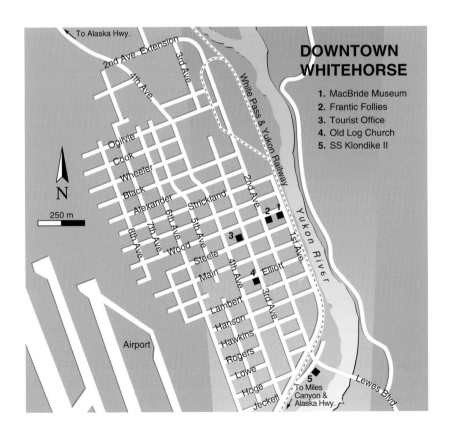

To Alaska Hwy.

DOWNTOWN WHITEHORSE

1. MacBride Museum
2. Frantic Follies
3. Tourist Office
4. Old Log Church
5. SS Klondike II

N

250 m

Airport

Yukon River

White Pass & Yukon Railway

To Miles Canyon & Alaska Hwy.

Lewes Blvd.

porary rest area after prospectors survived the two major obstacles of MILES CANYON and the Whitehorse Rapids on their way to the gold fields. In the canyon, the Yukon River's wickedest rapids capsized many boats, prompting the ingenious use of horse-drawn cars on a log tramway to circumvent the white water. (You can still see signs of the route.) Indeed, it was the manelike whitecaps that suggested the name Whitehorse. A hydro dam has since domesticated the canyon. The same company that created the WHITE PASS & YUKON RAILWAY launched the British Yukon Navigation Company, which built and operated riverboats to Dawson until the 1950s. The stately S.S. *KLONDIKE II*, the very last working paddle wheeler to run the Yukon—powered by almost two logs on the boiler fire each minute—sits downtown at the foot of 2nd Avenue, landlocked but superbly restored as a national historic site.

With the railroad's arrival from Skagway in 1900, Whitehorse settled down as a community. Two decades later, after surfing the crests and troughs of a copper boom, the rail company began encouraging tourism and hunting using the city as a base, and in the mid-'30s set up an airline here for passengers, freight, and mail. World War II made the city a pivotal transportation center as North American military and civilian workers built a series of airfields across the north, the Alaska Highway, an oil pipeline from the Northwest Territories, and a refinery in Whitehorse.

By the time it became the territorial capital in 1953, the city was establishing itself as the hub of the highway system in the Canadian northwest: the Alcan to Fairbanks, which links with the Haines to the Panhandle, and the Klondike to Dawson, which links with the Dempster to Inuvik in the Northwest Territories. Other roads were constructed to service a boom in silver, copper, and lead-zinc mining in the territory.

All of these arteries were soon throbbing with a fresh infusion of tourists, whose number has continued to increase. Some now ride the WP&Y from Skagway to Fraser, B.C., and then board a motorcoach to Whitehorse—or do the bus-and-train trip in reverse. However they arrive, visitors come here for the combination of history and handsome surroundings. On the western shore of the Yukon, the city hunkers under a 200-foot plateau while 4,900-foot Grey Mountain looms to the east.

You might book a CITY TOUR that winds through the newly landscaped streets of the downtown, whose architecture can still reflect the gold rush, and such distinctive suburbs as forested Porter Creek and hilly Riverdale. Or make a YUKON INDIAN HOME VISIT and meet a typical Native family and tribal elders to learn a little of the culture and craftsmanship of the local Labarge and Tagish peoples. The OLD LOG CHURCH, 3rd Avenue and Elliott Street, is a turn-of-the-century Anglican chapel, which chronicles, in artifacts and photographs, the church's extensive missionary work. The group of log cabins that form the sod-roofed W.D. MACBRIDE CENTENNIAL MUSEUM, downtown at 1st Avenue and Wood Street, includes a dwelling once occupied by the real-life inspiration of Robert Service's *The Cremation of Sam McGee*—whose fiery end came at a scenic spot not far from Whitehorse, "on the marge of LAKE LABARGE."

Another destination outside the city, which one major cruise-ship company includes in its tours, is the YUKON WILDLIFE PRESERVE. Danny Nowlan and his German wife, Uli, began stocking the 700-acre game and bird sanctuary more than a quarter-century ago to protect and display Dall sheep, mountain goat, moose, mule deer, elk, woodland caribou, wood bison, and the far-northern musk-ox. Of the squat but powerful musk-oxen, several of whom were born on the farm, Uli Nowlan says, "Their sense of play is to knock over trees. That's why we figure there are no trees in the Arctic."

A different kind of wildlife is on show back in town. FRANTIC FOLLIES, in the Westmark Whitehorse Hotel at 2nd Avenue and Wood Street, is a high-stepping vaudeville revue with a Gay '90s theme that has been running for more than two decades. There's magic, can-can dancing, and—inevitably, in a city that trades so well on its history—the whooping-it-up wit of Robert Service.

SPORTING ADVENTURES

Sportfishing

The fish are big in Alaska—and they can be ferocious too. Consider the experience of Ron Dawson of Juneau, who flies his Piper Cub float plane to wonderful fly-fishing holes around the Panhandle. One summer he and a buddy settled down on Tracy Arm, a wilderness fjord about 50 miles southeast of Juneau, for a spot of halibut fishing. After hooking a 60-pounder, he had to rev up the engine and take off fast when a strong wind rose on the water. So fast that his friend was still hanging on for dear life to the fish dangling on a line outside the plane. The halibut, which didn't take kindly to this kind of fly-fishing, knocked half a dozen holes in the side of the Piper Cub before the pilot could land the plane—and the fish.

Cruise-ship companies offer their passengers fishing expeditions (as well as packing and shipping services) at several stops along the way in Alaska, especially in Southeast, where the cruise season parallels some of the best runs of sport fish. The whole state is an angler's Shangri-la: five species of salmon remain plentiful, the freshwater trout offer superb eating, the Arctic char and grayling are exotic catches, and the halibut are big enough to batter planes.

Normally halibut aren't quite that fearsome, but they—like many other species—can grow enormous. (Ron Dawson had to drag one 258-pounder behind his plane to shore, where he could deal with it.) While an official record is 440 pounds and 97.5 inches, marine biologists speculate that the white-bellied bottom fish could balloon to half a ton here. These flatfish tend to frequent the depths, from which they may demand an hour or several hours

Alaska, an angler's nirvana,
offers some of the world's best fishing.

of an angler's time to land. Using octopus and herring as lure, you can find halibut year-round; the waters off Sitka and Skagway are good spots.

Salmon offer some of the finest saltwater sportfishing, and you can tackle them by booking trips aboard mini-cruisers in many ports of call, including Ketchikan, Juneau, Sitka, and Skagway. Alaska has the biggest king salmon in the world, nearing 100 pounds—or more, if you believe the word of mouth. You can troll for these giants, known locally as tyee, chinook, and springs, in Southeast saltwalter, where whole or cut herring, spoons, and spinners attract them. More abundant are pinks, the smallest of salmon, averaging little more than 4 pounds. These humpbacks (named for the bump they develop while spawning) like spoons, spinners, herring, and blends of flashers and Hoochies. While sockeye or reds can be the tastiest salmon—and sizable, at about 6 to 12 pounds— they're also the trickiest to find and land in saltwater, though tiny plastic squid and Hoochies do work. For wet-fly fishing for sockeye on a seven-weight fly rod or medium-weight spinning gear, the Russian River area in the Kenai Peninsula is considered a classic, if crowded, location. Coho or silver salmon are swift and smart, average 7 to 10 pounds, and run from mid-summer to November. Trolling for them, you might use fresh herring or salmon roe (though the roe is so seductive that some jurisdictions might not allow it). Chum are the least desirable of salmon, despite sizes of up to 20 pounds, because of their reputation as feed for sled dogs—hence their nickname, dog salmon. Roaming as far afield as the High Arctic, they seldom take a lure.

Freshwater fish—which can be caught on independently arranged fishing jaunts as well as some saltwater tours in the South and Southeast—include native rainbow trout, the sea-going rainbows called steelhead, and the cutthroat. Try them on flies, lures, and eggs. All are excellent sport fish and terrific eating. Other angling possiblities include Dolly Varden, a kind of char that react to eggs, spoons, and flies; and the Arctic grayling, which go after just about anything, from small spinners to flies to smolt.

River Rafting

Running Alaskan rivers in inflatable rafts can be sport for everyone, independent of age, size, and even physical condition. Some of the runs offered to cruise-ship passengers are quiet and even soothing; others are breathtaking rides through a rapid's white water. All of them transport you—in more ways than one—through stunning landscapes where your unobtrusive presence might permit close-up views of wildlife and other natural wonders. Check with your tour organizers for the float trip that meets your needs. Some trips are restricted to those above 5 years old, others to those above 11.

Ask whether you should take a camera and what you should wear; warm clothes and thick wool socks (perhaps even an extra dry pair) are usually advised. Experienced rafting companies provide the rest of the gear, including the requisite life jackets and, if necessary, rainwear and rubber boots. The oarsmen are skilled and refuse to take chances with a boatload of passengers, yet manage to create exciting voyages that taste of adventure.

A sampling of some of the float trips offered:

On MENDENHALL LAKE near Juneau, a ten-person raft plies the calm iceberg-dotted waters—with a full-frontal view of Mendenhall Glacier—and heads into the glacier-fed Mendenhall River and its brief bouts of gently boiling rapids. Halfway through, there's a stop amid a mountain setting for a snack of such regional food as smoked salmon and reindeer sausage.

The CHILKAT RIVER trip, arranged from Skagway, floats you serenely through the 49,000 acres of the Chilkat Bald Eagle Preserve near Haines. As well as an abundance of eagles, the preserve affords the chance of spotting salmon-foraging grizzlies and wolves and the occasional moose and mountain goat. A picnic lunch is included.

KEYSTONE CANYON outside Valdez provides a thrilling one-hour, 4.5-mile rush through a breach in the Chugach Mountains, past 900-foot Bridal Veil Falls, along the glacially cold Lowe River. It was here in the canyon that guards from the infamous Alaska Syndicate shot five men from the competitive Alaska Home Railroad in the early 1900s.

DENALI NATIONAL PARK offers a choice of runs down the Nenana, one of the preserve's less-riotous rivers. A two-hour scenic float for the family down the broad and civilized Nenana provides wild-life-watching as you pass through 13 miles of valley, forest, and tundra among the Alaska Range mountains, ending in an explosion of white water. A two-hour, 11-mile rapids run propels you through a straight-sided canyon and a succession of rapids with such suggestive names as Splatter Rock and Royal Flush.

World Eskimo–Indian Olympics

Many of the 18 events sound like something out of the Marquis de Sade's fevered imagination: the Ear Pull, in which competitors twine dried seal gut around their ears and yank their heads back sharply, occasionally losing these organs in the process; the Ear Weight, which has them walking up to half a mile with a load of lead as heavy as a bowling ball hanging from their ears; and one of the most painful, Drop the Bomb, where an individual is picked up by wrists and ankles and his rigid body toted around until it collapses in agony.

If you happen to be in Fairbanks during the second-last weekend in July, you can witness all this—and lots of other unusual sports that depend more on strength and endurance than a high pain threshold. Since 1960, the World Eskimo–Indian Olympics has attracted thousands of spectators and international media each year to watch hundreds of men and women representing every Native group from across the state, Canada, Greenland, and Siberia.

Sports in this case include skinning seals and cutting up salmon, high-kicking and log-walking. All of which gives a hint of what inspired these centuries-old athletic contests: crucial life skills and perseverance, a combination that equals survival in the North's ferocious living conditions. Obviously, speed in cleaning fish and mammals was vital in vicious weather. Strolling a bumpy log slick with vegetable oil harks back to the time not long ago when Indians had to negotiate a slippery tree trunk that led to a fish-catching wheel far out in a frigid river. And high-kicking? The astonishing leaps of well over six feet to touch a suspended ball with the feet is a sporting version of the jumps Eskimo whalers made to communicate to shore that they'd captured a whale.

Those high kicks are ranked the hardest events, despite the challenges of other contests. Such as the Four-Man Carry, where an individual stumbles along with a quartet of 150-pounders circling his torso, in a feat that sends some competitors to hospitals with dislocated backs. Or the One-Hand Reach in which one hand stays on the floor, supporting the body in mid-air, while the other reaches up more than 4.5 feet to touch a sealskin ball. Or the Seal Hop, which has a contestant travelling 120 feet and more on nothing but knuckles and toes.

The fitness of these athletes is usually demonstrated dramatically each year during the tug-of-war between Native women and non-Native men. At this writing, the women have never lost.

Eskimo and Indian high-kickers can hurl their bodies six feet and more to touch a ball with their toes.

BRINGING ALASKA HOME

For more than a century, visitors have been coming to Alaska as tourists, and residents have willingly been offering them keepsakes to take back home. In the 19th century, visiting naturalist John Muir complained about the steamer passengers who arrived at the glacier named for him in Glacier Bay and "turned from the great thundering crystal world of ice to look curiously at the Indians that came alongside to sell trinkets." But most Alaskans were grateful for the opportunities that tourism provided a boom-and-bust economy, and Native people in particular sold everything from reindeer moccasins to the elaborate baskets that became a North American fad in the first decade of the 20th century.

Today there are many ways of keeping Alaska alive in your memory: buying meaningful souvenirs, taking still photographs or making videotapes, and reading about the state before, during, and after your cruise there.

SOUVENIRS

Perhaps the most meaningful Alaskan memorabilia you can bring back home are authentic traditional and contemporary Native art and crafts. The aboriginal peoples have been creating souvenirs—such as model kayaks—almost since the first European set foot on this land. And you can be assured that the works are genuine if they bear an emblem of a silver hand and the words "Authentic Native Handcraft from Alaska."

As detailed in *The Native Way (pages 118–26)*, Alaskan Natives have long been creating practical tools and works of art from wood, grasses, and seeds; the skins, quills, and intestines of animals; and bone, ivory, and even fossils. Only they can legally possess raw ivory from the walruses they hunt, or fossilized ivory from the tusks of mammoths and mastodons, but they are allowed to sell only ivory that has been handcrafted.

What are Native artists and craftspeople creating today? Well, don't overlook the exciting work many are doing in the modern idiom, transcending their heritage and stretching old styles to create contemporary—often multimedia—sculpture, paintings, prints, and jewelry. Others continue in the traditional modes, using traditional materials, such as the popular etched ivory called scrimshaw.

The Inupiat Eskimos of the Bering Sea and Arctic Ocean sculpt walrus ivory and baleen (whale bone); create masks of hide and baleen, and baskets of birch bark and baleen; fashion garments of local furs; and continue a craft that's at least 2,000 years old: the making of dolls for little girls. Some dolls of museum quality may take months to make, with faces and hands carved of wood, eyes of ivory and baleen, and hand-sewn parkas of fur.

A beautifully crafted miniature
Eskimo whale hunter.

The Southwestern Yup'ik Eskimos craft dolls too (their history recounts taboos limiting the occasions girls could play with them), along with miniature dog sleds and kayaks of local materials. They also carve walrus-ivory sculptures and spirit masks, as well as weaving fine baskets of beach grasses and hand-knitting scarves, sweaters, and other garments with age-old patterns, using *qiviut*, the warm, shrink-proof, and rare musk-ox underwool.

The Aleuts of the Aleutians and the Pribilofs use strong, sinewy rye grass to weave their superb small baskets and bigger, more practical ones. They also use feathers to make their famous birdskin parkas, and wood for their highly decorated visor hats. Athabaskan Indians in the Interior specialize in working with beads of seeds, shells, quills, and wood to adorn moccasins, mittens, jewelry, and garments made from furs and hides. Their other creations include dolls, baskets of willow root and birch bark, and carvings of wood and soapstone.

Southeast's Haida, Tlingit, and Tsimshian peoples are acclaimed for their totem poles and other wood carvings such as ceremonial masks; their silver jewelry, beadwork, and art prints; and their red-and-black felt blankets decorated with buttons and beads, and sometimes woven of mountain-goat wool and cedar bark.

NON-NATIVE SOUVENIRS

Meanwhile, authentic local souvenirs created by non-Native artists and craftspeople can be identified by the symbol of the circular figure of a bear and the words "Made in Alaska." Among the most popular items are gold-nugget jewelry and carved local jade, which comes in a variety of colors from the expected green to red, yellow, brown, and even black and white. The inspiring landscape can spur Alaskan artists to impressive heights in creating eminently collectable works in oil and watercolor or limited-edition prints.

Non-Native arts and crafts:

Prints and original paintings, along with the art of resident photographers, weavers, and potters working in local clay. Gold nuggets fashioned into pendants, rings, and earrings; and jewelry of blue topaz, hematite, and a trademarked stone called Arctic Opal. Art works of porcelain, lead crystal, Alaska coral, and stained glass. Carvings in ivory, jade, wood, and soapstone, as well as miniature totem poles and birch bowls. And a variety of souvenirs with Alaskan motifs, such as Christmas ornaments, belt buckles, collectors' pins, pewter figures on fool's gold, and painted gold pans.

Tools and other practicalities:

The semi-circular ulu (Oo-loo), a skinning and filleting knife, now made with a stainless-steel blade and handles of ivory, jade, and walnut; wallets and purses of fish-skin leather; and folding and rigid kayaks, in finished or kit form, which can be shipped home.

Clothing:

T-shirts featuring such local events as the Iditarod sled-dog race; sheepskin slippers, mittens, and earmuffs trimmed with farm-fox fur; slippers of beaver and seal, and seal and lamb; Eskimo-style summer and winter parkas; fur-trimmed and wool vests; and other garments of fur and leather.

Food:

Caribou and reindeer sausage; jams, jellies, sauces, and even candies made from local wild berries; smoked salmon and halibut, king crab and scallops—all of which can usually be packed and shipped to your home address anywhere in the world.

Printed materials:

Old local maps and nautical charts.

Russian souvenirs:

Nesting dolls, hand-painted icons dating back to the 17th century, lacquer boxes, Ural stone carvings, Ukrainian Easter eggs, and porcelain figurines.

BUYER BEWARE

The caveat for shoppers in Alaska is that not everything you buy will necessarily get to sit on your mantlepiece. Art or craft objects made from the body parts of wild animals are subject to international regulations regarding trade in endangered species, about which shopkeepers may not always be forthcoming.

Because these regulations govern goods crossing an international border, American citizens travelling directly from Alaska to the Lower 48 can acquire most souvenirs or art objects made from animal parts. The problem for Americans occurs if they attempt to carry their purchases through Canada. Then the regulations established under the Convention on International Trade in Endangered Species (CITES) will apply as they do to foreigners. The situation for Americans is further complicated by U.S. legislation regarding marine mammals and endangered species. Under these laws, certain goods that might be brought into Canada will not be allowed to re-enter the U.S. What's more, although Americans may use the Personal Exemption Certificate mentioned below to bring some restricted items through Canada, the limited number of certificates might create a problem. *The advice for American travellers entering Canada is simple: mail your animal-parts souvenirs home from Alaska.*

Although whale parts *are* restricted under CITES, Americans may purchase by-products of Alaskan whales taken for subsistence by natives and handcrafted. Walrus ivory or parts may be sold in interstate commerce only if they are part of an authentic Native handicraft; polishing or carving a signature on the ivory does not qualify. Under U.S. law, it is a felony to sell parts—such as feathers—of migratory birds. All wild birds, except ptarmigan and grouse, are protected.

Canadians returning to Canada from Alaska and other nationals who must cross an international border need to be more concerned about CITES regulations.

Products made from animals on the most-endangered species

list (CITES Appendix I) cannot be transported, unless you have an import and an export permit. Import permits, which must be obtained before you leave your own country, are given only if the item is to be used for educational purposes or for scientific research, or if it has been inherited and you can prove it is a family heirloom. In other words, an import permit for an Appendix I animal is almost impossible to obtain.

In Alaska, that means Canadians and other nationals crossing an international border must forgo souvenirs such as carved whales' teeth or carved baleen, and that old whale bone you found lying on a beach. You must also be careful not to buy elephant ivory, which *is* offered for sale in Alaska. Mastodon or mammoth ivory, however, can be imported. Since only an expert can sometimes distinguish between elephant and mastodon ivory, be very sure about what you are buying.

The importing to Canada of Appendix II and Appendix III animal products requires a CITES export permit if you are shipping the goods. Since 1993, tourists carrying items in their personal baggage have been allowed to bring them into Canada if they have a Personal Exemption Certificate, which can be obtained at no charge from the U.S. Fish and Wildlife Service offices in Ketchikan, Juneau, Sitka, Anchorage, Fairbanks, and Tok, as well as from Alaska Department of Fish and Game offices in Juneau, Ketchikan, Petersberg, Sitka, Haines, Douglas, Tok, and Fairbanks. A limited number of these certificates were available in 1993. The animals on these lists include bears, cats, river otters, and walruses.

Canadians can bring home carved walrus ivory if they have an export permit. In this case, and only in this case, Canadian officials will accept a certificate filled in at the place of purchase. The U.S. Fish and Wildlife Service supplies the larger gift stores with certificates labelled "Convention on International Trade in Endangered Species: Personal Property Exemption." The exemption applies only to goods carried in one's baggage, not to mailed goods. Americans who mail walrus ivory home do not need the certificate. Travellers from other countries should check their countries' regulations in this case.

Travellers entering British Columbia should be aware that the province prohibits traffic in bear gallbladders and paws.

Canada Customs has the power to seize any item for which proper permits are not available—and it does so, frequently. The Canadian Wildlife Service will not issue after-the-fact permits for Appendix I items. If the seized items are noteworthy, they will be given to a museum or school. Otherwise, they will be destroyed, which would make them a sad souvenir indeed.

(Canadians may apply for import permits to the Canadian Wildlife Service branch in their province or to the Adminstrator, CITES, Environment Canada, Ottawa, K1A 0H3.)

PHOTOGRAPHY

When Danny Lehman photographed Denali National Park for a *National Geographic* feature in 1992, he spent four months off and on in one of the world's grandest wildernesses and came back with 600 rolls of film to create a stunning portrait of the park. But he believes that cruise passengers need only do some thoughtful planning, expend a little time, and shoot intelligently—not extravagantly—to record images that will remain memorable.

Lehman, who regularly visits Alaska to photograph for the major cruise lines, has known both ships and the state since the start of his commercial and documentary career. He grew up in New Mexico, where he still lives, and earned a degree in business administration and then another in photography from the esteemed Brooks Institute. It was as a student that he worked on a tramp freighter off Africa for 25 cents an hour and as a young professional in 1975 took his first pictures of Alaska for what was then the Orient Overseas Line's *Universe*. On that initial assignment, he chronicled the wonders of Glacier Bay and began to learn some of the secrets of photographing the state.

Such as timing his shots to capture the singular light of this land. When we talked, he had just returned from a two-week Alaskan photo expedition for Princess Cruises. "I was up at 2:30 in the morning to catch the ship at sunrise in the Lynn Canal," he says. "Cruise passengers may miss the best scenery because they don't get up early enough or stay up late enough to shoot the magic of the sun glowing red on the mountain peaks. People should try to have a catnap and then take pictures—or simply see—the landscape at these special times, when the raking light of a sunrise or the alpenglow of sunset can be much more interesting than the blasting sunlight of midday." He frequently uses a polarizing filter when shooting water or glaciers or working in bright light. At other times, especially an hour after sunrise or an hour before sunset, he uses a warming filter to heat up the color and amplify the wakening or waning rays.

Danny Lehman advises checking your ship's itinerary to determine exactly when it will be at various key locations—on the first evening out from Vancouver, for instance, the Inside Passage offers some of the most spectacular scenery of the trip. You've already broken your routine to take this voyage, so bend it a bit more to be out on deck when others may be inside, "when it's just you and the scenery." Photographing from aboard ship should pose no particular problems because most of the scenery is distant and cruise vessels travel smoothly enough to accommodate shooting at such slow shutter speeds as 1/30th of a second.

Where the problems arise is in establishing context for a photo, such as showing how big a glacier really is. "If there's a kayak or another ship or even a loon in the water, you can include them in the photo to establish size. Glaciers can dwarf some of the hugest cruise ships on earth." Frame the picture so that the strong lines of the shore or a mountain range don't split the image into too-neat halves; "you can put more water at the bottom or more mountain at the top. And use an iceberg or the wake of a boat to create texture—or reflections in the water to create interest—in what might otherwise be the blank blue of the sea."

Photographing from a plane or helicopter presents its own challenges: "Don't brace yourself on the frame of the aircraft because you'll pick up vibrations; keep the camera cushioned in your arms. And you can ask the pilot if the windows lift up or slide back so you don't have to shoot through glass." If travelling on a tour bus that stops for a wildlife photo opportunity where you have to stay inside, have a rolled-up towel or piece of foam to cradle your camera while you use the frame of the bus as a steadying support.

Other tips? Filming a glacier, you don't need the sun directly behind your back because other light creates interesting cross-light or texture. Filming wildlife, recall his rule about being on the scene at odd times: most animals show themselves in early morning or late afternoon when the crowds have gone. Filming close-ups doesn't mean lugging an enormous telephoto lens around; an astonishing tableau of a moose in a mountain setting for his Denali feature in *National Geographic* was taken with an 85-millimeter lens. And an expensive camera isn't necessary. When Lehman becomes a tourist with wife Laurie and children, he takes along a simple Instamatic.

Before you leave on a cruise, he suggests, check the camera and the film you intend to use by shooting in a variety of situations and then have the images processed to make sure everything's working. (If you suspect your batteries might run out, bring spares.) During the trip, decide why you're taking pictures: "Ninety-five per cent of the time you want photos that bring back special memories, like a friend dancing with his wife on the stern deck at sunset. You can buy slides of beautiful scenics along the way, so include someone special in your landscape—a mountain isn't going to change much in 10,000 years, but your travelling companions will, and you'll have an enchanting record of them in Alaska." Including several different elements in a picture enhances interest: for instance, a sled-dog musher with a husky in front of a log cabin.

Back home again, realize that you can often take your negative film into customizing photo shops to have special photos specially handled rather than machine-printed. And when you decide to show your family and friends the fruits of your trip, remember that less is better. While Danny Lehman returned from Denali with 600 rolls of film, the final screening at *National Geographic* was a mere 80 images.

AND FOR THE VIDEO PHOTOGRAPHER . . .

Panasonic has a few sensible hints for cruise passengers using video cameras:

Drain and recharge the camcorder's battery before leaving on your trip; take along spare batteries and several blank tapes in case the shops along the way are closed. And bring a carrying case to protect the camera and hold supplies, lights, and other accessories.

Tape an establishing, wide-angle shot of a new setting—perhaps of an interesting sign in context—before going for close-ups. Then pan slowly and smoothly rather than taking the usual two-second bursts that most people shoot in fresh situations. If the camcorder comes with an image-steadying device, don't forget to use it.

Minimize your narration; identify what you're shooting but don't describe it in dull detail. Let the subjects of your video talk for themselves. And if you do decide to add narration afterward, you might consider scripting it.

Give a friend or fellow passenger a quick lesson in operating the camera and let them record you in the setting—too many people forget to include themselves in their videotaped vacations.

Most of all, don't glue your eye to the viewfinder. Tape the highlights of your trip, not every waking moment—so that you don't miss the actual experience of *being* in Alaska.

A CRUISE DIARY

The keeping of a journal at sea or on an overland journey is a centuries-old tradition. Voyagers have long endowed us with dramatic details of the discoveries of new lands, new species. In Alaska, recall German naturalist Georg Steller reporting that after the first important Russian sighting of America from the *Saint Peter*, Vitus Bering simply gazed at the land and shrugged his shoulders. Or consider William Dall, as part of the International Telegraph Expedition in the late 19th century, remarking on an Alaskan delicacy, "Duck roasted on a stick before a fire is quite another thing from the embalmed remains which hotels offer us."

A chronicle of a trip is a lifelong record of those moments that too often remain forgotten, lost with the passing of time. Recording them can sharpen our appreciation of the journey, focusing our attention on scenes and events and travelling companions in a way that the casual taking of photographs seldom does. Which moments to preserve? Well, the cruise diary that follows is yours; the details are your own. On its pages you might want to describe friends you've made aboard ship or wildlife you've spotted on land and sea, portray a calving glacier in words or a totem pole with a pencil sketch, recount your emotional responses to Alaska, or simply list everything you did, day by day.

We have prompted you with a sample first page, assuming that, like most cruise passengers, your voyage begins in Vancouver as you head north to Alaska. Ignore it, of course, if your itinerary is different or if you prefer to do your own thing. The rest of the pages are blank—a diary waiting to be written about what bids to be an adventure of a lifetime.

Day One

Aboard the _____

We sailed from _____ at _____ on _____

Our cabin number was _____ on _____ deck

Our cabin steward's name was _____

The weather was _____

We ate dinner at the _____ sitting, at table number _____

Our dining room steward's name was _____

Our tablemates were _____
_____
_____
_____

On board were _____ passengers, _____ officers and _____ crew

Our Captain was _____

First Impressions _____
_____
_____
_____
_____
_____
_____
_____
_____
_____
_____
_____
_____
_____
_____
_____

RECOMMENDED READING

General/Reference

Alaska Atlas & Gazetteer: Topo Maps of the Entire State (DeLorme Mapping, 1992)

Alaska Magazine, always fascinating (subscriptions: P.O. Box 10545, Des Moines, IA, 50340-0545)

Arctic Dreams: Imagination and Desire in a Northern Landscape, Barry Lopez (Scribner's, 1986)

Art of the Northern Tlingit, Aldona Jonaitis (University of Washington Press, 1986)

Coming into the Country, John McPhee (Farrar, Straus and Giroux, 1976)

Facts About Alaska: The Alaska Almanac (Alaska Northwest Books, 1990)

Looking at Indian Art of the Northwest Coast, Hilary Stewart (Douglas & McIntyre, 1979)

Looking at Totem Poles, Hilary Stewart (Douglas & McIntyre, 1993)

Ragged Islands: A Journey by Canoe Through the Inside Passage, Michael Poole (Douglas & McIntyre, 1991)

Raven Tells Stories: An Anthology of Alaskan Native Writing, Joseph Bruchac, editor (Greenfield Review Press, 1991)

Totem Poles of the Pacific Northwest Coast, Edward Malin (Timber Press, 1986)

History

The Cook Inlet Collection: Two Hundred Years of Selected Alaskan History, Morgan Sherwood, editor (Alaska Northwest Publishing Company, 1974)

George Vancouver: A Portrait of His Life, Alison Gifford (St. James Press, 1986)

Interpreting Alaska's History: An Anthology, Mary Childers Mangusso and Stephen W. Haycox, editors (Alaska Pacific University Press, Anchorage, 1989)

Mt. McKinley: The Pioneer Climbs, Terris Moore (The Mountaineers, for The University of Alaska, second edition, 1981)

Northwest Explorations, Gordon Speck (Binfords & Mort, 1954)

Two Voyages to Russian America, 1802–1807, G.I. Davydov (The Limestone Press, 1977)

Vancouver's Voyage: Charting of the Northwest Coast, 1791–1795, Robin Fisher (Douglas & McIntyre, Vancouver, 1992)

Nature

Alakshak: The Great Country, Art Wolfe and Art Davidson (Yolla Bolly Press; Douglas & McIntyre, 1989)

Alaska Whales and Whaling (Alaska Geographic, Vol. 5, No. 4, 1978)

Grizzly Cub: Five Years in the Life of a Bear, Rick McIntyre—for young readers (Alaska Northwest Publishing, 1990)

A Guide to the Birds of Alaska, Robert H. Armstrong (Alaska Northwest Books, 1991)

Marine Mammals of Eastern North Pacific and Arctic Waters, Delphine Haley, editor (Pacific Search Press, 1978)

Where the Whales Are, Patricia Corrigan (The Globe Pequot Press, 1991)

Wolves, Candace Savage (Douglas & McIntyre, 1988)

The World's Whales: The Complete Illustrated Guide, Stanley M. Minasian, Kenneth C. Balcomb III, Larry Foster (Smithsonian Books, 1984)

Mystery Novels

Blood Vessel, Paul Grescoe (Douglas & McIntyre, Vancouver, 1993), set in Alaska and on a cruise ship

A Cold Day for Murder (1993) and *A Fatal Thaw* (1992), in the Kate Shugak series by Dana Stabenow (Berkley Books)

Death Below Zero, S.H. Head (Comet, 1954)

Death of an Alaskan Princess, Bridget A. Smith (St. Martin's Press, 1988)

Deep Freeze (1992); *Frozen Franklin* (1990); *Big Dark* (1989); and *Cold Front* (1989), in the Prester John Riordan series by Sean Hanlon (Pocket Books)

INDEX